THE NEW CAMBRIDGE S

GENERAL EDITOR
Philip Brockbank

ASSOCIATE GENERAL EDITORS
Brian Gibbons, *Professor of English Literature, University of Zürich*
Robin Hood, *Senior Lecturer in English, University of York*


KING HENRY VIII


*Henry VIII* was one of Shakespeare's most popular plays in the eighteenth and nineteenth centuries when great actors took the roles of Queen Katherine and Cardinal Wolsey, and elaborate pageantry was much extended. It has not been staged frequently in the twentieth century, but a number of important recent productions have revealed the theatrical potential of a more complete text.

Professor Margeson considers and illustrates the stage history of the play, and gives a balanced account of the authorship controversy from the mid nineteenth century when John Fletcher's name was first put forward as a collaborator, to recent scholarship, which has not yet reached a consensus. The Introduction discusses the political and religious background of the play, its pageant-like structure and visual effects, and its varied ironies. The Commentary is detailed but concise, explaining difficult passages and contemporary references, and suggesting how the play might have been staged in an Elizabethan theatre, or might still be staged for a modern audience.

# THE NEW CAMBRIDGE SHAKESPEARE

*Romeo and Juliet*, edited by G. Blakemore Evans
*The Taming of the Shrew*, edited by Ann Thompson
*Othello*, edited by Norman Sanders
*King Richard II*, edited by Andrew Gurr
*A Midsummer Night's Dream*, edited by R. A. Foakes
*Hamlet*, edited by Philip Edwards
*Twelfth Night*, edited by Elizabeth Story Donno
*All's Well That Ends Well*, edited by Russell Fraser
*The Merchant of Venice*, edited by M. M. Mahood
*Much Ado About Nothing*, edited by F. H. Mares
*The Comedy of Errors*, edited by T. S. Dorsch
*Julius Caesar*, edited by Marvin Spevack
*The Second Part of King Henry IV*, edited by Giorgio Melchiori
*King John*, edited by L. A. Beaurline
*King Henry VIII*, edited by John Margeson

# KING HENRY VIII

*Edited by*

## JOHN MARGESON

*Emeritus Professor of English, University of Toronto*

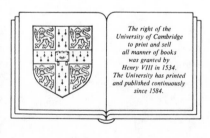

The right of the
University of Cambridge
to print and sell
all manner of books
was granted by
Henry VIII in 1534.
The University has printed
and published continuously
since 1584.

## CAMBRIDGE UNIVERSITY PRESS

*Cambridge*
*New York   Port Chester*
*Melbourne   Sydney*

Published by the Press Syndicate of the University of Cambridge
The Pitt Building, Trumpington Street, Cambridge CB2 1RP
40 West 20th Street, New York, NY 10011, USA
10 Stamford Road, Oakleigh, Melbourne 3166, Australia

First published 1990

Printed in Great Britain at
the University Press, Cambridge

*British Library cataloguing in publication data*

Shakespeare, William, *1564–1616*
[Henry VIII] King Henry VIII. – (The new
Cambridge Shakespeare)
I. [Henry VIII]   II. Title   III. Margeson,
John
822.3'3

*Library of Congress cataloguing in publication data*

Shakespeare, William, 1564–1616.
King Henry VIII / edited by John Margeson.
    p.    cm. – (The New Cambridge Shakespeare)
Bibliography: p.
ISBN 0-521-22876-x. – ISBN 0-521-29692-7 (pbk.)
1. Henry VIII, King of England, 1491–1547 – Drama.   I. Margeson,
J. M. R.   II. Title.   III. Series: Shakespeare, William, 1564–1616.
Works.   1984.   Cambridge University Press.
PR2817.A2M27   1989   822.3'3 – dc19   89-503   CIP

ISBN 0 521 22876 x   hard covers
ISBN 0 521 29692 7   paperback

# THE NEW CAMBRIDGE SHAKESPEARE

The *New Cambridge Shakespeare* succeeds *The New Shakespeare* which began publication in 1921 under the general editorship of Sir Arthur Quiller-Couch and John Dover Wilson, and was completed in the 1960s, with the assistance of G. I. Duthie, Alice Walker, Peter Ure and J. C. Maxwell. *The New Shakespeare* itself followed upon *The Cambridge Shakespeare*, 1863–6, edited by W. G. Clark, J. Glover and W. A. Wright.

*The New Shakespeare* won high esteem both for its scholarship and for its design, but shifts of critical taste and insight, recent Shakespearean research, and a changing sense of what is important in our understanding of the plays, have made it necessary to re-edit and redesign, not merely to revise, the series.

The *New Cambridge Shakespeare* aims to be of value to a new generation of playgoers and readers who wish to enjoy fuller access to Shakespeare's poetic and dramatic art. While offering ample academic guidance, it reflects current critical interests and is more attentive than some earlier editions have been to the realisation of the plays on the stage, and to their social and cultural settings. The text of each play has been freshly edited, with textual data made available to those users who wish to know why and how one published text differs from another. Although modernised, the edition conserves forms that appear to be expressive and characteristically Shakespearean, and it does not attempt to disguise the fact that the plays were written in a language other than that of our own time.

Illustrations are usually integrated into the critical and historical discussion of the play and include some reconstructions of early performances by C. Walter Hodges. Some editors have also made use of the advice and experience of Maurice Daniels, for many years a member of the Royal Shakespeare Company.

Each volume is addressed to the needs and problems of a particular text, and each therefore differs in style and emphasis from others in the series.

PHILIP BROCKBANK
*General Editor*

# CONTENTS

# ILLUSTRATIONS

Illustrations 1, 3, 4 and 5 are reproduced by permission of the Hulton Picture Library; illustrations 2, 9, 10 and 11 by permission of the Syndics of Cambridge University Library; illustrations 12, 13, 14 and 15 by permission of the

Shakespeare Centre Library, Stratford-upon-Avon; illustration 16 by courtesy of Angus McBean and the Shakespeare Centre Library, and illustration 17 by permission of Dominic Photography.

# PREFACE

Like any editor of a play of Shakespeare's, I am indebted to the rich treasure-house of previous scholarship and criticism, where gold can be found, as well as a little dross. I owe much to recent editors of *Henry VIII*, particularly to R. A. Foakes, and to J. C. Maxwell who did not like the play but whose scholarship is evident in every note. The editions by David Hoeniger and A. R. Humphreys have been valuable to me, and also an unpublished dissertation by Margaret Swayze on the stage history and critical reception of the play over several centuries.

I am obliged to Dr Maija Jansson and to the editors of *Shakespeare Quarterly* for permission to quote the previously unknown letter of Henry Bluett about the fire at the Globe theatre in 1613. Former colleagues and friends in the University of Toronto have encouraged me with comments and criticism; I am grateful also for the practical assistance given me by the Research Board of the University. Dr Levi Fox and his staff at the Shakespeare Centre Library in Stratford-upon-Avon have given me their time and assistance during visits and by correspondence. At the Cambridge University Press, Paul Chipchase has used his sharp eye and extensive knowledge of the plays to warn me of inconsistencies and possible errors.

A lively correspondence with C. Walter Hodges in relation to the Jacobean staging of the play has proved illuminating on several important issues. Beyond any other, I am grateful to Philip Brockbank for his encouragement and for his often disconcerting and stimulating observations.

J. M.

# ABBREVIATIONS AND CONVENTIONS

Shakespeare's plays, when cited in this edition, are abbreviated in a style modified slightly from that used in the *Harvard Concordance to Shakespeare*. Other editions of Shakespeare are abbreviated under the editor's surname (Foakes, Hoeniger) unless they are the work of more than one editor. In such cases, an abbreviated series name is used (Cam., Var. 1773). When more than one edition by the same editor is cited, later editions are discriminated with a raised figure (Rowe[3]). All quotations from Shakespeare, except those from *King Henry VIII*, use the lineation of *The Riverside Shakespeare*, under the general editorship of G. Blakemore Evans.

## 1. Shakespeare's plays

| | |
|---|---|
| *Ado* | *Much Ado About Nothing* |
| *Ant.* | *Antony and Cleopatra* |
| *AWW* | *All's Well That Ends Well* |
| *AYLI* | *As You Like It* |
| *Cor.* | *Coriolanus* |
| *Cym.* | *Cymbeline* |
| *Err.* | *The Comedy of Errors* |
| *Ham.* | *Hamlet* |
| *1H4* | *The First Part of King Henry the Fourth* |
| *2H4* | *The Second Part of King Henry the Fourth* |
| *H5* | *King Henry the Fifth* |
| *1H6* | *The First Part of King Henry the Sixth* |
| *2H6* | *The Second Part of King Henry the Sixth* |
| *3H6* | *The Third Part of King Henry the Sixth* |
| *H8* | *King Henry the Eighth* |
| *JC* | *Julius Caesar* |
| *John* | *King John* |
| *LLL* | *Love's Labour's Lost* |
| *Lear* | *King Lear* |
| *Mac.* | *Macbeth* |
| *MM* | *Measure for Measure* |
| *MND* | *A Midsummer Night's Dream* |
| *MV* | *The Merchant of Venice* |
| *Oth.* | *Othello* |
| *Per.* | *Pericles* |
| *R2* | *King Richard the Second* |
| *R3* | *King Richard the Third* |
| *Rom.* | *Romeo and Juliet* |
| *Shr.* | *The Taming of the Shrew* |
| *STM* | *Sir Thomas More* |
| *Temp.* | *The Tempest* |
| *TGV* | *The Two Gentlemen of Verona* |

| | |
|---|---|
| *Tim.* | *Timon of Athens* |
| *Tit.* | *Titus Andronicus* |
| *TN* | *Twelfth Night* |
| *TNK* | *The Two Noble Kinsmen* |
| *Tro.* | *Troilus and Cressida* |
| *Wiv.* | *The Merry Wives of Windsor* |
| *WT* | *The Winter's Tale* |

## 2. Other works cited and general references

| | |
|---|---|
| Abbott | E. A. Abbott, *A Shakespearian Grammar*, 1869 (references are to numbered paragraphs) |
| Cam. | *The Works of William Shakespeare*, ed. W. G. Clark and J. Glover, 9 vols., 1863–6 (Cambridge Shakespeare) |
| Capell | *Mr William Shakespeare, His Comedies, Histories, and Tragedies*, ed. Edward Capell, 1767–8 |
| Chambers, *ES* | E. K. Chambers, *The Elizabethan Stage*, 4 vols., 1923 |
| Collier | *The Works of William Shakespeare*, ed. J. Payne Collier, 1842–4 |
| conj. | conjecture |
| Dyce | *The Works of William Shakespeare*, ed. Alexander Dyce, 1857 |
| *ELH* | *ELH: A Journal of English Literary History* |
| F | *Mr William Shakespeares Comedies, Histories, and Tragedies*, 1623 (First Folio) |
| F2 | *Mr William Shakespeares Comedies, Histories, and Tragedies*, 1632 (Second Folio) |
| F3 | *Mr William Shakespeares Comedies, Histories, and Tragedies*, 1664 (Third Folio) |
| F4 | *Mr William Shakespeares Comedies, Histories, and Tragedies*, 1685 (Fourth Folio) |
| Foakes | *King Henry VIII*, ed. R. A. Foakes, 1957, 1964 (Arden Shakespeare) |
| Foxe, *Acts* | John Foxe, *The Acts and Monuments of Martyrs*, 2 vols., 1596 |
| Halle | *Henry VIII by Edward Hall*, ed. C. Whibley, 2 vols., 1904 (from Edward Halle, *The Union of the Two Noble...Families of Lancaster and York*, 1550) |
| Hanmer | *The Works of Shakespear*, ed. Thomas Hanmer, 1743–4 |
| Hinman | Charlton Hinman, *The Printing and Proof-Reading of the First Folio of Shakespeare*, 2 vols., 1963 |
| Hoeniger | *The Life of King Henry the Eighth*, ed. F. David Hoeniger, 1966 (Pelican Shakespeare) |
| Holinshed | Raphael Holinshed, *The Chronicles of England*, 1587 |
| Hoy, 1962 | Cyrus Hoy, 'The shares of Fletcher and his collaborators in the Beaumont and Fletcher canon VII', *SB* 15 (1962), 71–90 |
| Humphreys | *King Henry the Eighth*, ed. A. R. Humphreys, 1971 (New Penguin Shakespeare) |
| Johnson | *The Plays of William Shakespeare*, ed. Samuel Johnson, 1765 |
| Kittredge | *The Complete Works of Shakespeare*, ed. G. L. Kittredge, 1936 |
| Malone | *The Plays and Poems of William Shakespeare*, ed. Edmond Malone, 1790 |
| Maxwell | *King Henry the Eighth*, ed. J. C. Maxwell, 1962 (New Shakespeare) |
| Maxwell, Baldwin | Baldwin Maxwell, 'Fletcher and Shakespeare', in *Studies in Beaumont, Fletcher, and Massinger*, 1939 |

| | |
|---|---|
| *N&Q* | *Notes and Queries* |
| *OED* | *Oxford English Dictionary* |
| Onions | C. T. Onions, *A Shakespeare Glossary*, 1911, 1982 |
| *PBA* | *Proceedings of the British Academy* |
| *PMLA* | *Publications of the Modern Language Association of America* |
| Pooler | *The Famous History of the Life of King Henry VIII*, ed. C. K. Pooler, 1915, 1936 (Arden Shakespeare) |
| Pope | *The Works of Shakespear*, ed. Alexander Pope, 1723–5 |
| Rann | *The Dramatic Works of Shakespeare*, ed. Joseph Rann, 1786–94 |
| Rowe | *The Works of Mr William Shakespear*, ed. Nicholas Rowe, 1709 |
| Rowe[3] | *The Works of Mr William Shakespear*, ed. Nicholas Rowe, 3rd edn, 1714 |
| *SB* | *Studies in Bibliography* |
| SD | stage direction |
| SH | speech heading |
| Sisson | C. J. Sisson, *New Readings in Shakespeare*, 1956 |
| *SP* | *Studies in Philology* |
| *SQ* | *Shakespeare Quarterly* |
| *S.Sur.* | *Shakespeare Survey* |
| Theobald | *The Works of Shakespeare*, ed. Lewis Theobald, 1733 |
| Tilley | M. P. Tilley, *A Dictionary of the Proverbs in England in the Sixteenth and Seventeenth Centuries*, 1959 (references are to numbered proverbs) |
| *TLS* | *Times Literary Supplement* |
| Var. 1773 | *The Plays of William Shakespeare*, ed. Samuel Johnson and George Steevens, 1773 |
| Var. 1778 | *The Plays of William Shakespeare*, ed. Samuel Johnson and George Steevens, 2nd edn, 1778 |
| Vaughan | H. H. Vaughan, *New Readings and New Renderings of Shakespeare's Tragedies*, 1886 |
| Walker | W. S. Walker, *A Critical Examination of the Text of Shakespeare*, 3 vols., 1860 |
| Warburton | *The Works of Shakespear*, ed. William Warburton, 1747 |
| Wright | *The Works of William Shakespeare*, ed. William Aldis Wright, 1891–3 (Clarendon Shakespeare) |

Quotations from the Bible are taken from the Geneva version, 1560.

# INTRODUCTION

## Date and occasion

*King Henry VIII* will always be linked with the burning down of the first Globe theatre on 29 June 1613. As Sir Henry Wotton and several others of the time remark, it was during a performance of this play that the fire took place. Wotton's letter to Sir Edmund Bacon, written on 2 July 1613, is the fullest and best known account:

Now, to let matters of state sleep, I will entertain you at the present with what hath happened this week at the Bank's side. The King's players had a new play, called *All is true*, representing some principal pieces of the reign of Henry VIII, which was set forth with many extraordinary circumstances of pomp and majesty, even to the matting of the stage; the Knights of the Order, with their Georges and garters, the Guards with their embroidered coats, and the like: sufficient in truth within a while to make greatness very familiar, if not ridiculous. Now, King Henry making a masque at the Cardinal Wolsey's house, and certain chambers being shot off at his entry, some of the paper, or other stuff, wherewith one of them was stopped, did light on the thatch, where being thought at first but an idle smoke, and their eyes more attentive to the show, it kindled inwardly, and ran round like a train, consuming within less than an hour the whole house to the very grounds.

This was the fatal period of that virtuous fabric; wherein yet nothing did perish but wood and straw, and a few forsaken cloaks; only one man had his breeches set on fire, that would perhaps have broiled him, if he had not by the benefit of a provident wit put it out with bottle ale.[1]

Thomas Lorkin, writing on 30 June, speaks of the play as 'the play of Hen:8' and again notes the cause of the fire as 'shooting of certayne chambers in way of triumph'.[2]

Wotton calls it 'a new play', a phrase commonly used at the time to indicate a first performance, but he may have meant to describe a relatively new play, still attracting a lot of attention. This interpretation is borne out by a letter discovered by M. J. Cole and published in *Shakespeare Quarterly*.[3] It was written on 4 July 1613 by Henry Bluett, whom Cole describes as a young merchant in London, to Mr Richard Weeks:

On Tuesday last [29 June 1613] there was acted at the Globe a new play called *All is Triewe*, which had been acted not passing 2 or 3 times before. There came many people to see it insomuch that the house was very full, and as the play was almost ended the house was fired with shooting off a chamber which was stopped with towe which was blown up into the thatch of the house and so burned down to the ground. But the people escaped all without

---

[1] L. Pearsall Smith (ed.), *The Life and Letters of Sir Henry Wotton*, 2 vols., 1907, II, 32–3.
[2] Thomas Lorkin, in BL Harl. MS. 7002 f. 268 (quoted Pooler, p. vii).
[3] *SQ* 32 (1981), p. 352.

I

1　Portrait of Henry VIII by an unknown artist, probably painted about 1511. It shows him aged 20, the young king admired by More and Erasmus. He had married Katherine of Aragon two years before

hurt except one man who was scalded with the fire by adventuring in to save a child which otherwise had been burnt.

Again the play is called *All is True*, and it is described as one 'which had been acted not passing 2 or 3 times before', an important point which ought to settle the question of its 'newness'.[1] We learn that the play was popular, the house being crowded, and Wotton's account of the cause of the fire is confirmed by Bluett. The interesting difference is that Bluett remarks that the 'shooting off a chamber' happened 'as the play was almost ended', whereas Wotton gives a strong indication that it occurred near the end of the first act: 'King Henry making a masque at the Cardinal Wolseys house, and certain chambers being shot off at his entry'. There is no way of reconciling these two statements. Bluett adds one small dramatic incident that is in contrast with Wotton's light-hearted account of the man who 'had his breeches set on fire', though of course they may be writing about the same man, Bluett explaining why the man had ventured in. It is worth noting the presence of children in the audience – at least, of one child.

It seems certain from these letters that while the play was indeed new, the occasion of the fire may have been the third or fourth performance. Records indicate that new plays were rarely given a number of performances on successive days but that they were presented at intervals of several days or a week. One other question which may or may not have something to do with its date is its relationship to Samuel Rowley's *When You See Me You Know Me*, a romantic chronicle play of the old-fashioned kind, which shows Henry as a popular hero, disregards chronology, is often fiercely anti-papist, and spends much time on the antics of two fools, Patch and Will Summers. The Prologue to *Henry VIII* stresses the play's truth to history and points out that the audience will be disappointed if they have 'come to hear a merry bawdy play' or 'to see a fellow / In a long motley coat guarded with yellow'. Rowley's play was first acted in 1604 at Easter and printed in 1605 and 1613, but, as Foakes points out, was probably revived on the stage in 1613.[2]

Many scholars from Spedding onward have linked the play with the celebrations for the marriage on 14 February 1613 between Princess Elizabeth and one of the notable champions of Protestantism in Germany, Prince Frederick, the Elector Palatine. Court records show that a number of plays, six by Shakespeare, were called for from the King's Men during the festivities at court, but *Henry VIII* (or *All is True*) was not among them.[3] This does not vitiate the argument that Shakespeare and his company may have considered it as a play to be put forward with the others as a possible choice, or as a colourful show with topical overtones that would do well in the popular theatre during the same period or immediately after.

As Foakes has demonstrated, the wedding attracted special attention in the country because of the death of Prince Henry, the young and hopeful heir to the throne, in November 1612. After a period of mourning, there were large-scale

---

[1] See Foakes, p. xxix.
[2] *Ibid.*, p. xxix.
[3] E. K. Chambers, *William Shakespeare*, 1930, II, 343; Maxwell, p. x.

displays of pageantry and much festivity for the wedding in February, as if to make up for the great sorrow of the court and the nation over the young prince's death. Foakes adds that in the general atmosphere of suspicion of Spain and Catholic conspiracy that existed in 1613, there was a widespread hope, evident in many documents, that the marriage would bring about a strong alliance with the German Protestant princes, to England's advantage.[1] Much was made also by pamphleteers and poets of the identity between the names of the bride and the glorious queen of the recent past. Certainly the christening scene at the end of *Henry VIII* makes a strong dramatic point of the naming of the child Elizabeth by Archbishop Cranmer. As Foakes observes, 'A play on the downfall of Wolsey, the last great Catholic statesman of England, on the rise of Cranmer, and the birth of "that now triumphant Saint our late Queene *Elizabeth*" would have been very appropriate at such a time.'[2]

The play is not anti-papist in the way that Rowley's *When You See Me* is, but ultimately tolerant and reconciling in its portrayal of the falls of Wolsey and Katherine. It concludes with a visionary prophecy from Cranmer not only of the peace and security of Queen Elizabeth's reign, but also of the idealised hopes, still felt by some in 1613, for the reign of James I. These themes of the reconciling of the divisions of the past in the hopes of the future, in the birth of new generations which would undertake this task, and even of 'new nations', make the play appropriate to a marriage which was also an alliance and which revived hopes that had been lost at the time of Prince Henry's death.[3]

Most scholars, whether they agree with the link between *Henry VIII* and the wedding celebrations of February 1613, accept the long-held view that the play was written late in 1612 or early in 1613. The language of the play and its versification (so far as these are Shakespeare's) indicate the last stage of Shakespeare's career, the period of the late romances. Perhaps only *The Two Noble Kinsmen*, a collaboration with Fletcher, comes later, but that was not included in the Folio.

## Authorship

Heminges and Condell, the editors of the First Folio and actors in Shakespeare's company, the King's Men, printed *Henry VIII* as the final play in the long series of Shakespeare's history plays. No one doubted Shakespeare's authorship until the middle of the nineteenth century, though there had been questions asked about the Prologue and the Epilogue, and whether the section on King James in Cranmer's prophecy had not been added later to an Elizabethan play.[4] In 1850, however,

---

[1] Foakes, p. xxxi.

[2] *Ibid.*, p. xxxi. Tyrone Guthrie made effective use of this identity of names when he produced *Henry VIII* at the Old Vic at the time of Queen Elizabeth II's coronation in 1953.

[3] Bernard Harris, 'What's past is prologue: *Cymbeline* and *Henry VIII*', in John Russell Brown and Bernard Harris (eds.), *Later Shakespeare*, 1966, p. 232; Frances Yates, *Shakespeare's Last Plays: A New Approach*, 1975, p. 67.

[4] See Maxwell, pp. xii–xiii.

James Spedding announced his dissatisfaction with the idea that Shakespeare had written the whole of *Henry VIII* and suggested that he must have had a collaborator, probably John Fletcher. About the same time, Samuel Hickson revealed that he had independently come to the same conclusion, and that his division of the play between collaborators was almost identical with that of Spedding.[1]

Spedding claimed that the design of the play was not worthy of Shakespeare's craftsmanship; he also said that he had become aware of two distinct styles in the play, in part through a suggestion from Tennyson:

> The resemblance of the style, in some parts of the play, to Fletcher's, was pointed out to me several years ago by Alfred Tennyson...and long before that, the general distinctions between Shakespeare's manner and Fletcher's had been admirably explained by Charles Lamb in his note on the Two Noble Kinsmen, and by Mr Spalding in his Essay.[2]

One style, he claimed, was syntactically difficult and charged with images, full of vigour and freshness, the other easy, familiar, 'diffuse and languid'. He then devised metrical tests based on the occurrence of feminine and masculine endings, the use of an extra accented syllable at the end of a line, and the number of run-on lines and end-stopped lines, all of which proved conclusively, in his view, that there were two distinct kinds of prosody in the play, one Shakespeare's and the other most probably Fletcher's. He divided the play between the two on this basis, scene by scene, with the following result:

| Shakespeare: | 1.1 and 1.2 | Fletcher: | Prologue and Epilogue |
|---|---|---|---|
| | 2.3 and 2.4 | | 1.3 and 1.4 |
| | 3.2.1–203 | | 2.1 and 2.2 |
| | 5.1 | | 3.1 and 3.2.204–459 |
| | | | 4.1 and 4.2 |
| | | | 5.2, 5.3 and 5.4 |

This division gives Fletcher over two-thirds of the play on the basis of the number of lines; it is also assumed that each author was responsible for complete scenes, with the single exception of 3.2. The table is worth quoting because it has been accepted by many editors and scholars since Spedding's time, although the evidence for dual authorship is now largely of a different kind from Spedding's and various modifications have been made in the traditional division.

The evidence for Fletcher's hand in the play (or the hand of any other playwright of the time) is entirely internal since there is no external evidence of any kind pointing to his contribution. The external evidence that does exist seems to show Shakespeare's authorship clearly. *Henry VIII* was included in the First Folio with Shakespeare's other plays, which are declared to be 'absolute in their numbers, as he conceived them'. The Folio editors, Heminges and Condell, would certainly have known, Peter Alexander observes, if Fletcher had written the major portion of

[1] James Spedding, 'Who wrote Shakespeare's *Henry VIII?*', *Gentleman's Magazine* (Aug. 1850), pp. 115–24; (Oct. 1850), pp. 381–2; Samuel Hickson, *N&Q* (24 Aug. 1850), p. 198, and subsequent issues.

[2] Spedding, *Gentleman's Magazine* (Oct. 1850), p. 382.

the play: they were managing the King's Men at the time of its composition and would have been responsible for paying him for his share.[1] *The Two Noble Kinsmen*, ascribed to Shakespeare and Fletcher on the title page of the 1634 quarto, was apparently close in date to *Henry VIII* but was not included by Heminges and Condell in the Folio.[2]

However, Spedding's hypothesis was widely accepted, as we have noted. His argument was cogently presented, and was supported by carefully worked-out metrical data from particular scenes. Spedding disliked the play, finding that it lacked a clear moral design, and did not believe that Shakespeare could have written the whole of it at the end of his career, even though he recognised that certain scenes showed the master's hand. Following Spedding, Farnham and Thorndike began to study the linguistic data which seemed to strengthen the case he had put forward.[3]

Early scepticism about the theory found supporters in Baldwin Maxwell, Peter Alexander and G. Wilson Knight. Maxwell in his essay 'Fletcher and Shakespeare' (1923) doubted if the scenes assigned to Fletcher were entirely his.[4] He gave examples of his own tests – for instance, the immediate repetition of single words or of words with a modifying phrase, where the Fletcher scenes of *Henry VIII* showed far fewer examples than scenes from Fletcher's known works. He also laid much stress on the use of sources. The scenes assigned to Fletcher make as close a verbal use of Holinshed as the scenes given to Shakespeare, but in *Bonduca*, Fletcher's only historical play, there is no verbal borrowing whatever from Holinshed or Tacitus, its obvious sources. This argument was to be repeated and developed further by Geoffrey Bullough and R. A. Foakes.

Peter Alexander argued strongly in his 'Conjectural history, or Shakespeare's *Henry VIII*' (1930) against the manipulation of evidence by those who wished to make conjectures about the authorship and provenance of literary works, and used *Henry VIII* as an example. He pointed out that the differences of style in the play have an important dramatic function in relation to widely differing speeches and situations, and yet these very differences are made the basis for disintegration.[5] In a careful analysis of Spedding's evidence, he showed how the so-called peculiarities of style in the scenes given to Fletcher can be paralleled in Shakespeare's late plays in varying proportions from play to play. Spedding, he claimed, never considers how metrical variations arise in the development of Shakespeare's verse. Alexander also gave considerable weight to the external evidence pointing to Shake-

[1] Peter Alexander, 'Conjectural history, or Shakespeare's *Henry VIII*', *Essays and Studies* 16 (1930), 118.

[2] *Cardenio*, a lost play, was entered under Shakespeare's and Fletcher's names in the Stationers' Register, 9 September 1653, by Humphrey Moseley (Chambers, *Shakespeare*, I, 538). Moseley is not highly regarded for the accuracy of his ascriptions (Baldwin Maxwell, p. 57).

[3] W. E. Farnham, 'Colloquial contractions in Beaumont, Fletcher, Massinger and Shakespeare as a test of authorship', *PMLA* 31 (1916), 326–58; A. H. Thorndike, *The Influence of Beaumont and Fletcher on Shakspere*, 1901.

[4] Baldwin Maxwell, p. 17.

[5] Alexander, 'Conjectural history', pp. 110–11.

speare, and saw in the play themes and attitudes characteristic of Shakespeare.

Wilson Knight in *Principles of Shakespearean Production* (1936) and particularly in *The Crown of Life* (1948) stressed the unity of the play and its special relationship with Shakespeare's last plays. Like Alexander, Knight saw the different styles in the play as deliberate variations for dramatic purposes which he found paralleled in other of Shakespeare's plays.[1] His analysis of structure is closely related to his analysis of central themes, themes which he found elsewhere in Shakespeare but nowhere in Fletcher.

Although the kind of evidence presented by Spedding was cast seriously in doubt by Alexander and other critics, many scholars continued to believe that the play was not solely by Shakespeare and were assiduous in collecting other evidence, stylistic and linguistic, of a more convincing kind. The most persuasive of these, in terms of the evidence presented, have been A. C. Partridge (1949, 1964) and Cyrus Hoy (1962).[2] Partridge uses the Spedding division of the play as a basis for comparison and points to characteristic linguistic habits of the two authors. In particular, he cites the use of the auxiliary verb 'do' as a mere expletive and the common use of 'hath' in the Shakespearean scenes, whereas Fletcher avoids 'do' and prefers 'has' to 'hath'. Partridge also stresses Shakespeare's use of 'you' where Fletcher uses 'ye', and Shakespeare's preference for 'them' as against Fletcher's use of the clipped form ''em'. Partridge notes differences between the often tortured syntax in the Shakespearean scenes and the more orderly syntax of the passages assigned to Fletcher. However, he is inclined to give more of the play to Shakespeare than Spedding and Hickson had done in Acts 3 to 5; for example, he gives 4.2 to Shakespeare, and also Cranmer's final speech in 5.5 (5.4 in this edition).[3] He speculates that Shakespeare had left an unfinished play with his company on his retirement which Fletcher was asked to complete when it was required for production, a theory which he believes is better than the less probable theory of 'simultaneous collaboration'.[4]

Cyrus Hoy's work on the play is firmly based on a thorough linguistic study of all of Fletcher's non-collaborative plays and of Shakespeare's later plays. Hoy observes that the linguistic practices of authors involve questions about the nature of the manuscript behind the printed text, the possibility of scribal interference where the copy for the printer is not the author's foul papers, and the habits of the compositors of the printed text where these are known.[5] He finds that the linguistic practices of Shakespeare and Fletcher are often similar, but that the most noteworthy differences occur in their use of 'hath' and 'has', 'you' and 'ye', and 'them' and ''em'. Hoy and Partridge agree on these usages, but Hoy's work is based on a larger body of evidence.

[1] G. Wilson Knight, *The Crown of Life*, 1948, p. 263.
[2] A. C. Partridge, *The Problem of Henry VIII Re-Opened*, 1949; *Orthography in Shakespeare and Elizabethan Drama*, 1964. Cyrus Hoy, 'The shares of Fletcher and his collaborators in the Beaumont and Fletcher canon', *SB* 8 (1956), 129–46; *SB* 15 (1962), 71–90.
[3] Partridge, *Orthography*, p. 161.
[4] *Ibid.*, p. 162.
[5] Hoy, 1962, p. 73.

Hoy also observes, on the basis of Foakes's and Hinman's studies of the compositors' work on the text, that Compositor B, who set rather less than half the play, is known to be inclined to alter 'ye' to 'you', so that there may be fewer 'ye's than one might expect in a scene ascribed to Fletcher.

From his study of linguistic preferences by the two authors, Hoy supports some of the traditional ascriptions and alters others. Thus he thinks that 1.3 and 1.4 are probably Fletcher's because of the frequent use of "em' even though there is no clear evidence from 'ye' and 'you'. However, he gives 2.1 and 2.2 to Shakespeare because the 'ye's occur grouped in clusters of two or three lines, as if a few lines here and there were interpolated or rewritten by Fletcher. Act 3, Scene 1 presents, he thinks, the clearest evidence of Fletcher's hand, but 3.2 is probably entirely Shakespeare's because again the 'ye's occur in a cluster. The same argument applies to both scenes of Act 4, which Hoy assigns to Shakespeare. In Act 5, Hoy agrees that Scene 1 is Shakespeare's, but is inclined to think that Scenes 2 to 4 are Fletcher's because of the general spread of 'ye's throughout each scene, although he does note a majority of 'you's in 5.2 and 5.3. Since Compositor X, who is not known to prefer one form to the other, set this act, no argument can be based on the compositor.

In sum, Hoy would tentatively ascribe to Shakespeare ten of the sixteen scenes (or 1,848 lines) and six to Fletcher (736 lines), thus reducing Fletcher's share of the play from over two-thirds in the traditional division to less than one-third. He also appends some non-linguistic evidence, pointing out that there are clear signs of Fletcher's modes of syntax and rhetorical habits in the six scenes which linguistic evidence shows are probably his. He believes that 'the truth about Fletcher's share in *Henry VIII* is to be found where truth generally is: midway between the extreme views that have traditionally been held regarding it'.[1] Hoy does not develop a theory of how collaboration may have worked, beyond the suggestion that Fletcher touched up certain of Shakespeare's scenes and added a few more of his own.

Non-linguistic tests for authorship based on style, structure, characterisation and the use of imagery have tended to cancel one another out because of their widely differing conclusions and their apparently subjective nature. Probably the most objective of these tests involves a comparison of the handling of sources by Shakespeare and Fletcher, though here too there are differences of opinion. A comparison is difficult since Fletcher wrote only one history play, *Bonduca*. As already mentioned, Baldwin Maxwell has shown that there is no verbal borrowing in *Bonduca* from its sources in Holinshed and Tacitus, but close borrowing from Holinshed and Foxe occurs throughout *Henry VIII* in the Shakespearean manner. Maxwell's conclusion is that 'a comparison of *Henry VIII* with its sources argues strongly against Fletcher's participation'.[2] However, R. A. Law argues

---

[1] *Ibid.*, p. 79. In a 1962 'Postscript' to his edition of the play, R. A. Foakes, who had argued on a variety of grounds for the likelihood of Shakespeare's sole authorship, accepts the importance of Hoy's evidence and quotes Hoy's measured conclusion.

[2] Baldwin Maxwell, p. 58.

2  Henry VIII making Pope Clement his footstool: an engraved frontispiece from John Foxe's *Acts and
Monuments* (1583), which gives the popular Protestant view of Henry's triumph over Pope Clement.
The king receives the Word of God from Cranmer, while papal representatives recoil in horror

for Fletcher's share, noting that there are distinct differences in the handling of
source material in the scenes ascribed to the two supposed authors. Law maintains
that Shakespeare modifies his source material to clarify motivation, strengthen
characterisation and increase dramatic power, whereas Fletcher uses the sources
in a pedestrian way, without development of character or other signs of dramatic
imagination.[1]

[1]  R. A. Law, 'The double authorship of *Henry VIII*', *SP* 56 (1959), 486–7.

In the view of R. A. Foakes, there is much evidence in *Henry VIII* of a close reading of Holinshed and Foxe, often of material in widely separated sections of the chronicles which is then used in a single scene. This evidence of close reading, the compression of chronology for dramatic purpose, and the reshaping of material to bring out aspects of character are all in keeping with what we know of Shakespeare's practice and not typical of Fletcher. In any theory of collaboration, Foakes observes, 'it would have to be assumed that each author read independently not merely the sections in the histories relevant to the scenes he wrote, but all the material on the reign of Henry'.[1] Bullough reaches a very similar conclusion in his study of the sources of the play.[2]

The argument of Spedding and some of his followers that metrical analysis could differentiate between two distinct styles in the play has been largely discounted. The argument from style is on stronger ground when it is concerned with syntax and rhetorical practice. Like Spedding, A. C. Partridge compares the 'difficult syntactical progression of Shakespeare' in the early scenes with the 'clarity of Fletcher' in certain later scenes[3] and claims that Shakespeare neglects grammatical relationships for the sake of ideas and images: 'Few dramatists, except Shakespeare, could have drafted such structurally entangled accounts of events.'[4] However, after a number of examples, Partridge admits the possibility that complications of syntax may be the result of heightened feeling in particular scenes. Hoy likewise finds indications of Fletcher's syntactical and rhetorical habits in the scenes where there is clear evidence of his linguistic preferences. He gives a number of examples of Fletcher's favourite line structures, the use of repetition with different modifiers ('O very mad, exceeding mad, in love too', 1.4.28), the use of a second subject after the verb, and what he calls 'rhetorical cascades'.[5]

Other scholars have claimed that the different styles apparent in the play are functional and dramatically appropriate to the scenes where they are used. Alexander argues that the play would have been 'intolerably monotonous' had it been written throughout in the manner of Buckingham's farewell,[6] and Wilson Knight recognises three major variations in the style of the play, each with a particular dramatic function.[7] Northrop Frye points out that the low-keyed quality of the writing in much of the play is appropriate to its nature as pageant, that 'obtrusively magnificent poetry in the text accompanying such spectacle' would violate decorum.[8]

The division of critical opinion is as marked with respect to structure as it is over the question of style. Most of those critics who find serious faults in the play's

---

[1] Foakes, p. xxiii.

[2] Geoffrey Bullough, *Narrative and Dramatic Sources of Shakespeare*, IV (1962), 449.

[3] Partridge, *Orthography*, p. 147.

[4] *Ibid.*, p. 158.

[5] Hoy, 1962, pp. 82–4.

[6] Alexander, 'Conjectural history', pp. 110–11.

[7] Knight, *Crown of Life*, p. 261.

[8] Northrop Frye, 'Romance as masque', in C. McG. Kay and H. E. Jacobs (eds.), *Shakespeare's Romances Reconsidered*, 1978, p. 31.

structure blame dual authorship and a lack of close collaboration between Fletcher and Shakespeare: a play by one author finished in haste by another, Spedding conjectured; a badly organised general plan deriving from Fletcher, according to Pooler;[1] a complete lack of cohesion between the parts in the view of J. C. Maxwell and R. A. Law.[2] Yet Hardin Craig and Wilson Knight find clear signs in *Henry VIII* of the traditional patterns of Shakespeare's histories. Other scholars like R. A. Foakes and Frances Yates see unity of design in the play deriving from major thematic concerns, as in Shakespeare's romances.

There have been few or none who have argued that there are any structural resemblances between *Henry VIII* and Fletcher's undoubted plays. *Bonduca* would seem to be a likely candidate, yet it proves on examination to have little in common with *Henry VIII*. In *Bonduca* there is very little dramatic preparation for subsequent action; in *Henry VIII* every major action is planned or forecast or rumoured beforehand. *Bonduca* provides little in the way of linkage between scene and scene, whereas *Henry VIII* uses many traditional devices for the purpose, and a new one – anonymous gossiping gentlemen (whom we also meet in *The Winter's Tale*). The multiple plot of *Bonduca* arises from three threads of action – the heroic plot, the love plot, and the comic underplot – which alternate on the stage but have only accidental relationships with one another. Yet every action in *Henry VIII*, even the comic scene of the porter and his man (5.3), bears some relation to the central themes of the play. The most difficult aspect of the structure to justify is the final act where Wolsey and Katherine are no longer part of the action and where Cranmer takes Wolsey's place, somewhat inadequately, at centre stage with Henry. It seems at this point that thematic material (the partnership of church and state, the succession, the future of England) has become dominant and that the momentum and suspense involved in a character's reaction to events have become subordinate. Nevertheless, the characteristic use of parallel situations, contrasts of character and attitude, cross-reference and linkage with what has gone before (almost completely absent in *Bonduca*) are as important in the fifth act as they are earlier in the play.

Discussions of the style and dramatic craftsmaship of *Henry VIII* have obviously not resulted in any widely accepted conclusions; only linguistic criteria seem to have much importance in the continuing debate about the authorship of the play. Much recent criticism has left the question of authorship behind as something unlikely to be resolved and has concentrated on other matters such as the masque-like qualities of the play, its use of music, dance and spectacle.[3] The ironies of the play, by no means a strong point in elaborate eighteenth- and nineteenth-century productions, have also been noted and analysed.[4] There is an awareness in recent criticism of the dramatic integrity of *Henry VIII* rather than a desire to emphasise its dramatic faults and moral incoherence and then to explain them by a theory of

[1] Pooler, p. xxiii.
[2] Maxwell, p. xxxii; Law, 'The double authorship', p. 486.
[3] J. D. Cox, '*Henry VIII* and the masque', *ELH* 45 (1978), 390–409.
[4] Clifford Leech, *William Shakespeare, the Chronicles*, 1962, pp. 38–9.

3 Katherine of Aragon, Henry's queen from 1509 till 1531. The portrait is a formal one but suggests Katherine's strength of character

dual authorship. The varied interpretations of a number of recent staged presentations have demonstrated the potentialities that lie within its text so that it now appears less of an exception in the canon of Shakespeare's histories, tragedies and ironic comedies.[1]

If there was collaboration between Shakespeare and Fletcher, how did it work? Schoenbaum warns us that there is no general rule governing collaboration by Elizabethan playwrights: there were many reasons for collaboration and many different ways of going about it.[2] The problem seemed easy enough for Spedding: on the basis of his sense of disparate styles, he assigned whole scenes to one author or the other, and only one scene is divided, at a distinct point, between the two. He speculated that Shakespeare had conceived the idea of a much larger historical play on the reign of Henry VIII but had never completed it, and that Fletcher had filled out the small germ of a play left by Shakespeare, working hurriedly for the special occasion of Princess Elizabeth's wedding. But of course, as J. C. Maxwell has pointed out, there is no evidence at all either for the larger scheme of the play or for a hurried completion by Fletcher for a special occasion.[3]

Partridge also indulges in speculation, though in a less radical form. He suggests that Shakespeare blocked out the original play but left it unfinished when he retired to Stratford. Fletcher then revised many of the already written scenes and completed the play, 'perhaps with his [Shakespeare's] acquiescence'.[4] Partridge thinks the idea of 'simultaneous collaboration' by the two playwrights unlikely, though J. C. Maxwell adheres to this as most probable.[5]

By the time we reach Hoy, the picture has changed. Hoy's tentative division gives Shakespeare two-thirds of the play, by far the major part of it in terms of its dramatic form. Fletcher, he suggests, is responsible only for the light scenes of diversion with the masque at York Place (1.3 and 1.4), the domestic scene of Katherine with her women interrupted by the cardinals (3.1), the trial scene of Cranmer (5.2), and the two final scenes of the christening celebrations (5.3 and 5.4). He is doubtful about 1.3 and 1.4 because of the lack of clear 'ye–you' evidence, but finds some other evidence which suggests Fletcher's hand. As for collaboration, Hoy thinks that Fletcher worked on a few of the scenes on his own and that, in other scenes previously attributed to him, he did 'little more than interpolate a handful of lines of his own, or touch up after his fashion occasional passages of the original author's'.[6] Wisely he does not attempt to build a speculative model of collaboration on this foundation.

Like Foakes, I think one must take Hoy's contribution to the debate as the most carefully worked out evidence to date as to the actual fact of Fletcher's participation and also to its extent. The narrative plot, characters, the major confrontations, the

[1] See pp. 52–9 below.
[2] Samuel Schoenbaum, *Internal Evidence and Elizabethan Dramatic Authorship*, 1966, p. 226.
[3] Maxwell, p. xxvi.
[4] Partridge, *Orthography*, p. 162.
[5] Maxwell, p. xxvii.
[6] Hoy, 1962, p. 81.

interplay of ideas and the over-all pattern of the play – the alternation of sorrow and joy, as the Gentlemen observe – are Shakespeare's. The authorship question is unlikely to be settled to everyone's satisfaction unless startling new external evidence is uncovered at some future date. It is encouraging, therefore, to find more critical attention being given to the play in its own right in the last two decades rather than to problems of collaboration.

## Sources

The sources of *Henry VIII* have long been known to be Holinshed's *Chronicles of England* (1587 edition) and John Foxe's *Acts and Monuments*, which was first published in 1563 but often reprinted. Holinshed provided most of the material for the first four acts, and Foxe for the fifth act, apart from the final christening scene which is again from Holinshed. The chroniclers write extensively about the reign of Henry VIII, giving full descriptions of ceremonies, trials and meetings, and providing summaries of the qualities of major characters. Often what was said on certain occasions is reported as direct speech. Shakespeare (and I use his name in the discussion that follows for whichever author may have been responsible for a particular scene) has kept very close to the chronicle material, perhaps, as Geoffrey Bullough suggests, to make *All is True* as true as possible in contrast with Rowley's *When You See Me*. Yet facts and incidents have sometimes been drawn from quite widely separated sections of these chronicles, and the language used by Shakespeare occasionally echoes a phrase from Halle's *The Union of the Two Noble...  Families* (1550) and possibly from Speed's *History of Great Britain* (1611), as Foakes believes.[1] Several scenes or portions of scenes in the play have no known source and should be considered largely the invention of the dramatist, such as Katherine's plea for the common people and her attack upon Wolsey in 1.2, the litany of complaints against Wolsey by several disaffected nobles at the beginning of 2.2, and the details of Katherine's vision in 4.2. Elsewhere, brief statements in Holinshed or Foxe are developed into dramatic situations, hints about character are enlarged or strengthened, and minor characters are introduced for specific purposes.

Bullough calls Rowley's play *When You See Me You Know Me* Shakespeare's point of departure and notes several resemblances between the two plays, referring also to earlier scholars like D. Nichol Smith (1899) and K. Elze who edited Rowley's play in 1874.[2] Recent editors of *Henry VIII* like Maxwell and Foakes have seen little of importance linking the two, but Bullough may be right in thinking of Rowley's play as a starting point. There had been earlier plays on Wolsey at the end of Elizabeth's reign such as *Cardinal Wolsey* and *The First Part of Cardinal Wolsey*, apparently written by Chettle, Munday, Drayton and Smith according to Henslowe's record of payments, but nothing is known about them

---

[1] Foakes points particularly to 1.1.97, 2.4.76–7, and 2.4.87 ff. as from Halle, and 3.2.222–7 and 3.2.358 ff. from Speed. See Foakes, p. xxxv.

[2] Bullough, *Sources*, IV, 449.

beyond the titles.[1] The Prologue to *Henry VIII* makes a great point of being very different from plays full of spectacle, bawdry and merry clowns: 'fool and fight', a description which fits well the hodge-podge of popular elements brought together in *When You See Me*. This play, by contrast, is to be serious and concerned with great characters brought low to 'misery'; at the same time, it will be true to history.

*Thomas Lord Cromwell* (quarto, 1602 and 1613) is another play that lurks in the background of *Henry VIII*. There is no evidence of direct borrowing from this romantic and rambling biography, comic and serious by turn, but since according to the first quarto it had been performed by Shakespeare's company, Shakespeare may have remembered, for example, the portrayal of Gardiner as a proud and envious man, determined to bring down his high-flying rival, Cromwell, who was also a heretic and despoiler of the abbeys. Not only is the plot against Cranmer suggested but also Wolsey's plot against Buckingham: Gardiner puts pressure on two of his followers to act as false witnesses against Cromwell and rehearses the dangerous evidence they are to give. When Norfolk hears their testimony, he warns them: 'My friends, take heed of that which you have said, / Your soules must answer what your tongues reports.' Norfolk is far from being another Queen Katherine, but the germ of her protest is here.

One other slight inheritance from *Thomas Lord Cromwell* may be the use of 'merchants' and 'citizens' to give some sense of public opinion in a wider sense; thus the two merchants comment on the enmity between Gardiner and Cromwell in 4.3 and two citizens discuss reports of Cromwell's arrest in 5.4. Shakespeare did not need such a precedent but it remains an interesting parallel in a play concerned with the same period of history.

The shows and pageants of *Henry VIII* come very largely from Holinshed. Holinshed in turn derives his material from Halle, to whom he sometimes refers the reader for greater detail (p. 873).[2] In both chronicles, the political purpose of these shows is usually obvious – the welcome for a visiting monarch like the Emperor Charles V, or the celebration of a new treaty or alliance like the Field of the Cloth of Gold. In the play, Norfolk's description of the ceremonies on this latter occasion makes plain its ostensible purpose, although subsequent dialogue with Buckingham reveals more subtle manoeuvring. The masque at York Place, as the play presents it, is pure entertainment, a masque in the Italian manner noted by Holinshed and Halle in which disguised masquers take the ladies of the court out to dance and in which the king often took part, disguised among the masquers.

The festivities for Anne's coronation in Act 4 are of a different nature. After the early years of Henry's reign, there is a considerable falling off of elaborate shows and pageants, so far as can be judged from the chronicles and Revels Accounts. However, Anne's coronation was a large exception. Holinshed describes the coronation rites in great detail as a succession of shows on the river, in the city, and at

[1] W. W. Greg (ed.), *Henslowe's Diary*, 2 vols., 1904–8, II, 218.
[2] This and subsequent page references are to the 1587 edition of Holinshed's *The Chronicles of England*.

ANNA · REGINA ·

4   Anne Boleyn, from an engraving after Holbein. The richness of her head-dress and jewels suggests her magnificence during her brief period as Henry's queen

court. The processions were designed to show the monarch or his consort to the people as part of the traditional ritual, and the play captures this civic involvement by using the three Gentlemen as observers of the procession. The last major show in the play, the christening of Elizabeth, is in Holinshed's description (pp. 934–5) a relatively private function at court, with only the lord mayor and aldermen present to represent the city. Shakespeare, however, has turned this occasion also into a popular festival.

Shakespeare's dramatisation of the chronicles' narrative is marked, as so often in the history plays, by a sharp eye for theatrical confrontations and opportunities to express lively or powerful emotion. The play shows also that Shakespeare is aware of latent possibilities within the chronicle material for ironic contrasts, from the most subtle to the most blatantly theatrical. In the first scene, for example, some of Buckingham's motives for detesting Wolsey's underhand dealings at home and abroad are revealed, not through description but in a passionate conversation between Buckingham, Norfolk and Abergavenny, a conversation interrupted by Wolsey passing over the stage with secretaries, page, and members of the guard. Though nothing is said, it is a moment of high tension between implacable enemies. In 1.2, the king has Buckingham's surveyor brought before him so that he can hear the treasonable information for himself, and he grows increasingly angry as he listens, in spite of Katherine's cautions and warnings. The passage in Holinshed is very different, since Henry merely reads the document that Wolsey brings him. Another more striking example of the transformation of narrative material occurs in 3.2 where the king plays with Wolsey ironically before giving him the damning evidence against him, rather than leaving it to the Dukes of Norfolk and Suffolk as in the chronicle. One further minor example is a significant one. Foxe describes how Cranmer was left outside the locked council chamber among pages and servingmen where he is seen by Dr Butts; Dr Butts then reports what he has seen to the king, but the king does not see for himself. In the play, Dr Butts brings Henry to the window above the scene without telling him beforehand so that Henry's surprise and immediate angry reaction have strong dramatic force.

Very marked shaping of the diffuse narrative material of the chronicles is evident in the way parallels and contrasts are drawn between the tragic falls of one group of characters from high place to wretchedness and the rise of others from lowly place to high favour. Thus Buckingham in the first scene is arrogant in his pride, sure of his ability to win the king's ear, but when he next appears, he is making an emotional speech on the way to the scaffold, standing between guards with halberds, on a stage that images his isolation. Wolsey likewise is revealed at the height of his power in a series of early scenes so that the dramatic impact of his fall in a single long scene (3.2) is greatly heightened. Instead of troops of sycophantic followers, at the end of the scene Wolsey has only one left. By concentrating the diverse material of the chronicles, the dramatist stresses the similarities between the falls of Buckingham and Wolsey, adds a third fall to the pattern, that of Katherine, which has its resonance in pathos rather than tragic irony, and counterpoints Katherine's isolation in her final illness with the thronging crowds and acclaim of Anne's coronation. All of these events, including the rise of Cranmer to the high position once enjoyed by Wolsey, are reported in the chronicles, but the distinct shaping of the material, the patterning of the action, is not.

If there are passages in the play where one chronicle or the other appears to be

THOMAS
WOLSEY
Cardinall,
Archbifhope
of Yorke, and
Chaunceloure
of England,
Died Nou:29
1529

Non fecus unda mari paulatim accrefcit et alta
Neptuni frontem fupereminet; at fua tandem
Vis ruit, et pelago labens deuoluitur imo,
Quam tua te VUOLSEDE tumens evexit honoris
Aura, et fublimen fuper—extulit ardua regis
Culmina, fed tandem conuerfo CARDINE rerum
In fcopulos, rigidasqg extrufa est gloria fyrtes.
Terra olim corpus, tumuit, iam corpore tellus.

5  Cardinal Wolsey, from a contemporary engraving. The Latin inscription concerns the transience of earthly glory

closely followed, as in the almost formal debate between Katherine and Griffith over Wolsey's faults and virtues (4.2), there are many others where brief statements in the chronicles are expanded and new material is introduced. Katherine's independence of mind and determination to defend herself are apparent in Holinshed's account, but such invented incidents as her championship of the oppressed taxpayers in 1.2 and her annoyance at the messenger's rudeness in 4.2 add strength and individuality to her portrait. There is no hint in Holinshed of the religious fervour of the vision scene in 4.2. It has been argued that the idea of the vision, if not the detailed substance of it, was derived by the dramatist from a funeral oration by Charles de Sainte Marthe for Margaret of Navarre, published in 1550, in which Margaret is said to have had such a dream before her death.[1] The dream was of 'une très-belle femme' who showed Margaret a crown of flowers with which she would be crowned after her death. Although there is a marked resemblance in the imagery of the two dreams, the main difficulty lies in determining how Shakespeare might have come across this relatively obscure work. The comforting aspect of Katherine's dream and its timing just before her death may have been suggested by Holinshed's account of the dream of Anne Bullen in which Morpheus appears in the guise of her grandfather to forewarn her of her death but to tell her also of the future happiness of England under Elizabeth, whose reign 'should be established in tranquillitie and peace' (p. 940).

Henry is not the moral or emotional centre of the play, but he is the centre of authority and the link between all the other characters, since his relationships with Buckingham, Katherine, Wolsey, Anne and Cranmer are crucial for each of them. The chronicles portray Henry as a strong and vigorous king, the king who in the end defied the papacy and determined England's future. Shakespeare has followed their account, adding to the portrait such human qualities as impulsiveness, a hot temper, and some of the mannerisms of speech and habit that Rowley had depicted in the folk-hero king of *When You See Me*. Henry's motivation with respect to the divorce is highly ambiguous in the play and has a distinct ironic tone. Holinshed states that the cardinal was widely blamed for arousing the scruple in Henry's conscience concerning his marriage to his late brother's wife, the cardinal having done this as an act of revenge against the Emperor Charles V for not fulfilling his promises to him (p. 906). Charles was, after all, Katherine's nephew. Holinshed also reports Henry's long speech to the ecclesiastical court on the history of his troubled conscience but makes no judgement upon it. There is no mention in Holinshed of Henry's new affection for Anne until after the account of the divorce trial, and no mention either of the title and pension bestowed upon Anne until after the story of Wolsey's fall. Holinshed is therefore unambiguous in presenting Henry's problem of conscience as a genuine factor in determining his actions, though he also makes it plain that Wolsey had something to do with stirring up Henry's doubts in the first place.

[1]  E. E. Duncan-Jones, 'Queen Katherine's vision and Queen Margaret's dream', *N&Q* ns 8 (1961), 142–3.

The play, by contrast, suggests that Henry's early encounter with Anne and his lust after her beauty have as much to do with encouraging any tenderness of conscience as the manoeuvrings of Wolsey. Henry meets Anne for the first time during the masque at Cardinal Wolsey's house (1.4) and there is no doubt that he is smitten. When rumours begin to circulate about a possible separation or divorce between Henry and Katherine, in the talk of the Gentlemen (2.1) and among the nobles (2.2), Wolsey is blamed for arousing Henry's conscience, but this interpretation is devastatingly undercut by Suffolk's aside, 'No, his conscience / Has crept too near another lady' (2.2.16–17). Foxe reports a similar rumour among the common people, but in defence of his hero, he makes it plain that such talk was malicious and ill-informed. Foxe states that 'the mouthes of the common people, & in especiall of women, and such other as fauored the Queene, and talked to their pleasure' were engaged in 'foolish communication' in saying 'that the king would for his owne pleasure haue an other wife'.[1]

Henry's fullest account of his struggles with conscience occurs during the divorce trial when he addresses the court after Katherine's unexpected withdrawal (2.4). But this apparently thoughtful and serious speech, which includes a tribute to Katherine and describes his love for her, is given an ironic context by the placing immediately before it of the little scene of Anne and the Old Lady, during which the Lord Chamberlain brings Anne news of her new title and a pension. The Old Lady's bawdy remarks are a telling reminder to the audience of Henry's lust for youth and beauty, already evident from the masque at York Place. Henry's haste to marry Anne secretly before the ecclesiastical court has completed its deliberations and announced the divorce is another indication of the way Shakespeare has sharpened the irony of Henry's protestations and self-justification. The play does not demolish Henry's argument about his difficulties with conscience, but it shows more clearly than the chronicles that more than one interpretation could be placed on his actions.

As for the other characters, Anne Bullen is conceived by the dramatist largely as a foil for Katherine and as an obstacle to Wolsey's ambitions, neither role being a part of the chronicle accounts. The two invented scenes in which Anne appears give her sufficient reality as a lively and graceful young woman for the purpose of the play. Shakespeare's discretion about Anne is like Holinshed's, giving no hint of frivolity of mind and no hint of scandals to come. Shakespeare added little to the portrait of Cranmer drawn by Foxe, but the closeness of his relationship with Henry and his dependence upon him are contrasted sharply with Wolsey's dominating position and manipulation of the king in the early scenes.

Undoubtedly the writer (or writers) of *Henry VIII* followed his sources closely. Yet this use of source material can scarcely be called pedestrian or a mere time-saving device for a play needed in a hurry. The dramatist chose a limited number of characters and events from the large and crowded canvas of the chronicles to create a significant pattern, to demonstrate contrasts and similarities between

---

[1] Foxe, I, 957.

6  The masque at Cardinal Wolsey's house (Act 1, Scene 4) as it might have been played at the Globe theatre on 29 June 1613, drawn by C. Walter Hodges. The fire in the thatch, caused by the firing of chambers, is just taking hold

characters and their fateful progress, and to portray a working out of events that allowed a glimpse of providential order. The historical time sequence has not been altered in any major way but there is a concentration of events within a narrower compass and some adjustment of the order of events. The historical facts could not be changed because of their closeness in time, but in the process of selection and interpretation, the dramatist has shown a wise economy and a good eye for the telling detail.

## Divided critics

*Henry VIII* has suffered from critical neglect during much of its existence, largely because in the age of burgeoning criticism from the mid nineteenth century onward most scholarly interest in the play has been devoted to the question of its authorship. Before the nineteenth century, the play had attracted the interest of several commentators because of its continuing popularity on the stage. Pepys had noted the crowds thronging to it in the winter of 1663–4. In the same period, John Downes was impressed by the new costumes made for all the characters and by Betterton's performance as the king.[1]

Nicholas Rowe, the first major editor of Shakespeare's works, wrote about the play in his biography of Shakespeare, the 'Account of the Life' prefixed to the 1709 edition. Although admitting the fault of a complete absence of the unities of time and place, as in other of Shakespeare's histories, he nevertheless praises Shakespeare very highly for his handling of the 'Manners of his Characters' in the play – that is, the appropriateness of their actions and speeches to their place in the world and the situations in which they find themselves.[2] Rowe admires Shakespeare's portraits of Henry VIII and Cardinal Wolsey, agreeing, however, that the author has toned down Henry's faults to some extent, perhaps out of respect to the memory of Queen Elizabeth. There is only brief mention of the playwright's success in picturing the distresses of Queen Katherine.

In contrast, Samuel Johnson finds the high point of the play in Katherine's tragic fate. In his notes for *Henry VIII*, he places it 'deservedly' in the second class of Shakespeare's histories, along with *King John* and *Richard III*.[3] It has held the stage, he believes, because of 'the splendour of its pageantry'. His admiration is reserved, however, for the scenes in which the queen appears, particularly 4.2, which he regards as 'above any other part of Shakespeare's tragedies, and perhaps above any scene of any other poet'. It is the tenderness and pathos of the scene that move him so deeply. Johnson may almost be said to anticipate the nineteenth-century scholars who denied Shakespeare's full authorship when he writes: 'But the genius of Shakespeare comes in and goes out with Catherine. Every other part may be easily conceived and easily written.'

As already suggested, a major divide in critical judgement sprang up after Sped-

[1] C. M. Ingleby *et al.* (ed.), *The Shakespeare Allusion-Book*, 1932, II, 394, 437.

[2] Nicholas Rowe, *The Works of Mr William Shakespear*, 1709, repr. 1967, pp. xxix–xxx.

[3] *Samuel Johnson: Notes to Shakespeare*, ed. A. Sherbo, 1957, II, 65–6.

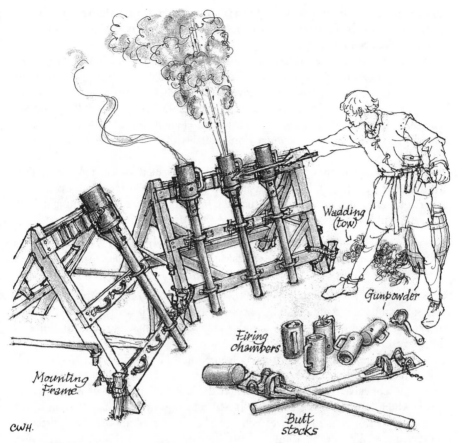

In the illustration: Wadding (tow), Gunpowder, Firing chambers, Mounting Frame, Butt stocks, CWH.

7   Chambers set off (Act 1, Scene 4), by C. Walter Hodges. The firing of chambers outside theatre buildings for an important entry scene, or the sound effects of war, may well have been achieved, as Walter Hodges has pointed out, through the use of removable firing chambers from small breech-loading cannon

ding and Hickson advanced the claim that Shakespeare could have written only a portion of the play, a divide that has persisted to this day. Discussions of the play's structure, characterisation, political ideas and imagery inevitably became bound up with each critic's opinion on whether Shakespeare wrote the whole of it or collaborated with some other playwright.

Those like Spedding who were convinced of the play's dual authorship could find little of merit in its dramatic expression, with the exception of three or four scenes which they assigned to Shakespeare. Many nineteenth-century critics found that it was altogether incoherent in its moral design. As Spedding himself put it, the play offers 'little else than the ultimate triumph of wrong'. In no other play of Shakespeare's does it happen that 'the moral sympathy of the spectator is not carried along with the main current of action to the end'.[1] Spedding's theory of a hasty completion by Fletcher of a play begun by Shakespeare explains, in his view, its unsatisfactory nature.

By contrast, Peter Alexander, who saw no reason to doubt Shakespeare's sole authorship, found much to praise both in the structural design of the play and in its development of major themes. He shows how its structure can be seen as a series of strongly contrasted variations on a single theme, the vanity of worldly greatness. The play is unified not only by this structural element but also by its prevailing atmosphere of tolerance and compassion, a quality that links it with Shakespeare's romances.[2]

Extreme positions have been taken up by advocates for each party. Arthur Symons, for example, in his introduction to the play in the Henry Irving Shakespeare of 1922 states unequivocally that 'the whole play is radically wanting in both dramatic and moral coherence':

Our sympathy is arbitrarily demanded and arbitrarily countermanded. We are expected to weep for the undeserved sorrows of Katherine in one act, and to rejoice over the triumphs of her rival, the cause of all those sorrows, in another.[3]

One might doubt that Anne was the efficient 'cause of all those sorrows'. Nevertheless Symons found it impossible to believe that at the climax of his career Shakespeare had anything to do with 'a blunder so headlong, final, and self-annulling' as this play.[4]

At the other end of the spectrum, Wilson Knight has claimed that *Henry VIII* is one of the supreme examples of Shakespeare's art. He considers the play to be 'massively conceived and constructed' on the basis of a series of pageants and rituals which have both royal (national) and religious significance. Certain of the rituals are communal in nature, echoing the deep aspirations, the boisterous energy, the virility of the whole society.[5] *Henry VIII* is, he believes, the most explicitly Christian of Shakespeare's plays because of its emphasis on justice, truth and charity, and is thus the appropriate fulfilment of the histories and romances.[6]

Most scholars would disavow such extreme positions, but it has proved difficult to approach the play without some consideration of the authorship question. In recent decades, some have pushed the problem into the background or disregarded it altogether in an endeavour to look at the play freshly and consider it on its own merits, particularly in the context of the theatre and social climate of the age that produced it. This approach, in my judgement, has strengthened the very sensible view that *Henry VIII* has a dramatic integrity of its own, a unified conception behinds its apparent diversity of action which can be revealed effec-

[1] Spedding, *Gentleman's Magazine* (Oct. 1850), p. 117.
[2] Alexander, 'Conjectural history', p. 114.
[3] *The Works of William Shakespeare*, ed. Sir Henry Irving and F. A. Marshall, 1922, XIII–XIV, 88.
[4] *Ibid.*
[5] Knight, *Crown of Life*, p. 320.
[6] *Ibid.*, p. 321.

tively in stage performances. Nevertheless it is not yet a view that is universally accepted, and a wide division of opinion regarding the merits of the play continues to exist.

Fairly typical of those who find little of interest and quite marked dramatic weaknesses in *Henry VIII* is J. C. Maxwell. He is convinced by the evidence that Fletcher had a large part in its composition. Maxwell agrees that the play has had a long history of popular success on the stage, but in his view 'true dramatic life' is almost entirely absent from it. He finds a lack of 'momentousness' in the way the events are presented and notes the difficulties scholars have had in finding any substance in its general direction or meaning. The treatment of Henry as the central figure is particularly unsatisfactory: different views of his conscience, his love for Katherine and for Anne, his decisions and judgements, are laid side by side without any conclusions being reached. Likewise in scenes involving Katherine, 'no unified impression, not even a complex one' emerges.[1]

Although Clifford Leech finds more of interest in the play than Maxwell does, he makes a similar judgement on its lack of any clear sense of direction. 'We do not have the sense that as the play proceeds we are approaching an increasingly complex view of the characters and the situation, penetrating successively to more remote levels of significance: rather, we seem to be given a series of alternations between different views of the characters and situation.'[2] The varied responses aroused by the play are due, he believes, to a pervading scepticism which is characteristic of Fletcher. Leech finds a dominant theme in the operation of mutability and the fall of worldly glory. There is a counter-current moving toward some great destiny, but this movement is undercut by shabby intrigues, human littleness, deception and self-deception. Cranmer's prophecy at the end is, Leech believes, a mere dream when set against the realities of the life presented in the play and the well-known history of subsequent years, even though those years had some achievements to mark them and a degree of splendour. Rather than being the summation of Shakespeare's history play cycles, this one has 'no political lesson to offer'; good and bad characters have equally unfortunate ends, and the hope registered in the conclusion must be seen as a desperately qualified one.[3]

Although unsatisfactory to such scholars as Maxwell and Leech, the play has not lacked its champions, among them Geoffrey Bullough and R. A. Foakes. Bullough lays particular emphasis on *Henry VIII*'s connection with Shakespeare's earlier history plays, unlike Leech seeing it as a fitting conclusion that marked the end of the old order and revealed how the long series of power struggles was finally resolved in the Tudor regime. Henry himself has many human faults, but he overcomes difficulties and grows in wisdom and benevolence as the action proceeds. The play is 'a resplendent Finale, ritualistically expanding through conflict into grace and happy augury'.[4]

---

[1] Maxwell, p. xxxvi.
[2] Leech, *The Chronicles*, p. 34.
[3] *Ibid.*, p. 39.
[4] Bullough, *Sources*, IV, 450.

The most complete defence of *Henry VIII*'s unity, coherence and dramatic resourcefulness is to be found in R. A. Foakes's introduction to the Arden edition of 1957 (revised 1964). Foakes links the play primarily with Shakespeare's romances rather than with the history plays or the tragedies. Not only does it belong in date with the last plays; like them, it shows a wide prospect of life in which good and evil, suffering and joy all have their place. In these plays, he observes, 'the total effect, the almost visionary whole, is more important than what happens to the individual, or the development of character'.[1] Each play represents a different experiment in its structure but Foakes admits that none is entirely successful in overcoming the problems which the nature of the material imposed.

Foakes claims that the play's structure is based on the four trials involving Buckingham, Katherine, Wolsey and Cranmer, which have private as well as public dimensions. There is a complex pattern of parallels and contrasts in terms of suffering and joy, linked both with these trials and with the abundant pageantry which has a marked functional role. Foakes takes note of two major themes: justice, particularly the contrast between earthly and divine justice, and steadfastness or patience in adversity.[2] He admits the ambiguity in the portrait of Henry, but regards it as a natural strain in the portrait of a 'human and fallible' ruler who becomes more confident of his authority during the course of the action. The play's complexity is especially evident in the multiple levels of commentary, from ordinary citizens and gentlemen of the court to the great nobles and the central figures themselves: through such commentary, a whole range of different perspectives on motive and character and the meaning of events is presented, but without loss of the 'visionary whole'.[3]

Although Foakes was by no means the first to link the celebratory aspects of the play with the wedding festivities for Princess Elizabeth and the Elector Ferdinand, he provided a larger body of evidence demonstrating widespread contemporary interest in the wedding and specific parallels drawn between the princess and her namesake, the great queen. Other scholars such as Frances Yates and Glynne Wickham have made further suggestions about the topicality of the play, and its relevance to political and religious issues that were of lively interest to the court of James I. Howard Felperin and Alexander Leggatt are less interested in the play's topical concerns than in the mythical dimension given to English history, the attempt by the dramatist to explore beneath the actual mix of historical events and personages an obscure but nevertheless fundamental design or purpose.

In *Shakespeare's Last Plays*, Yates argues that there was a notable revival of Elizabethan ideals and causes in the early years of James's reign, many of the hopes for Protestant reform centring upon the young Prince Henry until the great disappointment of his early death. She links *Henry VIII* with *Cymbeline* as pointing to some great promise for the nation in the forthcoming marriage of Princess Elizabeth. The play, in her view, 'reflects the Foxian apocalyptic view of English

---

[1] Foakes, p. xli.
[2] *Ibid.*, p. lix.
[3] *Ibid.*, p. lv.

1 Enter Cranmer.
2 'Your grace must
  wait till you be
  called for.'
3 Enter Doctor Butts
  ('This is a piece of
  malice... The
  king shall under-
  stand it presently.'
4 Enter the King and
  Butts at a window
  above.

5 '...Draw the curtain close:
  We shall hear more anon.'
6 'Your grace may
  enter now.'
7 Enter the Guard.

8 Gardiner: '...How much are we bound
  to heaven in...thanks, that gave
  us such a prince.'
9 King: 'I charge you embrace...
  this man.'
  Gardiner: 'With a true heart...I
  do it.'

8   A possible staging of the council scene, Act 5, Scene 2, at the Blackfriars theatre, by C. Walter
Hodges. Although evidence is lacking, it seems likely that the King's Men would have played *Henry
VIII* on the smaller stage at Blackfriars after the Globe had burned down

history as a conflict between the royal-imperial power and the papal power, with justice, order and peace on the side of the former, injustice and war on the side of the latter'.[1]

Glynne Wickham also notes the topicality of *Henry VIII* but lays more emphasis on James's vision of himself as a peacemaker, reconciling Catholic and Protestant nations in Europe. Wickham reminds us that another of the suitors for Princess Elizabeth, one favoured by Queen Anne, was Philip III of Spain.[2] The vision of peace finds its echo in the reconciling and forgiving atmosphere of the play. Its structure is governed, Wickham believes, by a single unifying purpose – to redeem the slanders cast on the name of Katherine of Aragon in 1531 so that some of the shadows of the past arising out of religious conflict might be overcome.[3] In this process, Henry VIII and Anne Bullen are not specifically blamed for what happened; the blame falls upon Wolsey and the pope. Once some of the cruelties of the past have been forgiven, a messianic goal becomes possible.

Different approaches to topicality in drama and poetry always show the difficulty of comprehending the background knowledge and particular interests of a theatrical or reading audience in another age. Nevertheless the attempt to recover the social and cultural context of a play like *Henry VIII*, though necessarily tentative and partial, remains a worthwhile task.

Howard Felperin's discussion of *Henry VIII* in *Shakespearean Romance* (1972) is concerned with genre rather than with specific historical reference. In his view, English history is shaped in the play into patterns determined to a large extent by older narrative structures. The model of the Bible as divine comedy is followed as the action moves through tragic events to a culmination in peace, justice and spiritual freedom. Each of the tragic stories within the play is a 'fortunate fall' leading to spiritual wealth in place of worldly prosperity.[4] Felperin sees the influence of another traditional form, the Morality play, noting Wolsey's part as Lucifer or the Vice, Katherine as Henry's good angel, and Henry as one of a long line of sinning or misguided kings. The influence of the romance is also apparent, especially in the ending of the play which is the golden world of dream and wish-fulfilment. A major difficulty with the play, he believes, is that the reality principle involved in history is not reconciled with the opposite pole of idealism which romance projects. Shakespeare could not free himself from the context of what really happened: far too much is censored out or glossed over.[5] In this respect, Felperin supports Clifford Leech.

Alexander Leggatt also makes much of the tension between ideal vision and reality in *Henry VIII*, but he sees this tension as a constant factor in Shakespeare's history plays, carried further here than in most, if not all, of the others. Cranmer's

---

[1] Yates, *Shakespeare's Last Plays*, p. 70.
[2] Glynne Wickham, 'The dramatic structure of Shakespeare's *King Henry the Eighth*', *PBA* 70 (1984), 151 n.
[3] *Ibid.*, p. 165.
[4] H. Felperin, *Shakespearean Romance*, 1972, pp. 201–2.
[5] *Ibid.*, p. 209.

prophecy, which has presented difficulties for many critics, he compares with similar royal compliments and visions of the future in older Elizabethan plays. However, the prophecy is not a mere appendage; it has a structural function, drawing together images and ideas from earlier scenes and providing a culmination for the argument as it reveals a providential order in the disorderly world of history. The processes of history as they are shown to us in the action of the play are extraordinarily complex and difficult to fathom, the motives of the characters are mixed, and our judgements of events and characters remain uncertain or 'split'.[1] Yet hints of design or purpose form an undercurrent which finally emerges at the end.

The topicality of *Henry VIII* is seen by Leggatt chiefly in its portrayal of the new relationship between church and state that develops with the downfall of Wolsey and the establishment of Henry's authority. The coming to the fore of Cranmer will ensure that 'God shall be truly known.'[2] Because of the play's insistence on the shaping power of the imagination in prophetic vision, in the power of music, in the art of the play, Leggatt concludes that '*Henry VIII* is the work of a writer fresh from *The Winter's Tale* and *The Tempest*.'[3]

A particular interest of several recent critics has been the relationship of *Henry VIII* to the court masque and the romance. Music, dance, tableaux, processions have been recognised from classical times as vital elements in drama, often playing an important role in the total effect of a dramatic performance. Jacobean playwrights such as Webster and Ford, not to mention Beaumont, Fletcher and the later Shakespeare, made substantial use of such elements, already present in Elizabethan drama, to play sophisticated games with dramatic illusion, to provide different levels of commentary, and to give dramatic point to ironic situations, especially ironic reversals like the wedding celebrations at the end of Middleton's *Women Beware Women*. These playwrights were also influenced by the elaborate court masques in which shows and dances, costumes and scenic devices formed part of an allegorical whole. Recent studies have shown that masquing, particularly at the Jacobean and Stuart court, often had political implications and promoted specific messages from the king to his court at large, or from the poet and groups of courtiers to the king.[4]

J. D. Cox and Northrop Frye have both looked at *Henry VIII* from the point of view of the court masque, though Frye considers the romance as equally important in its background. Cox believes that the play is 'an experiment in adapting the principles of the court masque to the dramatic tradition of the public theatres'; the masque elements explain the extensive use of royal spectacle and pageantry.[5] As

---

[1] Alexander Leggatt, '"Henry VIII" and the ideal England', *S.Sur.* 38 (1985), 135.

[2] *Ibid.*, p. 137.

[3] *Ibid.*, p. 143.

[4] Roy Strong, *Art and Power, Renaissance Festivals 1450–1650*, 1984; Stephen Orgel, *The Illusion of Power: Political Theatre in the English Renaissance*, 1975; Martin Butler, *Royal Slaves? The Stuart Court and the Theatres* (*Renaissance Drama Newsletter*, Supplement Two, 1984).

[5] J. D. Cox, '*Henry VIII* and the masque', *ELH* 45, (1978), 391.

9  Henry gives the incriminating papers to Wolsey, Act 3, Scene 2. This illustration from Rowe's edition of Shakespeare (1714) suggests a stage setting but there is no evidence that it represents an actual production. The three nobles at the back are dressed in the fashion of eighteenth-century courtiers

in Jonson's masques, order and royalty are equated: only royal power can quell the forces of disorder. In *Henry VIII*, the anti-masque elements appear in Wolsey, who is associated with devils, whose power shadows the king's own power, and whose shows are extravagant, flimsy and ultimately deceptive. In the true masque of 1.4, Henry brings a company of masquers to entertain the cardinal's guests; he wears a shepherd's garb, a costume which Cox believes signifies Henry's role as shepherd of his people and as head of the church.[1]

In adapting the conventions of a new form, Cox maintains, Shakespeare always qualifies them by playing them off against the conventions of an older form. In *Henry VIII*, the masque form is given an injection of realism from such older forms as the political Morality and the history play, so that ideal images are deliberately qualified or undercut. Unlike Felperin, who regards such ambiguity as a weakness, Cox believes this interplay of conventions to be a source of strength.[2]

In Frye's essay 'Romance as masque' (1978), the masque is described as an idealising mirror held up to its audience, a mirror reflecting the cosmology of a stratified society. The darker, less orderly aspects of society and human nature are presented through the anti-masque so that the masque form is essentially a polarity between order and disorder. Romance depends on a similar polarity between blocking worlds and the world of desire and fulfilment, but the blocking worlds sometimes develop tragic action before they are overcome. Frye makes the wheel of Fortune the dominant force in *Henry VIII*, though it is uncertain whether Henry controls it or is merely 'a part of its machinery'; hence it is unnecessary to judge Henry from a moral point of view.[3] Frye sees opposed and unreconciled elements within the play, but he regards them as part of the corrosive irony which runs through it, an irony that has almost a comic dimension. The play becomes 'a sinister sacrificial dance in which the most conspicuous figure becomes the next victim'; apart from the king, of course, who is master of ceremonies.[4] The dance of the spirits and the prophecy of Cranmer belong generically to the masque proper, as opposed to the anti-masque. They suggest a transcendent realm beyond the glories and trials of this world, a world in which Anne and Cranmer are also doomed to suffer.

Frye believes that *Henry VIII* has a much greater dramatic integrity than it is usually given credit for – the integrity of the dramatic spectacle in a play which is 'deeply serious, even tragic'. Its most impressive characteristic is the way it reverses our normal standards of reality and illusion:

Nothing could be more immediately real than the ups and downs of fortune in King Henry's court, nothing more illusory than a prophecy of a future three reigns away, or the sick fancies of a dying woman. But what the play presents is a sense of reality and illusion quite the opposite of this.[5]

[1]  *Ibid.*, p. 399.
[2]  *Ibid.*, p. 407.
[3]  Frye, 'Romance as masque', p. 31.
[4]  *Ibid.*, p. 33.
[5]  *Ibid.*, p. 32.

Perceptions of *Henry VIII* have changed markedly since the eighteenth century, when it was regarded simply as one of Shakespeare's history plays, notable chiefly for two or three outstanding character parts and for the scope it gave to pageantry. Johnson had noted the exceptional tenderness and pathos of Katherine's last scene, and Hazlitt and Charles Knight typically had commented on the great characters, Buckingham, Wolsey and Katherine. However, the theory of dual authorship, raised in the mid nineteenth century, reflected the discomfort of scholars at the time over the absence of any political lesson or clear moral stance in the play, as well as its faults in dramatic structure and its seemingly varied styles. Victorian critics judged the play harshly for these defects, placing much of the responsibility upon Fletcher, and only a few joined Swinburne in asserting a general unity of theme and atmosphere.

In the early twentieth century, as we have seen, the vigorous debate over the qualities of the play continued, but there was a greater emphasis on structure, theme and imagery, and less on the presence or absence of moral purpose. It was regarded primarily as a history play, either (at one extreme) exceptionally faulty in dramatic craftsmanship, or (at the other) triumphantly summing up all Shakespeare's earlier histories. Later in the century, however, corresponding to the more moderate conclusions of scholars working on the authorship question, critics too began to regard the play in a more objective way. It was now thought of, by Foakes and others, as an experimental form, a history play modified in important respects by the romance and the court masque, and a play closely related to the political and social context of its own time.

Recent criticism has raised an additional question which has not yet been answered, or which demonstrates perhaps that the debate over the play is not yet over. Is the conceptual form, both structure and texture, of *Henry VIII* determined by its historic context, the special public occasion which had something to do with its origin and the political and religious issues that divided England in Henry's reign and still troubled the reign of James? Is the play a form of discourse related to and dependent upon its audience's perceptions of such issues, as Yates, Wickham and others propose? Or are these contextual matters peripheral to the generic qualities of Morality, history play, romance and masque that have been joined in a single work? There are those who maintain that *Henry VIII* as a pageant or 'show' is a kind of drama not so much mimetic as processional, organised through spectacle and ritual. The masque-like elements, Cox and Frye have pointed out, suggest an idealised society or state of existence, whereas the anti-masque patterns and figures subvert the play's dominant orthodoxies. There seems to be little inclination at the moment to dismiss *Henry VIII* as a play having no dramatic life and no substantial interest for the playgoer or reader.

### The unity of the play

Most questions about the structure, characters, pageantry and patterns of ideas in *Henry VIII* can be reduced to the single question: is it a complex play with an underlying unity, or is it a very simple play, a collection of lively shows and un-related emotional scenes produced as entertainment for a special occasion? There have been many who have supported the latter view, but in recent years a number have developed cogent arguments for the former. My own view, based on several notable stage performances as well as the text itself, is that it is more complex than once was thought and derives its special qualities from its nature as a new mode of drama, somewhere in the area between history play and romance. It has an ironic structure and tone, and becomes expressive drama through its extensive use of pageantry, music and dance.

In the First Folio of 1623, Heminges and Condell placed *Henry VIII* as the last of the history plays, apparently seeing it as a fitting conclusion to the long series of Shakespeare's histories. Chronology makes it the right play to end the series, but it could not have been written while Elizabeth was still on the throne because of its portrayal of her father and comment on issues of some sensitivity to Elizabeth's privy council. The play also appears to reach a fulfilment of important themes in the earlier histories, where there was a looking forward to a time of peace and promise, the ending of the struggles for the throne and a release from the long cycles of civil war.

In formal terms, *Henry VIII* is an old-fashioned history play, concentrating much of the historical narrative into a short compass, highlighting several major characters (like the three parts of *Henry VI* and the two parts of *Henry IV*), and making use of the central figure of a king to link episodes together. What is lacking is the momentum given to the narrative line in earlier plays by powerful motives like ambition or revenge. No one seeks to overthrow Henry VIII in this play or to organise a re-bellion; Wolsey is powerful and ambitious for himself but there is no conspiracy to bring him down; and jealousy and revenge are not stirred up by Henry's sudden shift of favour from Katherine to Anne Bullen. Hence there are no armed insurrections, no rival armies, no ultimate decisions by means of murder or battle. *Henry VIII* is remarkable in being a history play without corpses.

We have moved in this play into a Renaissance court where the authority of the monarch is not questioned, and where political rivalries, favourites and their factions have replaced competing armies. The narrative line, not the most important structural element here, consists largely of Henry's attempt to establish firmly his dynastic succession by begetting a male heir. This attempt involves a separation from Katherine, his wife of twenty years, and a second marriage to the most desirable woman he encounters. His long-standing chief minister, Cardinal Wolsey, at first helps him and then hinders him in his plans, and the king's discovery of Wolsey's underhand dealings leads to his complete disgrace. The pathetic fate of Katherine is balanced against the rise of Anne Bullen, and a new favourite, Archbishop Cranmer, takes Wolsey's place in the final act. It is a history play in which a powerful king can be deceived or misled, but his will cannot be denied.

Several very interesting political issues are raised in the play, issues Shakespeare had touched on in earlier histories, but related now to the changed conditions of a

10  Act 2, Scene 4 in J. P. Kemble's sumptuous production at Covent Garden in 1816, by G. H. Harlow. Sarah Siddons played Queen Katherine, with J. P. Kemble as Wolsey (seated, left), and Charles Kemble as Cromwell (centre)

contemporary court. Religious controversy, though understated in comparison with other plays and pamphlets of the time and very muted in relation to Foxe's *Acts and Monuments*, is tied unmistakably to the question of the power of the papacy over the English church and the king himself, as in *King John*, though now in the context of German Protestantism. Henry's discovery of Wolsey's tortuous schemes to achieve the papal throne at the expense of his duty to the king, his rapid throwing off of Wolsey's influence, and his choice of Cranmer as his ecclesiastical guide for the future display his increasing confidence and authority in matters of church and state.

*Henry VIII* is also a dramatic demonstration of the processes of power at a Renaissance court, how a favourite possessing the king's ear wields enormous influence and seeks every possible means to maintain that influence, including getting rid of possible rivals. As the First Gentleman observes early in the play, 'whoever the king favours, / The cardinal instantly will find employment, / And far enough from court too' (2.1.47–9). Those out of favour have little chance of success, though they may, like Buckingham, hope that 'from a mouth of honour' they can inform the king about 'This Ipswich fellow's insolence' (1.1.137–8). The play is as much about falls from favour as it is about rising: the falls are no mere retirement from the cabinet to the back benches but more like a sentence of death, an execution for Buckingham, and illness leading to death brought on by disgrace or abandonment for Wolsey and Katherine.

The appearance of factions, groups of friends or supporters around a favourite, or in opposition to a favourite, is another element in the political context Shakespeare supplies.[1] In the opening scene, it becomes plain that Buckingham, Abergavenny and Norfolk all oppose Wolsey's overweening power as the king's favourite but Norfolk is convinced that Buckingham is using the wrong tactics, as events soon prove. Later there are several consultations among the growing faction opposed to Wolsey – Norfolk, Suffolk, the Lord Chamberlain and Surrey – and although they are not instrumental in bringing Wolsey down, they are immediately ready to take advantage of the changed situation. The appearance of new factions is noted by the Gentlemen in a brief but telling conversation after Anne's coronation (4.1.103–10), and the opening of the fifth act represents Gardiner and Lovell talking late at night about the group around the king – Cranmer, Cromwell and Anne – without whom the king will do nothing. Shakespeare's political realism is evident in his presentation of these rival groups in Henry's court, and there is little doubt that they reflect also upon the court of James in 1613.

Henry VIII is the first of Shakespeare's kings who belongs to the new model of an absolute monarch in a modern state, not dependent on the loyalty of great nobles with armies of their own, though he may need to retain the good will of the citizens at large. He is responsible for the welfare of the state and for justice to the individual, just as the citizen is responsible to the king in terms of loyalty and duty.

---

[1] I was alerted to the part played by favourites and factions in *Henry VIII* by the historian Eric Ives in a paper read to the International Shakespeare Conference at Stratford-upon-Avon, August 1984.

Katherine frames her appeal to Henry on behalf of his subjects on the basis of such mutual responsibility, claiming that the injustice they have suffered 'breaks / The sides of loyalty' (1.2.27–8). Henry acts at once, noting that 'We must not rend our subjects from our laws / And stick them in our will' (1.2.93–4). However, he is not so concerned about justice a few minutes later when he hears the surveyor's carefully rehearsed evidence against Buckingham, and he disregards Katherine's warnings about the source of the evidence as he allows his anger to overcome his judgement.

The scene illustrates how easily a monarch can be fooled through flattery by a favourite or chief minister who is pursuing ends of his own. Henry is thoroughly deceived by Wolsey whom he trusts completely, and although others at court and in the country recognise what is going on, no one has the influence or the direct evidence to convince Henry of the truth until, ironically, Wolsey betrays himself. Jonson and Chapman also addressed such issues of absolutism and justice, Jonson in his Roman tragedies and Chapman in his tragedies set in modern France. Tiberius, Jonson's utterly corrrupt tyrant in *Sejanus*, is flattered and manipulated by the ambitious Sejanus until Tiberius eventually suspects the truth and gets rid of him. Francis I, in Chapman's *Tragedy of Chabot*, is deceived by his chancellor and a court faction into believing that the virtuous admiral, Chabot, has acted dishonestly for his own advantage.

A useful scene for defining the political stance of *Henry VIII* is the council's examination of Cranmer and Henry's sudden intervention in Act 5. Although Cranmer is presented as a good, almost saintly man and although the council has proceeded against him on the instigation of the envious Bishop Gardiner, the effect on the councillors when Cranmer produces Henry's ring is both comic and satiric, an effect enhanced when Henry himself enters. They are instantly swayed by the royal will and, apart from Gardiner, rush to embrace the king's favourite archbishop. There are similarly satiric scenes in *Sejanus* when the letter of Tiberius is read to the Senate, and in Chapman's *Tragedy of Chabot* when the judges find Chabot guilty, believing this to be the king's will, and shortly afterwards find his accuser guilty in an equally hurried trial when they discover the king has changed his mind. Likewise in *The Tragedy of Byron*, the courtiers pretend not to see Byron and D'Auvergne as the king's favour is withdrawn from them, and Henry's councillors rush ahead of him in suggesting methods of peremptory justice against Byron.

There are two characters in *Henry VIII* who stand out against absolute royal power. Katherine is by far the more important. She strongly repudiates Henry's doubts about the legitimacy of their marriage, refuses to accept Wolsey as both accuser and judge (since it is an ecclesiastical court) and in the end refuses to accept the jurisdiction of the court. There is little hope of her winning such an unequal contest, but although she is isolated and worn down by the continuing pressures, she keeps her independent spirit to the end. The second rebel against royal authority is that unlikable man, Bishop Gardiner, Cranmer's chief opponent. He is highly suspicious of Cranmer's heretical tendencies and refuses to accept his influence over the king, which he links with Cromwell's and Anne Bullen's. The plot against Cranmer fails, but Gardiner is noticeably tardy in moving to embrace Cranmer, as the king has ordered all his councillors to do. It is a significant moment.[1]

The historical and political context of the play ends with Cranmer's prophecy of the future glorious reigns of Elizabeth and James, a prophecy certainly appropriate to the occasion, Elizabeth's christening, but a little at odds with the doubts and qualifications about royal power expressed earlier in the play. The prophecy is scarcely an exercise in irony, even though irony abounds in the play and even though some members of the contemporary audience may have had doubts about the complete fulfilment of the prophecy in their own time. The prophecy says nothing at all about Henry's reign except that the begetting of the child will prove to be a great blessing for the nation. As a pageant of future peace, prosperity and contentment, it expresses a vision of an ideal state where the monarch rules in wisdom and virtue for the welfare of all the people. 'God shall be truly known' and greatness will depend upon honour and virtue, not upon birth. Rather than being an accurate forecast of things to come, it expresses, like many city pageants and courtly masques, the ideal against which reality can be measured.

The history play as Shakespeare, Marlowe and others developed it made use of certain formal conventions and a structure which ranged from the tightly controlled to the expansive and episodic. Each of Shakespeare's history plays can be thought of as an experiment in scope and form, and *Henry VIII* is an example of further exploration. However, it is also one of the plays written at the end of Shakespeare's career and it would be surprising if it had escaped altogether the influence of the new dramaturgy of the romances and their thematic concerns.

On the surface at least, *Henry VIII* seems to have little in common with *The Winter's Tale* and *The Tempest*. It is concerned with historical personages in a historical time scheme acting out a series of well-recorded events: in no way can it have the freedom of movement through time and space which the romances display. It is true that family relationships are a central issue, at least between husband and wife, and when the husband deserts one wife and marries another, a child is born of whom great things are promised. But there is no suggestion of the recurrent narrative pattern of the romances where the loss of a loved one is eventually overcome in a return, a recognition scene, a restoration of the closest family ties. *Henry VIII* is history and the basic events cannot be altered to provide for a different outcome. Nor is there scope for a mythological retelling of the story, the sort of thing remoteness allowed in the tales of Macbeth and King Lear as well as Cymbeline. What is possible, and common enough in history plays, is the shaping of events into deliberate patterns, the exploration of character, and through such means an interpretation of meaning.

---

[1] J. D. Spikes notes that Foxe had portrayed Bishop Gardiner as a villainous character who tried to get rid of Elizabeth, and that several popular plays enlarged upon this portrait, among them *Thomas Lord Cromwell, Sir Thomas Wyat* and *If You Know Not Me* ('The Jacobean history play and the myth of the elect nation', *Renaissance Drama* 8 (1977), 133).

It is in such shaping that critics have seen an influence from the romances. Within the play, there are three tragic falls from high place in sequence, ranging from well-deserved punishment to the totally undeserved (the debate in miniature about tragic falls and responsibility begun in *A Mirror for Magistrates* and continued in many subsequent tragic history plays). But for each individual, the play moves beyond the misery of the fall to some signs of spiritual growth, and for Katherine a spiritual blessing. The tone of forgiveness and reconciliation that results is in keeping with the similar atmosphere of the romances, with Prospero's statement in *The Tempest* that 'The rarer action is / In virtue than in vengeance' (5.1.27–8). *Henry VIII* progresses through individual tragedies to a comic triumph at the end involving the larger community. In *Pericles, The Winter's Tale* and *The Tempest*, the note of hope for the future sounds in the coming together of new generations in marriage. In *Henry VIII* it is the birth and christening of a child.

One of the characteristics of both the romance and the masque is an opposition between destructive forces and forces of order. The destructive forces in *Henry VIII* are concentrated in one character, Cardinal Wolsey – his arrogant oppression of citizens and unwanted rivals, his pride and greed, and above all his subordination of his country's needs to ambitious schemes for personal aggrandisement. The images his enemies use in condemning him are drawn from insects, animals, and demons and witchcraft. He is called a 'keech' (the rolled-up fat of a slaughtered animal), a 'butcher's cur', a 'holy fox or wolf or both', 'spider-like', a devil creating 'a new hell in himself'. Yet Henry also embodies obstacles that have to be overcome, particularly at the beginning of the play. He depends much on Wolsey, is blind to his scheming, and his judgement is all too easily clouded by his hasty temper and moodiness. The opposing forces of harmony and order are revealed in Katherine's persistence in virtue and love, crowned by her vision of eternity. They emerge also in Henry's growing maturity as he throws off Wolsey's influence and accepts Cranmer's guidance, and likewise in Cranmer's humility and grace which make him the proper vehicle for a vision of an idealised future society.

Shakespeare's romances often make use of visual and aural effects, not devised simply as spectacle but with specific dramatic functions and operating often on a symbolic level. The songs and country dances in Act 4 of *The Winter's Tale*, the interrupted banquet in *The Tempest*, and the solemn music introducing visionary scenes in *Pericles* and *Cymbeline* are familiar examples. In *Henry VIII*, a lively social ritual of banquet and masque in 1.4 creates a convivial atmosphere appropriate to courtship and seduction. In contrast are the harsh rituals of accusations, examinations and trials which belong to the iron world of political conflict and power. Shakespeare makes no use of magic or sorcery in *Henry VIII* but the supernatural makes its presence felt in the vision scene and again in the prophecy of Cranmer which appears to be divinely inspired. It does not require much imagination to see Cranmer as the good wizard presiding over a happy ending once the evil wizard, Wolsey, has been unmasked and deprived of his power. His 'witchcraft / Over the king in's tongue' is now vanished forever (3.2.18–19). Katherine, imprisoned at

Kimbolton, is the lost princess, but it is her fate to be rescued only for the next world by a heavenly messenger.

The mixture of elements in *Henry VIII* makes it difficult to categorise. Although it is a history play in subject matter and time scheme, the romance element appears in the shaping of this material, the use of symbolic pageantry and rituals, and the movement of the play toward vision or dream. It may help us to understand the play's design by looking more closely at the way the separate pageants are linked in their significance and how pageant, ritual and vision are related to the play's various ironies.

The pageantry of *Henry VIII* derives, as we have seen, from the chronicles but in the play it is made very much a part of the dramatic fabric. In the chronicles, masques and pageants were recorded in detail as revels of the court, and frequently they were shown to have a political purpose, to welcome royal visitors and ambassadors from abroad and to impress them with a display of Renaissance 'magnificence'. Other shows were not courtly since they involved the guilds and city corporations, as when a sovereign was welcomed to one of his own cities. A coronation procession, in particular, was a rite whose purpose was to show the monarch to the people.[1] The chronicles recorded other ritual occasions, too, such as state trials and public executions, where an accused or a condemned prisoner performed a central role in a much more sombre drama.

A contemporary audience would recognise many of these traditional elements in *Henry VIII*. In the design of the play, the sequence of rituals and shows is developed with considerable subtlety to reveal different aspects of authority in the state, the ceremonial occasions designed to buttress that authority, and yet also to point to significant flaws or weaknesses behind the splendid shows, even to deny their validity. The pageantry is closely related to the developing plot.

The ceremonies of the Field of the Cloth of Gold, as Norfolk describes them in the opening scene, represent a conspicuous display of wealth and power by the two kings, with a marked competitive element built into it, like the welcome for the emperor in Greene's *Friar Bacon and Friar Bungay*. There is an obvious political purpose to the great spectacle since it celebrates the signing of a treaty of friendship. But the dark underside is revealed as Norfolk and Buckingham discuss not only the crippling expenses incurred by the participants but also the way in which Wolsey had managed the whole enterprise for his personal advantage, with little thought either for his king or for the kingdom.

The banquet and masque at York Place in 1.4 are revels of the traditional courtly kind. They display Wolsey's wealth, his lavish hospitality (which his guests duly admire) and his high favour with the king, all marks of the lofty point of prosperity from which he is doomed to fall later in the play. The masque proper is a dance between disguised masquers and the ladies of the court, without a spoken text apart from the brief introduction by the Lord Chamberlain as 'presenter', and

[1] M. C. Bradbrook, 'Shakespeare and the multiple theatres of Jacobean London', in *The Elizabethan Theatre*, VI, ed. G. R. Hibbard, 1978, p. 89.

11  Queen Katherine's vision (Act 4, Scene 2), with Mrs Kean as Katherine, in Charles Kean's 1855 production, which was noted for its antiquarian detail and its spectacular scene setting, as here. In a revival in 1858, Ellen Terry is reputed to have been the top angel on the concealed ladder

is thus typical of Tudor masquing, though not of masques at the court of James. Besides giving us a view of Wolsey and his relation to Henry, the scene moves the plot forward when Henry chooses Anne Bullen as his partner. Whatever allegorical significance the shepherds' costumes may have had at the beginning of the masque, they take on a distinct colouring of sexuality before the end.

Royal and ecclesiastical power are still on display and make a striking visual point in following scenes – Buckingham on his way to execution (2.1) and the divorce hearing in which Henry and Katherine attend a court presided over by the cardinals (2.4). These are ritualistic scenes of accusation and condemnation. Buckingham's speech is in effect a scaffold speech as he makes his last testament, standing between armed guards close to the threatening axe with the edge turned towards him.[1] In the ecclesiastical court, with its elaborate iconography of church and state, Katherine finds herself the central figure, like an accused prisoner, though it is her marriage to Henry that is being considered. Just as the history play pattern of *Henry VIII* shows the triumph of one character in counterpoint against the tragic fall of another, so the pageantry demonstrates visually the splendour of royal favour and the isolation and despair of those who have lost it.

A graphic example can be found in Wolsey's progress. When the procession enters Blackfriars for the ecclesiastical court, Wolsey appears with all the trappings of his position as lord chancellor and as a cardinal of the church. Vergers carry silver wands, gentlemen bear silver 'pillars', and other officers bear the great seal, sword and silver mace. But a few scenes later, he has only his memories of former grandeur as he laments:

> No sun shall ever usher forth mine honours,
> Or gild again the noble troops that waited
> Upon my smiles.                                                       (3.2.410–12)

The gold and silver imagery of the Field of the Cloth of Gold and the procession into Blackfriars becomes a symbol of the worldly wealth and power that have been lost, and religious imagery begins tentatively to take its place:

> Cromwell, I charge thee, fling away ambition,
> By that sin fell the angels; how can man then,
> The image of his maker, hope to win by it?                           (3.2.440–2)

The two scenes of Act 4 are both centred upon pageants – Anne's coronation and Katherine's vision – that illuminate the meaning of the play through being placed side by side. The splendid coronation procession is commented upon by the Gentlemen who give the names and rank of the principal persons (like modern television presenters). Stage directions place much emphasis on costume and ornament, especially gold and silver, the emblems of title and wealth. The Marquess of Dorset bears *a sceptre of gold* and on his head *a demi-coronal of gold*; the Earl of Surrey carries *the rod of silver with the dove* and is himself *crowned with an earl's coro-*

---

[1] Compare Byron's speech from an actual scaffold in Chapman's *The Tragedy of Charles Duke of Byron* (1608).

*net* (4.1.36 SD). When the queen appears, the Second Gentleman describes her beauty in erotic language so that we are reminded of Henry's instant attraction to her during the masque at York Place in 1.4:

> Our king has all the Indies in his arms,
> And more, and richer, when he strains that lady;
> I cannot blame his conscience. (4.1.45–7)

The procession moves off to another feast at York Place and Anne now appears to have won all the prizes.

Immediately after the coronation scene, the audience is transported to Kimbolton where Katherine endures house arrest, without her due place in the king's love, without rank, wealth or influence. Instead of the noisy acclaim of crowds, flourishes of trumpets and the singing of choristers, she has just two faithful attendants and the quiet music of (most probably) viols and recorders. Her dream is a vision of heavenly beings, in costumes of white and gold for purity and steadfastness, dancing a graceful measure as they invite her to a banquet and offer a garland for her head. It is a courtly masque with a vital difference: a spiritual world has manifested itself, questioning the value of worldly glory, the symbols of status, power and wealth so prominent in the previous scene.[1]

The last of the major scenes of pageantry is the procession for the christening of Elizabeth, with its comic prologue by the Porter, and Cranmer's visionary epilogue. The Porter's prologue describes the noise and excitement of the entire community. Images of sexuality and fertility are a popular version of what a christening is all about:

Bless me, what a fry of fornication is at door! On my Christian conscience, this one christening will beget a thousand, here will be father, godfather, and all together. (5.3.32–4)

The continuity of life suggested by birth and christening is stressed when the royal procession enters: dynastic succession is all important as the monarchy demonstrates its continuity with the past to buttress its claim on the future. The prominent display of christening gifts vies with splendid costume and insignia of rank as the Princess Elizabeth is proclaimed by Garter King of Arms.

Cranmer's prophecy which follows has much to say about glorious reigns in the future. Yet it is also a religious vision, drawing upon images from the Old and New Testaments: the Queen of Sheba, 'covetous of wisdom and fair virtue', foes shaking 'like a field of beaten corn', every man eating 'in safety / Under his own vine what he plants' (5.4.23–34). The image of King James flourishing 'like a mountain cedar' and reaching out his branches to 'all the plains about him' is taken from the prophet Ezekiel. In particular, the birth of a child bringing hopes of a renewed golden age or a providential restoration of an unfallen world is a powerful image drawing upon Old Testament prophecies of a messiah, the New Testament gospels, and the Fourth Eclogue of Virgil, so often linked during the Renaissance

---

[1] Alan Brissenden, *Shakespeare and the Dance*, 1981, p. 106.

with the religious imagery of a messiah. In his prophecy, the worldly and the spiritual, which are distinguished from each other earlier in the play, are harmonised.

Much of the pageantry of *Henry VIII* has a celebratory quality, as hundreds of performances over several centuries have shown. Yet as we have seen, the pageants in their dramatic contexts also expose the vanities of power and wealth, and some of the ceremonies and rituals reveal the arbitrary cruelties of authority. The play has an ironic quality as essential to its meaning as celebration.

Although *Henry VIII* is not continuously ironic in the way that *Troilus and Cressida* is, nevertheless the action, the characters and much of the dialogue are given an ironic colouring which creates a degree of scepticism in the audience about protestations of innocence or conscience and a sense that more than one interpretation of words and deeds is possible. Irony is apparent in the structure of *Henry VIII*, it is also theatrically active as dramatic irony in specific scenes, and it affects much of the play through such devices as diverse observation and commentary, since almost everyone in the play becomes involved in watching others and speculating about their reactions or motives. The first two scenes demonstrate admirably how the irony works in structural terms. In the first, the audience hears Buckingham's charges against Wolsey, which add up to treason against the state, but it is Buckingham who is arrested at the end of the scene. In the second scene, Henry thanks Wolsey for his great concern and care in unmasking treason; the audience then watches a corrupted witness skilfully managed by Wolsey describing in some detail the alleged treasonable outbursts of Buckingham. Katherine's warnings about the witness, disregarded by Henry, serve to point the irony.

Another example occurs in a later pair of episodes. In 2.2, Henry talks to the two cardinals about the difficulties he is having with his conscience over his marriage to Katherine and concludes with a brief lament for the loss of Katherine:

> Would it not grieve an able man to leave
> So sweet a bedfellow? But conscience, conscience;
> O 'tis a tender place, and I must leave her.                    (2.2.140–2)

The scene immediately following undercuts this lament, indeed the whole conversation with the cardinals, by presenting the Lord Chamberlain bringing news to Anne Bullen of her new title and a handsome pension. The Old Lady's bawdy remarks make clear the implications of this transaction.

Dramatic irony is powerful in several episodes in the play, the kind of irony that depends on the ignorance of one or more characters on stage as to the true state of affairs while others know the truth, as does the audience. The most notable of these episodes concerns the fall of Wolsey in a large scene at the centre of the play. The scene is remarkable for its watching and listening groups as well as for the tension between the central characters, Henry and Wolsey. Knowing something of what has reached the king (Wolsey's letter to the pope), the nobles watch Wolsey's strange behaviour as he converses with Cromwell and then talks to himself, though Wolsey does not yet know that his letter has gone astray. When the king enters, he tells the nobles, and hence the audience, of the further evidence he has discovered of Wolsey's duplicity – the inventory of Wolsey's vast wealth accidentally placed among the other papers Wolsey had sent him that morning. He then calls for Wolsey, who has walked aside, and proceeds to tease him, with a nice play on the words 'audit' and 'inventory' in relation to Wolsey's supposed devotion to spiritual blessings:

> Good my lord,
> You are full of heavenly stuff, and bear the inventory
> Of your best graces in your mind, the which
> You were now running o'er; you have scarce time
> To steal from spiritual leisure a brief span
> To keep your earthly audit. . .                         (3.2.136–41)

Henry's demand for a full public statement from Wolsey of his loyalty to his master, the bonds of duty and gratitude to the one who has given him so much, is an elaborate test of Wolsey's ability to deliver fine speeches which conceal his true purposes, a test in other words of Wolsey's hypocrisy. He then gives the puzzled and very worried Wolsey the incriminating papers and departs with the nobles, not waiting for the dénouement as Wolsey discovers the real truth of his situation.

There is similar dramatic irony in the scenes in Act 5 involving Gardiner's plan to remove Cranmer from office and have him put on trial, Henry's awareness of the plot, and the examination of Cranmer by the council. The watching and overhearing in these scenes are part of a current of comment, rumour and speculation running throughout the play, which creates a third form of irony, a general atmosphere of detachment and scepticism.[1] Most of the big scenes of crisis or celebration have their watchers and listeners: Buckingham's final speeches before he goes to the scaffold, Katherine's trial before the ecclesiastical court, Henry's testing of Wolsey at the time of his overthrow, Anne's coronation, and the council's high-handed treatment of Cranmer. The listeners on most of these occasions make their own assessment of what they see and hear and try to judge what lies behind outward appearance. The nobles, like the Gentlemen, are intensely curious about Henry's motives for attempting to divorce Katherine, and their comments raise doubts in the audience's mind about his public protestations of conscience and scruple.

A general scepticism about motive and character is focused principally upon Buckingham, Wolsey and Henry, since Katherine and Cranmer are much less problematic. Did Buckingham make the statements he was alleged to have made? We are never really sure, though we suspect that the witnesses have been bribed. The debate between Katherine and Griffith in 4.2 about Wolsey after his death highlights the difficulty of accepting any simple version (such as complete villainy) of an individual's character and purpose. Its very formality stresses the double-sidedness of human nature.

---

[1] Pierre Sahel, 'The strangeness of a dramatic style: rumour in "Henry VIII"', *S.Sur.* 38 (1985), 146–8.

12    Henry Irving as Cardinal Wolsey at the Lyceum Theatre, 1892. Playing opposite Ellen Terry, who
took the part of Katherine, Irving made Wolsey one of his most famous roles

The openness of view regarding character applies also to the interpretation of events, almost as a principle of uncertainty. It is not at all certain, for example, whether the tragic falls in their stately succession are completely arbitrary or whether they have a significant place in some larger pattern. Deserved retribution may account for the fall of Wolsey, but not for that of Katherine and doubtfully for Buckingham's. Because of the attention given to human motives like ambition and lust, the goddess Fortune does not appear to dominate the action, even though it is the most eminent who are most vulnerable, to be picked off in turn. Is Henry in control of events, or is he merely the agent of a more powerful force? Though Wolsey manipulates him at first, Henry seems increasingly dominant as the play proceeds, but at the end he is shunted to one side by Cranmer's vision of the glorious reigns beyond his own, and beyond that of the forgotten Mary. Through-out, the historical process appears to be uncertain in direction and often highly devious as the rivalries of court factions and the king's mixed motives of sexual desire and dynastic succession interact. Only towards the end of the play are the harsh realities of the power game transcended in Katherine's vision of a super-natural realm where virtue is rewarded and in Cranmer's vision of a transformed society on earth.

The diverse events and conflicting emotional situations of the play lead event-ually to a conclusion fulfilling hope and desire. Nevertheless, it is the ironic inter-play of these different elements throughout that creates a series of parallels and contrasts and provides a thread of unity. The pageantry is by no means wholly ironic but it is often placed in an ironic context. Though lacking the unity of a single developing action, or the unity of a dominating character, *Henry VIII* has a wholeness about it of a rich and complex kind.

Certainly it is susceptible of many different interpretations – as an exploration of developing royal power, as the tragedy of two great opposites, Katherine and Wolsey, or as a thoroughly ironic account of a historical period of momentous decision. The history of stage performances suggests that it has been difficult for directors to find a balance between these elements, and there has consequently been much cutting of the text and much alteration of the already extensive stage directions. It may be that the play lacks just such a balance, a clear focus that would allow a proper place for each element within it. Simply because of the variety of characters, events and ideas and the refusal of the play to provide forthright interpretations, critics and producers alike have been able to emphasise particular aspects that appeal to them while neglecting others. Yet if *Henry VIII* is seen as at once an exposure and a celebration of royal power, a conflict between worldly and eternal values, then its integrity as a play can be respected.

## The verse of the play

Discussion of some oddities of the verse of *Henry VIII* had occurred before Spedding made his analysis, as Pooler notes in the introduction to his edition. After Spedding, it has been one of the curious aspects of the authorship controversy that whereas one party has regarded the variations in style and prosody as a clear indication of not very satisfactory collaboration between two or three playwrights, the other party has seen these variations as a sign of a single playwright's craftsmanship in adjusting style to dramatic purpose, very much in Shakespeare's manner in *King John, Richard II* and *1* and *2 Henry IV*. For Spedding, as we have already noted, the structure of the verse was 'full of mannerism' and the expression was 'diffuse and languid' in the scenes he believed Fletcher had written, compared with the 'close-packed expression' and seemingly careless but controlled metre of the Shakespearean passages.[1] Wilson Knight, by contrast, regarded the stylistic variations in the play as having very distinct dramatic purposes, 'complex syntax and metaphorical expression' for the divided consciousness troubled by inner conflict; a much simpler form of expression 'where the speaker functions as a unit'.[2]

The variations in the verse patterns in *Henry VIII*, like the diction and figurative speech, are not so clearly linked with character as they are, for example, in *1 Henry IV*; rather, they are related to differing emotional or mental states appropriate to each situation. In the first scene of Act 1, for instance, Norfolk attempting to describe the wonders of the Field of the Cloth of Gold is given verse of great complexity which seeks, among other things, to match the rapid alternation of gorgeous shows from each royal party with similar balance and antithesis, and similar wealth of allusion in the expression. A little later in the same scene, as Buckingham gives vent to his frustration and anger against Wolsey, Norfolk reasons with him in a much simpler, straightforward way, the verse expressing in its movement some of the urgency of his warnings. Buckingham's anger is embodied in long, cumulative sentences, constantly interrupted by parentheses and questions which add more details to the total picture, and they display a heated rhetorical pressure that gives a vivid sense of the state of his mind.

We next see Buckingham after his trial, saying farewell to his friends and the small public gathering, and he speaks here in a totally different manner from his speeches of the first scene. Now there is a flow of long sentences without rhetorical questions or parentheses. The iambic pattern of the verse is more regular, and the pauses do not interrupt the line structure so much as support it. The rhythm of grief and resignation is different from the rhythm of anger.

There are similar strongly marked variations in rhythm, diction, and rhetorical organisation in Wolsey's speeches in court and council scenes and in the scene of his fall from favour, the taunting of the lords, and the introspection that follows. The clever, apparently rational but always manipulative speeches of the court scenes are dignified in tone and rhythmically controlled. They move at the measured pace of the skilled performer. Yet after his fall, when the lords come for the great seal and proceed to mock and accuse him (3.2), his manner of speech changes rapidly to brief and bitter exclamations, angry reciprocal taunts, longer

[1] Spedding, *Gentleman's Magazine* (Aug. 1850), p. 117.
[2] Knight, *Crown of Life*, p. 263.

periods of dignified defence, and short ironic or sarcastic comments. When he is left alone, the introspection begins, and with it a quiet. elegiac tone and what critics have called a falling rhythm, light syllables at the ends of lines as stresses fall away. His dialogue with Cromwell is carried on in the same manner, though there are one or two outbursts which briefly interrupt the even tone.

It appears, then, that there are distinct adjustments of verse rhythms, syntax, and diction from one dramatic situation to another, appropriate sometimes to speakers and their particular reactions, but appropriate also to the tensions and significance of the action in a wider sense. Linguistic evidence now suggests that we cannot link these adjustments and variations to sudden shifts from the work of one playwright to that of another since many of them occur in scenes now thought to have been written by Shakespeare alone. In more general terms, although there is strong feeling in a number of passages expressed in the rhetoric of high passion, it is the quieter and more reflective style that in the end is most characteristic of the play and seems to express its essential nature.

## Stage history

The stage history of *Henry VIII* begins with the famous occasion on 29 June 1613 when the Globe theatre burned down during a performance. Personal letters which survive tell us rather more about this early production than we might otherwise have known. Henry Bluett reports that it was a new play 'acted not passing 2 or 3 times before' and that 'the house was very full', a comment that may attest to its popularity, though new plays were often popular because they were new. Sir Henry Wotton had not seen the play but he suggests in a letter that its pageantry had made a considerable impression: it was 'set forth with many extra-ordinary circumstances of pomp and majesty, even to the matting of the stage . . .' and he continues with comments on the splendid costumes of the Knights of the Order and the Royal Guard.[1] Only one other performance has been recorded before the closing of the theatres, that called for by George Villiers, Duke of Buckingham, at a critical time in his career (July 1628), and he apparently left the theatre after Buckingham was led off to execution.[2]

After the Restoration, *Henry VIII* was soon put on the stage again and remained one of the fairly limited number of Shakespearean plays frequently performed. Pepys heard of a much talked-about production at the end of 1663 and went to see it early in the new year. However, he was not much impressed: 'though I went with resolution to like it, it is so simple a thing made up of a great many patches, that, besides the shows and processions in it, there is nothing in the world good or well done'. He liked a performance in December 1668 much better: 'was mightily pleased, better than I ever expected, with the history and shows of it'.[3] Both

---

[1] For these letters, see pp. 1–3 above.
[2] Chambers, *William Shakespeare*, II, 347.
[3] *Shakespeare Allusion-Book*, II, 394, 430.

comments suggest that pageantry was an important ingredient in its popular success, though Pepys also liked its 'history'.

John Downes, an actor and book-keeper in Davenant's theatre from 1662 until 1706, gives us one reason for the interest the play had aroused: 'This Play, by Order of Sir *William Davenant*, was all new Cloath'd in proper Habits', and there were 'new Scenes' as well. Downes's most intriguing and often quoted observation concerns the continuity of the acting tradition, in spite of the interregnum of the Commonwealth years:

The part of the King was so right and justly done by Mr *Betterton*, he being Instructed in it by Sir *William*, who had it from Old Mr *Lowen*, that had his Instructions from Mr *Shakespear* himself, that I dare and will aver, none can, or will come near him in this Age, in the performance of that part. . .[1]

Downes praised an actor called Harris in the role of Wolsey as scarcely inferior, but it is clear that the part of Henry was regarded as the major role in the play, as it was to remain for many years ahead.

The stage history of *Henry VIII* in the eighteenth century is one of continuing popularity (C. B. Hogan has counted 262 performances between 1701 and 1800) and still greater emphasis on spectacle and pageantry.[2] Spectacle was enhanced through splendour of costume in the processional scenes and by adding to the participants and attendants in the great ceremonies. The coronation procession of Anne Bullen was especially notable in 1727 when Colley Cibber revived the play as part of the celebrations for the coronation of George II; Cibber added a pageant of the Queen's Champion, challenging all comers in Westminster Hall. As Cibber said of his theatre in 1728: 'They have invented, and adorn'd a Spectacle that for Forty Days together has brought more Money to the House than the best Play that ever was writ.'[3] The scene of the Queen's Champion was played as a sequel to other quite unrelated plays 'and exhibited, that one Season, 75 times', as an early historian of the theatre noted.[4]

At Garrick's Theatre Royal in Drury Lane, the 1762 production of the play required 137 participants for the coronation procession, including musicians, drummers, choristers and attendants; similar emphasis on costume, ornament, and numerous participants was provided for the masque scene in Act 1, the divorce trial in Act 2, and the christening scene at the end. Katherine's vision, however, was not staged: the queen slept quietly while solemn music was played.[5]

Such pageantry meant of necessity cuts in the text of the play and the removal of subsidiary characters. In the acting text of Garrick's 1762 production, the Gentlemen are left out; much of 3.1, the cardinals' visit to Katherine, is omitted,

[1] *Roscius Anglicanus*, 1708, quoted *Shakespeare Allusion-Book*, II, 437–8.
[2] C. B. Hogan, *Shakespeare in the Theatre 1701–1800*, 2 vols., 1952–7, II, 717.
[3] G. C. D. Odell, *Shakespeare from Betterton to Irving*, 2 vols., 1921, I, 307.
[4] W. R. Chetwood, quoted by Odell, I, 307.
[5] *King Henry the Eighth with the Coronation of Anne Bullen. . .As it is performed at the Theatre-Royal in Drury Lane*, 1762.

13  Two sketches of scenes from Henry Irving's production at the Lyceum Theatre in 1892
*a* Buckingham (Forbes-Robertson) and Wolsey (Irving) stare at each other in Act 1, Scene 1
*b* The elaborate multi-level staging of the coronation procession of Anne Bullen (Violet Vanbrugh)

and the comic scene of the Porter in Act 5 is made very brief. Large speeches elsewhere in the play are also reduced. J. P. Kemble's 1804 production carried the cutting process still further by leaving out 3.1 entirely, the comic scene in Act 5, and the part of Dr Butts.[1] Kemble surprisingly also left out the coronation scene,

[1]  *Shakespeare's King Henry the Eighth, A Historical Play revised by J. P. Kemble . . . as acted at The Theatre Royal Covent Garden*, 1804.

14   The spectacular qualities of Victorian stage production were carried over into the twentieth
century by Herbert Beerbohm Tree at His Majesty's Theatre in 1910. Buckingham (Henry Ainley)
says farewell from the barge (Act 2, Scene 1)

perhaps because of what C. B. Young calls 'financial stringency' at Drury Lane in
1788–9 when the play was first mounted.[1] Another probable reason is that Kemble
wished to stress the two major roles of Wolsey and Katherine. His sister, Sarah
Siddons, played Katherine as a tragic heroine and became famous for her interpretation.[2] Kemble himself took the role of Wolsey after his move to Covent
Garden in 1806. These two parts became dominant throughout the nineteenth
and into the early twentieth centuries; Henry Irving and Ellen Terry were perhaps
the most famous but by no means the last in the series.

Kemble was responsible for another major innovation in his work at Covent
Garden after 1811, an attempt at elaborate antiquarian realism in the play's
pageantry. 'The banquet', said a reviewer in *The Times* (October 1811), 'deserved
all the praise that can be given to costly elegance. It was the most dazzling stage
exhibition that we have ever seen.'[3] This was Tudor magnificence he was
describing, not 'elegance' in the Regency sense. Charles Kean went even further
in 1855, turning to the original chronicles, Cavendish's *Life of Wolsey*, old paintings
and museum artefacts for authentic detail.[4] Some of the effects were sensational

[1]   Maxwell, p. xlii.
[2]   Margaret I. Swayze, 'A History of the Literary Criticism and Stage Production of *Henry VIII*',
      unpublished doctoral thesis, University of Birmingham, 1973, p. 144. I am indebted to Swayze's wide
      survey of the stage history of *Henry VIII*.
[3]   Odell, II, 102.
[4]   Swayze, p. 152.

examples of stagecraft: Buckingham was carried off to execution in a barge with four oarsmen; Katherine's vision was embodied in a ladder of angels in a shaft of light; and the christening scene was introduced by a moving panorama of London as the lord mayor and his party might have seen it from the river on their way to Greenwich.[1] Henry Irving's new production in 1892 cut away still more of the text and concentrated almost entirely on the first three acts. Irving presented a reconstruction on stage of sixteenth-century London, not only in the council scenes but also in the street scenes where there were crowds of people in the street and at windows on three different levels.[2] Processions, costumes, dances, music were authentic in detail and splendid to eye and ear. Although Irving's production filled the theatres in London and New York (1893), it proved so expensive to mount that he lost money and did not repeat the experiment. But Beerbohm Tree's productions of 1910–12 were similarly elaborate, providing the kind of spectacular entertainment that theatre audiences had come to expect. Tree himself played Wolsey, one of his notable roles. The critic Desmond MacCarthy called Beerbohm Tree 'essentially a romantic actor, perhaps the last exuberant descendant of Romanticism flowering on the English stage'.[3] Tree concluded the play with a gorgeous coronation scene for Anne, yet to make room for this and other spectacular episodes, he cut 47 per cent of the lines of the play.[4]

The result of so much pageantry, very largely for its own sake (as Irving himself later admitted),[5] was that political issues such as the conflict between royal power and the papacy, and the more direct issue of the king's dependence on a royal favourite like Wolsey, were all but forgotten. The play was thrown badly out of balance by the reduction of Henry's role to a mere stereotype, the concentration on Wolsey and Katherine, and the sheer weight of the pageantry. Moreover there could be little interplay between one scene and another since the flow of action was greatly impeded by elaborate scene changes. Nevertheless the playing of Katherine and Wolsey by actors like Ellen Terry and Irving as supreme antagonists and ultimately tragic figures kept alive one vital component of the play's central action.

Twentieth-century productions, especially since the Second World War, have diverged remarkably from nineteenth-century traditions. These new productions have had several qualities in common – the return of Henry to a central place in the drama, a restoration of most of the complete text along with subsidiary characters that had been dropped, a flexible and often simple stage setting or multi-purpose set, and the reduction of pageantry to a mere shadow of its former dominance. One of the first to campaign for a new approach to the performance of *Henry VIII* was G. Wilson Knight. He wanted a complete text to be played on a single flexible stage set.[6] He insisted that there were four major characters in the play and that it moved through a series of three personal tragedies to a triumph for

[1] Odell, II, 333.
[2] Odell, II, 445.
[3] *Herbert Beerbohm Tree*, ed. Max Beerbohm, n.d. [1920], p. 219.
[4] M. R. Booth, *Victorian Spectacular Theatre 1850–1910*, 1981, p. 134.
[5] A. Hughes, *Henry Irving, Shakespearean*, 1981, p. 17.
[6] G. Wilson Knight, *Principles of Shakespearean Production*, 1936, p. 132.

15   Arthur Bourchier as Henry VIII in characteristic Holbein costume and pose, with Beerbohm Tree
as Wolsey and Violet Vanbrugh as Katherine in Tree's 1910 production (Act 1, Scene 2)

the king and the nation. 'The King', he said in a programme note to his own
production in 1934, 'is central throughout and to be sharply distinguished from
the conventional Henry VIII.' The climax of the play would be Cranmer's
prophecy: 'Cranmer's final prophecy at the christening of Elizabeth is the
justification of all that goes before.'[1]

   Tyrone Guthrie's single most important contribution to the play's performance
history was to demonstrate at Stratford-upon-Avon in 1949 and 1950 how a
single, carefully constructed stage set might allow the action of the play to flow as
rapidly as it had on the Elizabethan stage.[2] He replaced the cumbersome sets
and machinery of Victorian productions, which had aimed at realistic illusion, with
actors and stage business that gave a lively impression of the multifarious activities
of Tudor London.[3] Though the splendour of costumes and the colours of

---

[1] Professor Bruce Honeyford, who took part as a student in Wilson Knight's production of the play at
Hart House Theatre in Toronto, 23–25 April 1934, has kindly sent me his copy of the original
programme. He reports that Knight played Buckingham 'with quiet dignity', but in the final act took
the part of the Porter's man.

[2] The multi-purpose set designed by Tanya Moiseiwitsch and the thrust stage became the basis for
new theatres at Stratford, Ontario, Minneapolis and Chichester, and influenced stage design for
Shakespearean productions very widely elsewhere.

[3] Guthrie was not averse to topical allusion. In the 1953 London production, the Gentlemen waiting
for Anne's coronation procession looked at the sky, then covered their heads with newspapers, to the
delight of the audience, many of whom had waited in the cold and wet for Elizabeth II's coronation
procession.

16 The divorce trial (Act 2, Scene 4) in Tyrone Guthrie's 1950 production at Stratford-upon-Avon. Wolsey (on the left) was played by Andrew Cruickshank, Henry by Anthony Quayle, and Katherine by Gwen Ffrangcon-Davies. The permanent stage structure permitted rapid change of scenes and a continuous flow of action

banners created a richness of atmosphere in much of the play, the coronation procession and Katherine's vision were unseen in the theatre, being left to the audience's imagination. Another change was Guthrie's emphasis on the role of Henry, played with much vigour and many changes of mood by Anthony Quayle at Stratford and by Paul Rogers in London in 1953. Henry emerged as a temperamental, rash and impulsive individual, engaged in a struggle with Wolsey for authority in the realm. The use of an almost complete text, the restoration of characters like the Gentlemen, and the drawing out of dramatic tensions between four major characters instead of two gave new significance and dramatic vitality to the play.[1]

What had been learned through Guthrie's series of productions was not lost on subsequent directors such as Michael Benthall at the Old Vic in 1958 and Trevor Nunn at Stratford in 1969. Benthall used a permanent set to permit continuous action, and like Guthrie he gave Henry's role its proper importance. Yet he continued one old tradition by casting John Gielgud as Wolsey and Edith Evans as Katherine, so that these two roles were once more the starring parts. Like some of his nineteenth-century predecessors, he also cut the fifth act severely and rearranged it to bring all the action quickly to a close in the christening scene.[2]

Trevor Nunn's production at Stratford in 1969 and London in 1970 was more original. He used an austere set, a black box enlivened only with a back-drop model of Tudor London. Newspaper headlines (Buckingham Guilty – Duke speaks before he goes to the block) were flashed on a screen at the front of the stage between scenes, a Brechtian device many commentators found irritating and unnecessary. However, there were few doubts about the strength of the acting in the four major parts. Irving Wardle in *The Times* praised Donald Sinden who 'fully conveys the sense of a passionate nature that has never been checked', and gave equal praise to Brewster Mason for presenting an unusual Wolsey 'as sensuous as his master', conducting intrigues 'in a tone of unctuous geniality'.[3] Peggy Ashcroft as Katherine and Richard Pascoe as Buckingham were likewise given full marks by Philip Hope-Wallace in the *Guardian* for 'sober, simple and unforced acting'. The production demonstrated the importance of the changing relationships among these four characters, with Anne Bullen and Cranmer added for good measure. As in Guthrie's productions, the audience in the theatre was addressed and invited to participate, particularly in the final scene which Ronald Bryden in the *Observer* called 'a sonorous white hippie mass in which actors advance on the audience, chanting Cranmer's wishes for England's princess "peace, plenty, love, truth"'. Bryden also noted the importance of the play's production in the same season as Shakespeare's other late plays, revealing how often they are concerned with the same preoccupations.[4]

---

[1] A detailed account and considered judgement on Guthrie's 1949 production is given by Muriel St Clare Byrne in *S.Sur.* 3 (1950), 120–9.
[2] See Roy Walker's review, *S.Sur.* 12 (1959), 122–30.
[3] *The Times*, 10 October 1969. See also Robert Speaight in *SQ* 21 (1970), 440.
[4] *Observer*, 12 October 1969.

The BBC's 1978 film of the play is worthy of mention as one of the most successful of the filmed series. Although the director, Kevin Billington, had none of the restraints imposed by an actual stage, the courtly and elegant film set provided an appropriate background without being pedantic and without dominating the dramatic action. Thus the coronation procession, which might have been blown up into a great film spectacle, was glimpsed only briefly. In my view, the film achieved an admirable balance among the major characters: a gullible and passionate Henry (John Stride), a stolid, calculating Wolsey with something of the butcher's plebeian beefiness about him (Timothy West), an effective Buckingham, and a queenly Katherine (Claire Bloom), restrained but very moving in her final scene. The political issues of the play were given some substance in the production and there were striking contrasts between goodness and nobility of soul set apart from worldly concerns and the frequent hypocrisy and malice of those engaged in power struggles.

The most controversial production of *Henry VIII* in the late twentieth century was undoubtedly that of Howard Davies at Stratford-upon-Avon in 1983, perhaps the first to have credited Fletcher as Shakespeare's collaborator in the programme notes. Davies found certain ironies and contradictions in the text of the play and heightened them throughout his production. In a vaguely Tudor setting ('toytown fragments hanging from rails', said Robert Cushman),[1] courtliness was thrown aside by the king and the other masquers in their 'wildmen' costumes as they kicked the furniture out of the way and engaged the ladies of the court in an orgiastic dance, throwing them to the floor at the end. Buckingham's long speeches of farewell brought titters from the audience as the bored guards yawned openly and shifted their feet, in a scene which traditionally had given full weight to Buckingham's tragic fall. The Gentlemen were presented as servants about the court, commenting caustically on their betters, particularly in the coronation scene. Instead of a glittering procession, the audience saw the participants putting on their robes and ornaments, sometimes with difficulty, from a row of dummies in the robing-room. The incidental music, post-Kurt Weill, jazzy and decadent, accompanied the bustling actors as they moved on or off the stage and added further to the alienation from Tudor courtliness and ceremony. Philip Brockbank noted in a *TLS* review that 'the effect is to expose to view the duplicities and evasions usually cloaked in performance by mellifluence and magniloquence'.[2]

Most critics saw Davies's production as an attempt to stress the political issues of the play – the developing conflict between Henry and Wolsey and the determination of Henry to have his own way and rule with full authority. In Michael Billington's view, 'Mr Davies... tackled the piece as if it were a cynical anatomy of power politics', abandoning the traditional concept of the play as Tudor image-building. His production 'comes across as a republican revision of royalist propaganda'.[3] Of course there is also the question asked by Robert Cushman: 'if all

[1] *Observer*, 19 June 1983.
[2] *TLS*, 24 June 1983, p. 665.
[3] *Guardian*, 16 June 1983.

17  Henry and the two cardinals in Trevor Nunn's 1969 production for the Royal Shakespeare
Company. Henry was played by Donald Sinden, Wolsey by Brewster Mason, and Campeius by
Anthony Pedley

the ironies assumed by Mr Davies were really present in the text, would he have to
labour so hard to bring them to our attention?'[1] Another commentator, Irving
Wardle, saw a powerful momentum in the play, a 'sense of urgency' usually lacking
in productions of *Henry VIII*, centred upon the 'implacable accretion of centralised
national power'.[2]

Richard Griffiths's performance as Henry was a crucial element in the design.
As Wardle observed in his review, Griffiths 'is not the peremptory bull-like
autocrat of legend, but a slow-moving temperamentally withdrawn figure who at
first seems to be at the mercy of stronger surrounding personalities'. The
production made much of his erotic arousal by Anne Bullen's beauty in the
masque scene, but after this scene the play offers no opportunity for further
development of this aspect. By the end, he is the master-politician; he has

[1]  *Observer*, 19 June 1983.
[2]  *The Times*, 16 June 1983.

outmanoeuvred Wolsey and secured Cranmer as his willing ally. Opposite Henry, both John Thaw as Wolsey and Gemma Jones as Katherine presented strong performances. Gemma Jones maintained her strength of mind and queenly bearing, marked by occasional flashes of fire, until the end, and her vision was not undercut ironically. With its quiet music and the trailing costumes of the angelic figures, it appeared to be a scene from another play.

However, the positive note advanced by her spiritual serenity in the face of disaster remained a crucial problem in this production, which formed, as Philip Brockbank has phrased it, 'an inescapable indictment of the king, the Church, the law and even the divine will'.[1] The other positive and sometimes climactic moment of the play, Cranmer's prophecy, was treated here with mocking irony since Cranmer was presented as a whining individual, the 'accommodating keeper of the king's conscience', anxious only to be on the winning side.[2] There was a notable dramatic contrast in the final scenes between Cranmer and Bishop Gardiner who was played (by Oliver Ford Davies) as cunning and cruel but fiercely independent, a most unwilling servant to the king's commands.

Other performances in recent years have maintained the modern tradition of an almost complete text but have been straightforward in their approach, less innovative in their exploration of the play's significance. A production by the Norwich Players at the Maddermarket Theatre, Norwich, in 1986 was remarkably complete in terms of the major issues and many cross-currents that flow through the play, although it was presented in an intimate theatre on a very small stage. The anonymous actors made clear the relationships between a choleric and suspicious Henry, a Wolsey who was filled with steely resolve until the breaking point, and a cool, soft-spoken Katherine revealing an underlying strength of character. In spite of the small stage, the director (Ian Emmerson) managed to include a courtly dance for the masque scene, a coronation procession, and a stately measure for the vision. Cranmer's prophecy at the end carried conviction.[3]

At Stratford, Ontario, in 1986 John Neville included *Henry VIII* in a season of Shakespeare's last plays, like Trevor Nunn at Stratford-upon-Avon in 1969. It differed from the 1983 Royal Shakespeare Theatre production by stressing spiritual disorder in the kingdom rather than political disorder, and therefore, as the director Brian Rintoul observed in a programme note, 'at the end of the play the restoration to order is also spiritual and not political'. The director also suggested that Henry as a man of action is confronted by a crucial moral question, whether political and temporal affairs should come before spiritual issues, or vice versa. Leon Pownall played Henry as 'an insolent, energetic young king', impulsive, hot-tempered and inclined to bluster.[4] The other parts were equally strong. William Hutt as Wolsey dominated many scenes by his quiet, rather

[1] *TLS*, 24 June 1983, p. 665.
[2] Brockbank, *TLS*, p. 665.
[3] Since the production was not widely reviewed, I have used my own notes of the performance on 12 November 1986.
[4] Ray Conlogue, *Globe and Mail*, 26 May 1986.

sinister watchfulness as he awaited his opportunities. Michael Ratcliffe in the *Observer* noted that 'William Hutt plays Wolsey as a silky, superior intelligence; Elizabeth Shepherd tackles Queen Katharine as though it were a brand-new part and Shakespeare a contemporary writer; both are superb.'[1]

Staging on the smaller proscenium stage at Stratford was lavish in terms of costume, but there was less room for the pageantry of show and procession, so that more emphasis was necessarily placed, in the director's view, on the actors themselves. They were 'grittier' in their parts, more naturalistic.[2] Courtly music suggesting music of the period was important in creating atmosphere: thus the Orpheus song at the beginning of 3.1 was sung by a waiting-woman to the accompaniment of a lute, and this developed into a complex part-song in which the queen took part with spirit and enjoyment. Music, especially that of the vision scene, hinted at a resolution of the play's moral conflicts beyond intrigue, power struggles and worldly values.

Finally, the portrayal of Cranmer by David Brown as a strong and dignified character, showing little servility towards Henry but displaying a certain stiffness, even a hint of stubbornness, allowed the 'spiritual restoration' announced in his prophecy to make its full effect.[3]

If not fully rehabilitated as one of Shakespeare's major history plays, with a special significance in terms of the realities of power and the fate of the individual, or in terms of worldly values as against spiritual values, *Henry VIII* now appears able to stand on its own merits. Recent stage productions have shown it to be a play that need not depend for its appeal on spectacle and pageantry alone, or the acting of two or three great actors for whose sake much of the play is discarded as irrelevant. Like many of Shakespeare's plays, it contains much more than a simplistic portrayal of character or a single interpretation of events, and no one performance seems capable of encompassing all of it.

[1] *Observer*, 27 July 1986.
[2] Brian Rintoul, programme note.
[3] A personal recollection of Brown's portrayal of Cranmer.

# NOTE ON THE TEXT

The text of *Henry VIII* presents few problems to the editor and has aroused little debate, except over its possible relationship with putative authors. There is only one source for the text, the First Folio of 1623, where it concludes the series of Histories. The Folio text is a good one; there are comparatively few errors, the acts and scenes are clearly marked and the stage directions are set out very fully. The Folio text comes apparently from a fair copy, not the author's foul papers (or two authors' foul papers). As J. C. Maxwell points out, there are no unusual or characteristic habits of spelling or punctuation to suggest a particular scribe or an author.[1]

The copy-text used by the Folio compositors was probably not a prompt-book since there are several variations in speech headings which a book-keeper would be bound to tidy up. Many of the stage directions appear to have come from the playwright's script rather than from the book used in the theatre. Thus there are descriptive directions: *The* CARDINAL *in his passage fixeth his eye on* BUCKINGHAM, *and* BUCKINGHAM *on him, both full of disdain* (1.1.114); and vague or permissive directions: *Enter* BRANDON. . .*and two or three of the Guard* (1.1.197). The procession to the ecclesiastical court held at Blackfriars in 2.4 is outlined in the stage direction with particular details that sound like a playwright deter-mined to get it exactly right.

Spelling has been modernised, following the pattern of the New Cambridge Shakespeare. Punctuation is light, but where possible the Folio punctuation has been retained since it often appears to be related to the speaking voice. Changes or additions to stage directions are placed in square brackets. In the select col-lation, authority for the present reading is given first; other readings or con-jectures (if any) follow in their chronological order. Corrections of the lineation are in accord with changes made by Rowe and Pope in the eighteenth century, although there is speculation that some of the broken lines may represent the way the playwright wanted the lines spoken.

[1] Maxwell, p. 113.

*King Henry VIII*

# LIST OF CHARACTERS

HENRY VIII, *King of England*
KATHERINE, *Queen of England, later divorced*
CARDINAL WOLSEY
DUKE OF BUCKINGHAM
ANNE BULLEN, *maid-of-honour to Katherine, later Queen*
CRANMER, *Archbishop of Canterbury*
DUKE OF NORFOLK
DUKE OF SUFFOLK, *Charles Brandon, an intimate of Henry's*
EARL OF SURREY
CARDINAL CAMPEIUS
THOMAS CROMWELL, *in Wolsey's service, later privy councillor*
GARDINER, *Henry's secretary, later Bishop of Winchester*
BISHOP OF LINCOLN
LORD CHAMBERLAIN
LORD CHANCELLOR
LORD ABERGAVENNY
LORD SANDS (*Sir Walter Sands*)
SIR THOMAS LOVELL
SIR HENRY GUILFORD
SIR ANTHONY DENNY
SIR NICHOLAS VAUX
CAPUCHIUS, *ambassador from the Emperor Charles V*
GRIFFITH, *gentleman-usher to Queen Katherine*
DR BUTTS, *physician to the King*
PATIENCE, *Katherine's woman*
THREE GENTLEMEN
SURVEYOR *to the Duke of Buckingham*
BRANDON, *captain of the guard*
SERGEANT-AT-ARMS
DOOR-KEEPER
GARTER KING-AT-ARMS
OLD LADY
PORTER *and his* MAN
MESSENGER
PAGE *to Gardiner*
CRIER
SECRETARIES *to Wolsey*
SERVANT *to Wolsey*
SCRIBE
GENTLEMAN *to Katherine*
*Lords, ladies, bishops, judges, priests, vergers, women attending on the Queen, lord mayor, aldermen, citizens, scribes, officers, guards, servants, musicians, heavenly spirits*

SCENE: *London, Kimbolton*

**Notes**

The first list of characters was provided by Rowe in 1709, though it was incomplete.

LORD CHANCELLOR Although Cromwell tells Wolsey (3.2.393) that Sir Thomas More has been named lord chancellor in his place, in Act 5 any use of More's name is studiously avoided. Historically, the conspiracy against Cranmer took place in 1544 or 1545; Sir Thomas Audley, More's successor, was chancellor until he died in 1544, and Thomas Wriothesley (later Earl of Southampton) succeeded him.

LORD SANDS The compression of time in the play hides the fact that the trial and execution of Buckingham took place some years before the banquet at York Place or the meeting of Henry and Anne. Sir Walter Sands (as he was at the time of Buckingham's execution) was later elevated to the peerage and hence appears in 1.3 and 1.4 as Lord Sands, but in 2.1 as Sir Walter.

BRANDON The captain of the guard who enters at 1.1.197 may conceivably be Charles Brandon, Duke of Suffolk, called 'Charles' by the king in 5.1. However, it appears unlikely that Suffolk would fulfil this function, or speak in the tone that he does to Norfolk and Buckingham even though the arrest is a formal occasion. Holinshed names the captain as 'Sir Henrie Marneie'.

# THE FAMOUS HISTORY OF THE
# LIFE OF KING HENRY THE EIGHTH

THE PROLOGUE

I come no more to make you laugh; things now
That bear a weighty and a serious brow,
Sad, high, and working, full of state and woe;
Such noble scenes as draw the eye to flow
We now present. Those that can pity, here    5
May, if they think it well, let fall a tear,
The subject will deserve it. Such as give
Their money out of hope they may believe,
May here find truth too. Those that come to see
Only a show or two, and so agree    10
The play may pass, if they be still and willing,
I'll undertake may see away their shilling
Richly in two short hours. Only they
That come to hear a merry, bawdy play,
A noise of targets, or to see a fellow    15
In a long motley coat guarded with yellow,
Will be deceived. For, gentle hearers, know

**Prologue**

**Prologue** Dr Johnson suggested that both Prologue and Epilogue were by Ben Jonson, but there is no evidence for this conjecture. Peter Alexander argues incisively for Shakespeare's authorship, pointing to similar prologues and epilogues undoubtedly his ('Conjectural history, or Shakespeare's *Henry VIII*', *Essays and Studies* 16 (1930), 101).

**2 brow** countenance, appearance.

**3 Sad...working** Serious, important, and moving.

**3 state** lofty or impressive matters of state.

**9 truth** The Prologue insists on the historical truth of the play; the phrase 'chosen truth' (18) suggests that the serious import of events will be stressed. In his letter about the burning of the Globe, Wotton calls the play *All is True*, as does Henry Bluett (see p. 1 above).

**10 show** spectacle; also, 'foolery and fighting', as suggested at 19.

**12 shilling** Courtiers and gallants paid a shilling for the more expensive seats in the lords' room close to or above the stage: see Chambers, *ES*, II, 534.

**13 two short hours** Prologues often speak of two hours or three hours for the length of a play: these are probably round figures, as Foakes suggests.

**14 a merry...play** Such as Samuel Rowley's play about Henry VIII, *When You See Me You Know Me*, first played in 1604 or 1605, reprinted and perhaps revived on the stage in 1613.

**15 targets** shields; thus, 'the noise of swords against shields'. Rowley's play has a fight between Henry (in disguise) and Black Will.

**16 motley coat** A coat made of a cloth of mixed colours, typically worn by fools and jesters. Will Summers, Henry VIII's court jester, would have worn such a coat in Rowley's play.

**16 guarded** trimmed.

**17 deceived** disappointed

To rank our chosen truth with such a show
As fool and fight is, beside forfeiting
Our own brains and the opinion that we bring                    20
To make that only true we now intend,
Will leave us never an understanding friend.
Therefore, for goodness' sake, and as you are known
The first and happiest hearers of the town,
Be sad, as we would make ye. Think ye see                       25
The very persons of our noble story
As they were living; think you see them great,
And followed with the general throng and sweat
Of thousand friends; then, in a moment, see
How soon this mightiness meets misery:                          30
And if you can be merry then, I'll say
A man may weep upon his wedding day.


1.1 *Enter the* DUKE OF NORFOLK *at one door. At the other the* DUKE OF
BUCKINGHAM *and the* LORD ABERGAVENNY

BUCKINGHAM Good morrow, and well met. How have ye done
    Since last we saw in France?
NORFOLK                                          I thank your grace,
    Healthful, and ever since a fresh admirer
    Of what I saw there.
BUCKINGHAM                          An untimely ague

Act 1, Scene 1      1.1] *Actus Primus Scæna Prima* F

19–21 **beside...intend** besides losing all our
brain-work and the settled conviction we bring
with us to make what we present only the truth.
Pooler argues that 'opinion' means 'credit' or
'reputation' in this context, but the sense of convinced purpose – 'ready intention' (Foakes) –
seems closer to the mark.
    **24 first...hearers** A compliment by the
actors of the King's Men to the audience as the
foremost and most favourable audience the actors
could wish for.

**Act 1, Scene 1**
   1.1 F divides acts and scenes throughout.
   **0 SD** This long scene, apparently set in an
antechamber at court, is an effective means of
exposition. After the extravagant description of

the meeting of the two kings in France, it reveals
the bitter antagonism between Wolsey and certain
nobles, and moves rapidly towards Buckingham's
downfall. There is a clear reference to two doors
leading on to the stage, one on either side, and
this arrangement is apparent throughout the play
(thus 2.1.0 SD, 4.1.0 SD). A discovery space with
a curtain, probably between the two doors, is
revealed by the SD at 2.2.60, and an entry 'at a
window above' at 5.2.18 indicates the use of an
upper stage.
   **2 saw** saw each other.
   **3 fresh** untired.
   **4 ague** Holinshed reports that Buckingham
was present at the ceremonies of the Field of
the Cloth of Gold in June 1520, though he was
a reluctant participant because of the expense

Stayed me a prisoner in my chamber, when                    5
Those suns of glory, those two lights of men
Met in the vale of Andren.

NORFOLK                              'Twixt Guynes and Arde;
I was then present, saw them salute on horseback,
Beheld them when they lighted, how they clung
In their embracement, as they grew together,          10
Which had they, what four throned ones could have
    weighed
Such a compounded one?

BUCKINGHAM                          All the whole time
I was my chamber's prisoner.

NORFOLK                              Then you lost
The view of earthly glory: men might say
Till this time pomp was single, but now married          15
To one above itself. Each following day
Became the next day's master, till the last
Made former wonders, its. Today the French,
All clinquant all in gold, like heathen gods
Shone down the English; and tomorrow they          20
Made Britain India: every man that stood
Showed like a mine. Their dwarfish pages were
As cherubins, all gilt; the madams too,
Not used to toil, did almost sweat to bear
The pride upon them, that their very labour          25
Was to them as a painting. Now this masque
Was cried incomparable; and th'ensuing night
Made it a fool and beggar. The two kings,
Equal in lustre, were now best, now worst,

---

11] *Rowe*³; Which...they, / What...weigh'd F

involved (pp. 855 and 858). The dramatist in-
vents Buckingham's temporary illness to allow
Norfolk's vivid description and Buckingham's
reaction.

  **7 vale of Andren** The vale of Andren lies
between Guynes, at that time held by the English,
and Arde (or Ardres) held by the French.

  **9 lighted** alighted.

  **10 as** as if.

  **11 weighed** balanced.

  **15 single...married** Each king's pomp was
single but now they are married to form a pomp
greater than either king's pomp before (so

Johnson).

  **17 master** teacher.

  **19 clinquant** glittering.

  **21–2 India...mine** Foakes notes *1H4*
3.1.166–7: 'as bountiful / As mines of India'.

  **23 cherubins** Shakespeare's usual plural for
'cherubin', though 'cherubims' and 'cherubim'
were replacing it in the seventeenth century.

  **23 madams** noble ladies.

  **25 pride** ostentatious dress and ornaments.

  **26 as a painting** i.e. gave them colour as if
they had used cosmetics.

As presence did present them: him in eye                   30
Still him in praise, and being present both,
'Twas said they saw but one, and no discerner
Durst wag his tongue in censure. When these suns
(For so they phrase 'em) by their heralds challenged
The noble spirits to arms, they did perform               35
Beyond thought's compass, that former fabulous story
Being now seen possible enough, got credit
That Bevis was believed.

BUCKINGHAM                  O you go far.

NORFOLK  As I belong to worship, and affect
In honour honesty, the tract of every thing               40
Would by a good discourser lose some life
Which action's self was tongue to. All was royal;
To the disposing of it nought rebelled;
Order gave each thing view; the office did
Distinctly his full function.

BUCKINGHAM                        Who did guide,          45
I mean who set the body and the limbs
Of this great sport together?

NORFOLK                        As you guess:
One, certes, that promises no element
In such a business.

BUCKINGHAM              I pray you who, my lord?

---

33 censure. When] *Rowe;* censure, when F   42–7 All...together?] *Theobald; Buc.* All...together? F   47
NORFOLK As...guess:] F; (*Buck.*) as...guess? F4

**30 him in eye** The one who was present and
therefore in the eye of the beholder was always
the one to be praised. 'Still' = 'always'.

**33 censure** judgement.

**38 Bevis** Hero of the medieval romance, *Sir
Bevis of Hamtoun* (Southampton), mentioned
by Chaucer as one of the flowers of chivalry with
whom Sir Thopas is to be compared, and by
Drayton in *Poly-Olbion* (1613), II, 260 ff.
(Pooler).

**38 you go far** your imagination is running away
with you. The convolutions of the language with
conceits and paradoxes, and the later comments
of Buckingham and Abergavenny, suggest an
irony that calls into question the whole meaning
of the celebrations, particularly when it is revealed
that the treaty has been broken already.

**39 worship** good name, repute.

**39–40 affect...honesty** follow or love truth
according to my sense of honour.

**42–7 All was royal...together?** F gives all
these lines to Buckingham, although 42–5
appear to be part of Norfolk's speech. Most
editors follow Theobald in correcting the attribution.

**43 disposing** setting out, arrangement.

**44 office** (1) officer, (2) group of officials.

**45 Distinctly** Clearly, without any confusion.

**47 As you guess** Some editors follow F4 in
placing this phrase after 'together' at the end of
Buckingham's speech, with a question mark following. However, the F reading may be correct:
Norfolk assumes Buckingham can easily guess
the truth.

**48 element** part, share.

NORFOLK All this was ordered by the good discretion              50
　　　　Of the right reverend Cardinal of York.

BUCKINGHAM The devil speed him! No man's pie is freed
　　　　From his ambitious finger. What had he
　　　　To do in these fierce vanities? I wonder
　　　　That such a keech can with his very bulk            55
　　　　Take up the rays o'th'beneficial sun,
　　　　And keep it from the earth.

NORFOLK 　　　　　　　　　　　　Surely, sir,
　　　　There's in him stuff that puts him to these ends;
　　　　For being not propped by ancestry, whose grace
　　　　Chalks successors their way, not called upon        60
　　　　For high feats done to th'crown, neither allied
　　　　To eminent assistants, but spider-like
　　　　Out of his self-drawing web – O! gives us note,
　　　　The force of his own merit makes his way,
　　　　A gift that heaven gives for him, which buys        65
　　　　A place next to the king.

ABERGAVENNY 　　　　　　　　　　I cannot tell
　　　　What heaven hath given him: let some graver eye
　　　　Pierce into that, but I can see his pride
　　　　Peep through each part of him: whence has he that?
　　　　If not from hell, the devil is a niggard,           70
　　　　Or has given all before, and he begins
　　　　A new hell in himself.

---

63 web – O! gives us note,] F2; Web. O gives us note, F; web, he gives us note, *Capell;* web, 'a gives us note *Kittredge;* web, O, gives us note, *Foakes*　　65 gives...buys] F; gives, which for him buys *Hanmer;* gives to him, which buys *Rann, conj. Johnson*　　69–70 that? / ...hell] *Theobald;* that, / ...Hell? F

52–3 No...finger 'To have a finger in every pie' is proverbial for interfering and having influence everywhere (Tilley F228).

54 fierce vanities extravagant follies.

55 keech The fat of a slaughtered animal rolled up into a lump (*OED*). A reference to Wolsey's being a butcher's son: see 120 below.

58 stuff qualities of character, inner nature.

59 grace virtue.

60 Chalks Marks.

62 assistants supporters; possibly 'ministers of state' (see *Ham.* 2.2.166).

63 his...web the web he draws out of himself.

63 O! An expression of emotion in the midst of the sentence; however, a number of editors have considered the F 'O' as a misprint for 'a' (he) which occurs elsewhere in Shakespeare (*Ham.* 1.1.43), though not otherwise in this play.

63 gives us note tells us about it, i.e. that his own merit has brought about his advancement.

70 If...hell F places the question mark after 'hell' rather than after 'that'. The phrase follows naturally upon the question 'Whence has he that' but makes better sense introducing 'the devil is a niggard'. Lucifer fell from heaven because of his pride, and Abergavenny makes the point that Wolsey must have received his pride from the devil, or if the devil is selfish or has already given away all he had, then Wolsey is making a new hell from his own pride.

BUCKINGHAM                              Why the devil,
Upon this French going-out, took he upon him,
Without the privity o'th'king, t'appoint
Who should attend on him? He makes up the file          75
Of all the gentry; for the most part such
To whom as great a charge as little honour
He meant to lay upon: and his own letter,
The honourable board of council out,
Must fetch him in he papers.

ABERGAVENNY                               I do know             80
Kinsmen of mine, three at the least, that have
By this so sickened their estates that never
They shall abound as formerly.

BUCKINGHAM                            O many
Have broke their backs with laying manors on 'em
For this great journey. What did this vanity             85
But minister communication of
A most poor issue?

NORFOLK                       Grievingly I think,
The peace between the French and us not values
The cost that did conclude it.

BUCKINGHAM                          Every man,
After the hideous storm that followed, was             90

79–80 The...council out, / ...him in he papers.] *Capell*; The...Councell, out / ...him in, he Papers, F;
(The...Council out) / ...in him he papers. *Pope*; The...council, out / ...him in he papers. *Foakes*   87
issue?] *Pope*; issue. F

73 **French going-out** expedition into France.
74 **privity** participation, private knowledge.
75 **file** list.
76–7 **such To whom** i.e. those persons upon whom he meant to lay. 'To' is a redundant preposition.
78–80 **and his...he papers** and his own letter, the honourable board of council being disregarded, must fetch in whomever he puts on the list. There has been much argument about the punctuation and interpretation of this passage (see supplementary note). Holinshed reports that the peers who received such letters grudged the high expense of attending the king on 'such a costlie journie', 'without consent of the whole boord of the councell' and that Buckingham in particular was annoyed by the expense (p. 855).
80 **he papers** he sets down on paper (*OED* sv v 1).

83 **abound** live in prosperity.
84 Proverbial; see Tilley L452.
86–7 **minister...issue** Literally, 'arrange much talk to a very poor outcome', but a secondary idea carries on the image of wasteful expense, the transmission of impoverishment to a 'most poor issue', the heirs of those who have sold their manors. Foakes suggests 'communication' may also be a quibble on sexual intercourse and that 'poor issue' refers to bastard children.
87 **Grievingly** In a manner to cause trouble or pain; perhaps a coinage (Foakes).
88 **not values** does not equal in value.
90 **hideous storm** The meeting of the kings began on 7 June 1520. Holinshed mentions 'an hideous storme of wind and weather' on 18 June, 'that manie coniectured it did prognosticate trouble and hatred shortlie after to follow between princes' (pp. 860–1).

A thing inspired, and, not consulting, broke
Into a general prophecy; that this tempest
Dashing the garment of this peace, aboded
The sudden breach on't.
NORFOLK                          Which is budded out,
For France hath flawed the league, and hath attached    95
Our merchants' goods at Bordeaux.
ABERGAVENNY                          Is it therefore
Th'ambassador is silenced?
NORFOLK                          Marry is't.
ABERGAVENNY A proper title of a peace, and purchased
At a superfluous rate.
BUCKINGHAM                          Why all this business
Our reverend cardinal carried.
NORFOLK                          Like it your grace,    100
The state takes notice of the private difference
Betwixt you and the cardinal. I advise you –
And take it from a heart that wishes towards you
Honour and plenteous safety – that you read
The cardinal's malice and his potency    105
Together; to consider further that
What his high hatred would effect wants not
A minister in his power. You know his nature,
That he's revengeful; and I know his sword
Hath a sharp edge: it's long and't may be said    110
It reaches far, and where 'twill not extend,

96 Bordeaux] Burdeux F

91 **not consulting** not consulting together, independently.
92 **general** universal.
93 **Dashing** Violently spoiling; also in the sense of 'frustrating, bringing to nothing' the peace agreed upon.
93 **garment** The costly show celebrating the peace. Holinshed describes a splendid pavilion, prepared for a magnificent pageant, as blown down by the tempest.
93 **aboded** foreshadowed.
95 **attached** seized.
97 **silenced** This may be an echo of Halle's chronicle, as Foakes points out: 'the Ambassador was commaunded to kepe his house in silence, and not to come in presence, till he was sent for' (I, 243–4).

97 **Marry is't** Why of course it is.
98 **proper title** 'Proper' is used ironically for 'very fine' or 'admirable'. 'Title' is both the name which is 'a peace', and the legal title or agreed bargain which has been 'purchased' at an excessive cost.
100 **carried** managed, conducted.
100 **Like it your grace** May it please your grace (an apology for the advice that follows).
101 **state** the court; those closely connected with power and the political affairs of the realm.
104 **read** judge, estimate carefully.
107 **wants** lacks.
108 **minister** agent.

Thither he darts it. Bosom up my counsel,
You'll find it wholesome. Lo, where comes that rock
That I advise your shunning.

*Enter* CARDINAL WOLSEY, *the purse borne before him, certain of the
Guard, and two Secretaries with papers: the* CARDINAL *in his passage
fixeth his eye on* BUCKINGHAM, *and* BUCKINGHAM *on him, both
full of disdain*

WOLSEY The Duke of Buckingham's surveyor? Ha!                    115
    Where's his examination?
SECRETARY                          Here, so please you.
WOLSEY Is he in person ready?
SECRETARY                          Ay, please your grace.
WOLSEY Well, we shall then know more, and Buckingham
    Shall lessen this big look.
                                *Exeunt Cardinal and his train*
BUCKINGHAM This butcher's cur is venom-mouthed, and I          120
    Have not the power to muzzle him, therefore best
    Not wake him in his slumber. A beggar's book
    Outworths a noble's blood.
NORFOLK                          What, are you chafed?
    Ask God for temperance, that's th'appliance only
    Which your disease requires.
BUCKINGHAM                          I read in's looks            125
    Matter against me, and his eye reviled

115 surveyor? Ha!] Surveyor? Ha? F

113 **rock** The image is of a rock which may cause a shipwreck, Buckingham's.

114 SD The cardinal and his train enter by one door, pause on their way across the stage while Wolsey stares at Buckingham and asks a question of his secretary, and then go out by the other door. Buckingham and the others are no doubt forward on the stage and to one side. They do not appear to hear the exchange between Wolsey and his secretary.

114 SD **the purse** A special bag containing the great seal of England, part of the insignia of the lord chancellor.

115 **surveyor** overseer of the duke's estates.

120 **butcher's cur** Satirists attacking Wolsey made much of the fact that Wolsey's father was supposed to be a butcher. William Roy in *Rede me and be nott wrothe* (1528) speaks of him as 'the vyle butchers sonne' and again as 'the mastif Curre

bred in Ypswitch towne' (sig. aʼ). Skelton in 'Why come ye not to court' describes the fear of the barons 'For dread of the mastif cur / For dread of the butcher's dog', and comments scornfully on 'his greasy genealogy' (*Complete Poems*, ed. P. Henderson, 1931, pp. 347, 353).

122 **Not…slumber** Tilley notes a familiar proverb: 'It is evil waking of a sleeping dog' (Tilley W7).

122 **beggar's book** beggar's learning; again, a slighting reference to Wolsey's ancestry. Holinshed had written 'This Thomas Wolseie was a poore mans sonne of Ipswich…& there borne, and being but a child, verie apt to be learned' (p. 917). There may be a pun on 'bouk' = 'bulk', a massive body outweighing a noble's blood: compare 55 above (Foakes).

123 **chafed** fretted, angered.

124 **appliance** treatment; see *Ham.* 4.3.10.

Me as his abject object; at this instant
He bores me with some trick. He's gone to th'king:
I'll follow and out-stare him.

NORFOLK                                        Stay, my lord,
And let your reason with your choler question                         130
What 'tis you go about: to climb steep hills
Requires slow pace at first. Anger is like
A full hot horse, who being allowed his way,
Self-mettle tires him. Not a man in England
Can advise me like you: be to yourself                               135
As you would to your friend.

BUCKINGHAM                                I'll to the king,
And from a mouth of honour, quite cry down
This Ipswich fellow's insolence; or proclaim
There's difference in no persons.

NORFOLK                                          Be advised;
Heat not a furnace for your foe so hot                               140
That it do singe yourself. We may outrun
By violent swiftness that which we run at,
And lose by over-running. Know you not
The fire that mounts the liquor till't run o'er
In seeming to augment it, wastes it? Be advised:                    145
I say again there is no English soul
More stronger to direct you than yourself,
If with the sap of reason you would quench,
Or but allay the fire of passion.

BUCKINGHAM                                            Sir,
I am thankful to you, and I'll go along                              150
By your prescription: but this top-proud fellow,
Whom from the flow of gall I name not, but

---

127 **abject object** 'Abject' may mean 'reject-ed', hence 'despised', or it may mean 'degraded, despicable'. 'Object' is what is perceived by the eye.

128 **bores** deceives, mocks.

133 **full hot** high spirited.

134 **Self-mettle** His natural vigour. The expression is proverbial: 'A free horse will soon tire' (Tilley H642).

139 **difference** distinction of rank or breeding.

139 **Be advised** Be careful.

141–3 **We...over-running** One of a series of proverbial sayings in Norfolk's advice. This one suggests 'Make haste slowly', Erasmus's *Festina lente* (Tilley H192).

144 **mounts** raises.

144 **liquor** liquid.

147 **More stronger** A double comparative, often used by Shakespeare.

148 **sap** Any liquid, but perhaps with a hint of the life-giving fluid of plants and trees.

149 **allay** abate, moderate. *OED* notes that 'allay' as 'quell or put down' was often confused with 'allay' as 'alloy, temper, or qualify' from the fifteenth century onward and frequently in Shakespeare (see *Temp.* 1.2.393).

151 **top-proud** proud to the very height.

152 **from...gall** out of bitterness or rancour. The flow of gall or bile from the liver was related to the humour 'choler' in the body, and hence to wrath.

From sincere motions, by intelligence
And proofs as clear as founts in July when
We see each grain of gravel, I do know                        155
To be corrupt and treasonous.
NORFOLK                              Say not treasonous.
BUCKINGHAM To th'king I'll say't, and make my vouch as strong
    As shore of rock: attend. This holy fox,
    Or wolf, or both – for he is equal rav'nous
    As he is subtle, and as prone to mischief,               160
    As able to perform't, his mind and place
    Infecting one another, yea reciprocally –
    Only to show his pomp as well in France
    As here at home, suggests the king our master
    To this last costly treaty; th'interview                 165
    That swallowed so much treasure, and like a glass
    Did break i'th'wrenching.
NORFOLK                      Faith, and so it did.
BUCKINGHAM Pray give me favour, sir. This cunning cardinal
    The articles o'th'combination drew
    As himself pleased; and they were ratified               170
    As he cried 'Thus let be', to as much end
    As give a crutch to th'dead. But our court-cardinal
    Has done this, and 'tis well: for worthy Wolsey,
    Who cannot err, he did it. Now this follows
    (Which as I take it is a kind of puppy                    175
    To th'old dam treason), Charles the emperor

---

159–62 – for...reciprocally – ] *Capell;* (for...perform't), ...reciprocally, F     172 court-cardinal] *Pope;* Count-Cardinal F

**153 sincere** honest, pure.

**153 motions** motives

**153 intelligence** information privately or secretly gathered.

**157 vouch** assertion, allegation.

**158–60 fox...mischief** The animal references derive from proverbs (Tilley F629 and w601). 'Rav'nous' may suggest the biblical warning against false prophets 'which come to you in sheep's clothing, but inwardly they are ravening wolves' (Matt. 7.15). 'Subtle' echoes Ascham's *Scholemaster*: 'Yet shall he be as sutle as a Foxe, in breedyng of mischief' (1570, p. 76).

**159 equal** equally.

**161 place** high office.

**164 suggests** tempts.

**165 interview** formal meeting (of the kings).

**167 wrenching** rinsing; from dialect form of rinse, 'rinche' or 'renche' (*OED*); usually amended to 'rinsing' to make the meaning clear, following Pope. But the dialect form is a stronger word, and, as Foakes observes, there may be suggestion of 'wrenching' as 'distorting the truth' in relation to Buckingham's following lines.

**168 favour** leave, permission.

**169 combination** treaty.

**172 court-cardinal** The F 'Count-Cardinal' is difficult to justify and probably represents a misreading of *n* for *r*. Pope's emendation 'court' suggests the combination of power with church and is parallel with 'king-cardinal' at 2.2.18.

**176 dam** bitch.

Under pretence to see the queen his aunt
(For 'twas indeed his colour, but he came
To whisper Wolsey) here makes visitation;
His fears were that the interview betwixt                    180
England and France might through their amity
Breed him some prejudice, for from this league
Peeped harms that menaced him: privily
Deals with our cardinal, and as I trow,
Which I do well, for I am sure the emperor                   185
Paid ere he promised, whereby his suit was granted
Ere it was asked, but when the way was made
And paved with gold, the emperor thus desired
That he would please to alter the king's course
And break the foresaid peace. Let the king know,            190
As soon he shall by me, that thus the cardinal
Does buy and sell his honour as he pleases,
And for his own advantage.

NORFOLK                              I am sorry
To hear this of him, and could wish he were
Something mistaken in't.

BUCKINGHAM                          No, not a syllable:       195
I do pronounce him in that very shape
He shall appear in proof.

*Enter* BRANDON, *a Sergeant-at-Arms before him, and two or three of the*
*Guard*

BRANDON Your office, sergeant: execute it.

SERGEANT                                      Sir,
My lord the Duke of Buckingham, and Earl
Of Hereford, Stafford, and Northampton, I                    200

183 him: privily] *Foakes;* him. Privily F; him. He privily F2     200 Hereford] *Capell;* Hertford F

177 **his aunt** Holinshed notes (p. 856) that Queen Katherine was Charles's aunt. The passage following about Charles V's visit to England in May 1520 just before Henry's meeting with the French king is drawn in detail from Holinshed.

178 **colour** excuse, pretext.

179 **whisper** negotiate secretly with.

184 **trow** believe. The sentence is not completed.

192 **his honour** i.e. the king's honour.

195 **Something mistaken** Somewhat misjudged.

196 **pronounce** declare.

197 **proof** test, examination; or possibly 'experience'.

197 SD BRANDON Brandon seems to have the status of captain of the king's guard, although Holinshed reports that Sir Henrie Marnie acted as such at Buckingham's arrest. Foakes suggests that Shakespeare may have been thinking of the Duke of Suffolk, Charles Brandon; this seems unlikely, as Maxwell notes, when he is called Suffolk in the rest of the play.

200 **Hereford** Capell corrects the title from the source in Holinshed.

Arrest thee of high treason, in the name
Of our most sovereign king.
BUCKINGHAM                                    Lo you, my lord,
The net has fallen upon me; I shall perish
Under device and practice.
BRANDON                                    I am sorry
To see you ta'en from liberty, to look on                        205
The business present. 'Tis his highness' pleasure
You shall to th'Tower.
BUCKINGHAM                              It will help me nothing
To plead mine innocence, for that dye is on me
Which makes my whit'st part black. The will of heaven
Be done in this and all things: I obey.                          210
O my Lord Aberga'nny, fare you well.
BRANDON Nay, he must bear you company. The king
Is pleased you shall to th'Tower, till you know
How he determines further.
ABERGAVENNY                              As the duke said,
The will of heaven be done, and the king's pleasure             215
By me obeyed.
BRANDON            Here is a warrant from
The king t'attach Lord Montacute, and the bodies
Of the duke's confessor, John de la Car,
One Gilbert Perke, his chancellor –
BUCKINGHAM                                    So, so;
These are the limbs o'th'plot: no more, I hope.                 220
BRANDON A monk o'th'Chartreux.
BUCKINGHAM                        O Nicholas Hopkins?
BRANDON                                              He.

---

219 Perke] *Foakes* (Perk), *Maxwell* (Parke); Pecke F    219 chancellor] *Pope (from Theobald);* Councellour F    221
Nicholas] *Pope (from Theobald);* Michaell F

202 **Lo you** Look you.
204 **device and practice** stratagem and plot.
205 **look on** witness.
217 **attach** arrest.
219 **Gilbert Perke** Holinshed provides the
correction: 'sir Gilbert Perke priest, the dukes
chancellor'. As Foakes points out, the F 'Pecke'
is a likely misreading of 'Perke' because of the
similarity of *c* and *r* in Secretary hand. A chancellor was a secretary to a great lord. The F 'Councel-
lor' has been corrected to 'chancellor' by most
editors since Pope on the basis of Holinshed and
2.1.20 below.

221 **Nicholas** The F 'Michaell Hopkins' seems
to be at odds with the 'Nicholas Henton' of
1.2.147, though they are clearly meant to be one
person. Holinshed provides the answer (Pooler):
'a vaine prophesie which one Nicholas Hopkins, a
monke of an house of the Chartreux order beside
Bristow, called Henton, sometime his confessor
had opened unto him' (p. 863). The name
Michael instead of Nicholas may have occurred if
the abbreviation 'Nich.' were used in the MS.
and mistaken for 'Mich.' (Malone and Maxwell).

BUCKINGHAM My surveyor is false: the o'er-great cardinal
　　　　　Hath showed him gold; my life is spanned already:
　　　　　I am the shadow of poor Buckingham,
　　　　　Whose figure even this instant cloud puts on 　　　225
　　　　　By darkening my clear sun. My lords, farewell.

　　　　　　　　　　　　　　　　　　　　　　　*Exeunt*


**1.2** *Cornets. Enter* KING HENRY, *leaning on the* CARDINAL'*s shoulder,
the Nobles, and* SIR THOMAS LOVELL: *the* CARDINAL *places himself
under the King's feet on his right side.* [*Secretary attends the Cardinal*]

KING My life itself, and the best heart of it,
　　　Thanks you for this great care: I stood i'th'level
　　　Of a full-charged confederacy, and give thanks
　　　To you that choked it. Let be called before us
　　　That gentleman of Buckingham's; in person 　　　5
　　　I'll hear him his confessions justify,
　　　And point by point the treasons of his master
　　　He shall again relate.

*A noise within crying 'Room for the Queen' [who is] ushered by the Duke of
Norfolk. Enter the* QUEEN, NORFOLK *and* SUFFOLK: *she kneels.* KING
*riseth from his state, takes her up, kisses and placeth her by him*

KATHERINE Nay, we must longer kneel; I am a suitor.
KING Arise, and take place by us. Half your suit 　　　10
　　　Never name to us; you have half our power,

Act 1, Scene 2　　1.2] *Scena Secunda* F　　0 SD.3 *Secretary...Cardinal*] Foakes; *not in* F

223 **spanned** measured.
224 **shadow** mere semblance or appearance.
See *Ham.* 2.2.258–60.
225 **figure** form, shape.
225 **this instant cloud** this accusation.
226 **my clear sun** my glory. The phrase also
suggests the king's favour being darkened by a
cloud (Foakes). The passage is obscure in its
syntax, though the general sense is clear.

**Act 1, Scene 2**
0 SD The scene is a council chamber at court;
a throne for the king has been pushed forward
or brought in, raised on a dais so that the cardinal

is below the king on his right. The king's entry
leaning on the cardinal's shoulder is a clear signal
to the audience of his present dependence on
Wolsey.
2 **level** The mark aimed at, or the line of fire of
a gun (*OED* sv *sb* 9).
3 **full-charged** fully loaded.
3 **confederacy** conspiracy.
6 **justify** confirm.
8 SD.2 **ushered... Norfolk** The repetition of
'Norfolk' is a slight confusion in F's SD but does
not require amending.
8 SD.3 *state* chair of state, throne.

The other moiety ere you ask is given;
Repeat your will and take it.

KATHERINE                          Thank your majesty;
That you would love yourself, and in that love
Not unconsidered leave your honour nor                          15
The dignity of your office, is the point
Of my petition.

KING                          Lady mine, proceed.

KATHERINE I am solicited not by a few,
And those of true condition, that your subjects
Are in great grievance: there have been commissions            20
Sent down among 'em, which hath flawed the heart
Of all their loyalties; wherein although,
My good lord cardinal, they vent reproaches
Most bitterly on you as putter-on
Of these exactions, yet the king our master –                  25
Whose honour heaven shield from soil – even he escapes
    not
Language unmannerly, yea, such which breaks
The sides of loyalty, and almost appears
In loud rebellion.

NORFOLK                          Not almost appears,
It doth appear; for, upon these taxations,                      30
The clothiers all not able to maintain
The many to them longing, have put off
The spinsters, carders, fullers, weavers, who,
Unfit for other life, compelled by hunger
And lack of other means, in desperate manner                   35

---

12 **moiety** half.
13 **Repeat your will** State your wish.
18–29 There seems to be no hint in Holinshed or other sources of Katherine's championship of the common people. Shakespeare may
have invented it to show disorder in the kingdom
from Wolsey's exactions and to explain the antagonism between Wolsey and Katherine. The
image of the Good Queen belonged to earlier
drama, from the biblical *Godly Queen Hester* to
Shakespeare's *Richard II*. See especially Anne of
Bohemia in *Woodstock* (1591–4) who sells her
jewels to feed the poor and help the distressed
(2.3 and 3.1).
19 **condition** disposition.

20 **grievance** distress, state of oppression.
20 **commissions** Writs of authority for the
collection of taxes.
21 **flawed** broken.
26 **soil** tarnish.
27–8 **breaks...sides** bursts the bounds.
32 **to them longing** belonging to them, in
their employment.
32 **put off** dismissed.
33 **spinsters** spinners.
33 **carders** Those who comb the wool,
cleaning it for spinning.
33 **fullers** Those who beat the cloth to thicken
and clean it.

Daring th'event to th'teeth, are all in uproar,
And danger serves among them.

KING                                    Taxation?
Wherein? and what taxation? My lord cardinal,
You that are blamed for it alike with us,
Know you of this taxation?

WOLSEY                                  Please you, sir,          40
I know but of a single part in aught
Pertains to th'state; and front but in that file
Where others tell steps with me.

KATHERINE                               No, my lord?
You know no more than others? But you frame
Things that are known alike, which are not wholesome     45
To those which would not know them, and yet must
Perforce be their acquaintance. These exactions,
Whereof my sovereign would have note, they are
Most pestilent to th'hearing, and to bear 'em
The back is sacrifice to th'load. They say              50
They are devised by you, or else you suffer
Too hard an exclamation.

KING                                    Still exaction!
The nature of it, in what kind let's know,
Is this exaction?

KATHERINE               I am much too venturous
In tempting of your patience, but am boldened            55
Under your promised pardon. The subjects' grief
Comes through commissions, which compels from each
The sixth part of his substance, to be levied
Without delay; and the pretence for this
Is named your wars in France: this makes bold mouths,    60
Tongues spit their duties out, and cold hearts freeze

36 **Daring...teeth** Challenging the outcome with defiance. Holinshed describes the devising of the commissions by Wolsey on behalf of the council, the distress and uproar that followed, and the involvement of the Duke of Norfolk in putting down a rebellion in Suffolk. The king held a 'great councell' at Westminster to discover the cause of the trouble, but Wolsey, as Holinshed reports it, managed to escape most of the blame (pp. 891–2). Shakespeare has dramatised the issue by making it a confrontation between Katherine and Wolsey and a test of their influence over the king.

37 **danger...them** There are two possible meanings: 'they seem to welcome danger'; or 'mischief is working among them'. For the latter sense, see *JC* 2.1.17.
41 **a single part** one person's share.
42 **front...file** march first only in that file of men, i.e. in the most conspicuous position.
43 **tell steps** count steps, march in time.
45 **alike** to all alike.
48 **note** knowledge.
52 **exclamation** outcry of reproach.
53 **in what kind** of what form.
56 **grief** grievance.

Allegiance in them; their curses now
Live where their prayers did; and it's come to pass
This tractable obedience is a slave
To each incensèd will. I would your highness          65
Would give it quick consideration, for
There is no primer baseness.

KING                                                By my life,
This is against our pleasure.

WOLSEY                                             And for me,
I have no further gone in this than by
A single voice, and that not passed me but            70
By learned approbation of the judges. If I am
Traduced by ignorant tongues, which neither know
My faculties nor person, yet will be
The chronicles of my doing, let me say
'Tis but the fate of place, and the rough brake       75
That virtue must go through. We must not stint
Our necessary actions in the fear
To cope malicious censurers, which ever,
As ravenous fishes, do a vessel follow
That is new trimmed, but benefit no further           80
Than vainly longing. What we oft do best,
By sick interpreters, once weak ones, is
Not ours, or not allowed; what worst, as oft
Hitting a grosser quality, is cried up
For our best act. If we shall stand still,            85

---

67 baseness] F; business *Warburton* (*from Hanmer*)

---

64 **tractable** compliant; perhaps in the negative sense of 'easily swayed'.

65 **each...will** each individual's stirred-up passions.

67 **no primer baseness** no mischief of greater importance. Shakespeare uses 'prime' to mean 'of first importance', as in 3.2.162 and *Temp.* 1.2.426, but not elsewhere the comparative 'primer'. 'Baseness' is usually amended to 'business' but 'baseness' is a Shakespearean word and makes good sense (Foakes).

70 **single voice** unanimous vote.

73 **faculties** abilities.

75 **place** high office or rank.

75 **brake** thicket.

76 **stint** cease doing.

78 **cope** encounter.

80 **new trimmed** newly fitted out (and therefore unlikely to sink).

82 **sick** envious.

82 **weak** shallow, foolish. The passage means that interpreters of men's actions who at one time were uncertain and foolish but are now maliciously envious cannot accept as ours, nor approve, the things we do best.

83 **allowed** approved.

84 **Hitting...quality** Catching favour with a lower class of ignorant people. But the phrase is ambiguous since 'quality' may also mean 'disposition'; in this sense, it would mean 'falling in with an even lower or coarser side of themselves'.

In fear our motion will be mocked or carped at,
We should take root here where we sit,
Or sit state-statues only.

KING                                    Things done well,
And with a care, exempt themselves from fear;
Things done without example, in their issue          90
Are to be feared. Have you a precedent
Of this commission? I believe, not any.
We must not rend our subjects from our laws
And stick them in our will. Sixth part of each?
A trembling contribution; why, we take               95
From every tree lop, bark and part o'th'timber,
And though we leave it with a root, thus hacked,
The air will drink the sap. To every county
Where this is questioned, send our letters with
Free pardon to each man that has denied              100
The force of this commission. Pray look to't;
I put it to your care.

WOLSEY [*To the Secretary*]     A word with you.
Let there be letters writ to every shire
Of the king's grace and pardon. The grieved commons
Hardly conceive of me: let it be noised              105
That through our intercession this revokement
And pardon comes. I shall anon advise you
Further in the proceeding.

*Exit Secretary*

*Enter* SURVEYOR

KATHERINE I am sorry that the Duke of Buckingham
Is run in your displeasure.
KING                                    It grieves many.             110
The gentlemen is learn'd, and a most rare speaker,

102 SD *To...secretary*] *Rowe; not in* F

86 **motion** move or proposal.
88 **state-statues** statues set up in all the pano-
ply of office.
90 **example** precedent.
90 **issue** outcome.
93 **rend** Both 'rend' and 'stick' (94) suggest
force, 'rend' by tearing away and 'stick' by fixing
in position as with a sharp instrument.
94 **will** pleasure.

95 **trembling** fearful.
96 **lop** A small branch broken or pruned off.
101 **force** power.
104 **grace** mercy.
105 **Hardly conceive** Think harshly.
105 **noised** rumoured.
106 **revokement** act of revoking; apparently
Shakespeare's coinage.
110 **Is run in** Has aroused.

To nature none more bound; his training such
That he may furnish and instruct great teachers,
And never seek for aid out of himself; yet see,
When these so noble benefits shall prove                        115
Not well disposed, the mind growing once corrupt,
They turn to vicious forms, ten times more ugly
Than ever they were fair. This man so complete,
Who was enrolled 'mongst wonders, and when we
Almost with ravished listening could not find            120
His hour of speech a minute, he, my lady,
Hath into monstrous habits put the graces
That once were his, and is become as black
As if besmeared in hell. Sit by us, you shall hear
(This was his gentleman in trust) of him                        125
Things to strike honour sad. Bid him recount
The fore-recited practices, whereof
We cannot feel too little, hear too much.

WOLSEY Stand forth, and with bold spirit relate what you
    Most like a careful subject have collected            130
    Out of the Duke of Buckingham.

KING                                                  Speak freely.

SURVEYOR First, it was usual with him, every day
    It would infect his speech, that if the king
    Should without issue die, he'll carry it so
    To make the sceptre his. These very words            135
    I've heard him utter to his son-in-law,
    Lord Aberga'nny, to whom by oath he menaced
    Revenge upon the cardinal.

WOLSEY                                   Please your highness note
    This dangerous conception in this point,

---

139 This dangerous] F; His dangerous *Pope*    139–40 point, / ...wish to...person;] F; point: / ...wish to ...person, *Pope*

---

112 **bound** indebted; i.e. he has been given great gifts by nature.
114 **out of** beyond.
115–18 **When...fair** Proverbial. Maxwell notes *Sonnets* 94.13–14: 'For sweetest things turn sourest by their deeds: / Lilies that fester smell far worse than weeds.'
116 **disposed** regulated, directed; see 1.1.43 (Foakes).

118 **complete** accomplished (accented on the first syllable).
120 **ravished** enthralled, carried away; i.e. we were almost ravished with listening.
122 **habits** shapes, costumes.
127 **practices** intrigues.
130 **collected** gathered.
134 **carry** manage.

      Not friended by his wish to your high person;     140
      His will is most malignant, and it stretches
      Beyond you to your friends.
KATHERINE                My learn'd lord cardinal,
      Deliver all with charity.
KING                Speak on.
      How grounded he his title to the crown
      Upon our fail? To this point hast thou heard him   145
      At any time speak aught?
SURVEYOR           He was brought to this
      By a vain prophecy of Nicholas Henton.
KING What was that Henton?
SURVEYOR          Sir, a Chartreux friar,
      His confessor, who fed him every minute
      With words of sovereignty.
KING             How know'st thou this?   150
SURVEYOR Not long before your highness sped to France
      The duke being at the Rose, within the parish
      Saint Lawrence Poultney, did of me demand
      What was the speech among the Londoners
      Concerning the French journey. I replied,   155
      Men feared the French would prove perfidious,
      To the king's danger: presently the duke
      Said 'twas the fear indeed, and that he doubted
      'Twould prove the verity of certain words
      Spoke by a holy monk, 'that oft', says he,   160
      'Hath sent to me, wishing me to permit
      John de la Car, my chaplain, a choice hour
      To hear from him a matter of some moment:
      Whom after under the confession's seal

---

156 feared] *Pope;* feare F    164 confession's] *Theobald;* Commissions F

140 **friended** supported.
140 **his wish** i.e. that the king should die without issue.
143 **Deliver** Tell.
145 **fail** (1) failure to have issue, (2) death. Although the princess Mary was undoubtedly 'issue' of his marriage with Katherine, concern about her legitimacy and therefore about her ability to succeed him troubled Henry deeply, as a later passage indicates (2.4.168–84).
147 **Nicholas Henton** Nicholas Hopkins of Henton priory, and so properly Nicholas of Henton. See 1.1.221 n.

152 **Rose** The manor of the Rose, belonging to Buckingham.
156 **feared** F has 'feare', but the final *e* may represent a misreading of *d* in the scribe's MS.
157 **presently** at once.
158 **doubted** suspected.
162 **choice hour** suitable time.
163 **moment** importance.
164 **confession's** F has 'Commissions' which seems unlikely. Holinshed, from which this whole passage has been taken, provides the correction (p. 863).

He solemnly had sworn, that what he spoke                    165
My chaplain to no creature living but
To me should utter, with demure confidence
This pausingly ensued: "Neither the king, nor's heirs,
Tell you the duke, shall prosper; bid him strive
To [win] the love o'th'commonalty; the duke              170
Shall govern England."'
KATHERINE                    If I know you well,
You were the duke's surveyor, and lost your office
On the complaint o'th'tenants; take good heed
You charge not in your spleen a noble person
And spoil your nobler soul; I say, take heed;            175
Yes, heartily beseech you.
KING                              Let him on.
Go forward.
SURVEYOR            On my soul, I'll speak but truth.
I told my lord the duke, by th'devil's illusions
The monk might be deceived, and that 'twas dangerous
For him to ruminate on this so far, until                180
It forged him some design, which being believed
It was much like to do. He answered 'Tush,
It can do me no damage'; adding further
That had the king in his last sickness failed,
The cardinal's and Sir Thomas Lovell's heads            185
Should have gone off.
KING                              Ha? What, so rank? Ah ha!
There's mischief in this man; canst thou say further?
SURVEYOR I can, my liege.
KING                         Proceed.
SURVEYOR                         Being at Greenwich,
After your highness had reproved the duke

---

170 win] *Sisson; not in* F; *gain* F4    176–7 Let...forward] *As Pope; one line in* F    180 For him] *Rowe;* For this F

167 **demure confidence** grave assurance.
168 **pausingly** with pauses. *OED* gives only this example.
170 **commonalty** common people.
174 **spleen** Any passion, here suggesting malice or envy.
175 **spoil** ruin
175 **nobler** The soul is nobler in its essence than the nobility of rank.
178 **illusions** deceptions.

180 **For him** F 'For this' cannot be justified; possibly the compositor saw the second 'this' before he came to it. Alternatively the first two words of the line may have been marked for deletion since the line has an extra foot.
181–2 **which...do** once the prophecy was believed, it might lead him to forge a plot.
184 **failed** died.
186 **rank** foul, corrupt.

               About Sir William Bulmer –

KING                             I remember          190
               Of such a time: being my sworn servant,
               The duke retained him his. But on; what hence?

SURVEYOR 'If', quoth he, 'I for this had been committed,
               As to the Tower I thought, I would have played
               The part my father meant to act upon      195
               Th'usurper Richard, who being at Salisbury,
               Made suit to come in's presence; which if granted,
               As he made semblance of his duty, would
               Have put his knife into him.

KING                        A giant traitor.

WOLSEY Now, madam, may his highness live in freedom    200
               And this man out of prison?

KATHERINE                God mend all.

KING There's something more would out of thee; what say'st?

SURVEYOR After 'the duke his father', with the 'knife',
               He stretched him, and with one hand on his dagger,
               Another spread on's breast, mounting his eyes,    205
               He did discharge a horrible oath, whose tenor
               Was, were he evil used, he would outgo
               His father by as much as a performance
               Does an irresolute purpose.

KING                       There's his period,
               To sheathe his knife in us: he is attached,      210
               Call him to present trial. If he may
               Find mercy in the law, 'tis his; if none,
               Let him not seek't of us. By day and night,
               He's traitor to th'height.

                                       *Exeunt*

---

190 Bulmer] *Wright;* Blumer F    190–1 Bulmer – I remember / Of] *Pope;* Blumer. / I remember of F

190 **Bulmer** The Folios have 'Blumer' but both Halle and Holinshed spell the name 'Bulmer'.

198 **semblance** fair show, appearance.

204 **stretched him** straightened himself.

205 **mounting** raising.

207 **evil used** badly treated.

207 **outgo** surpass.

209 **period** goal; but also suggesting the end of Buckingham.

210 **attached** arrested.

211 **present** immediate.

213 **By day and night** A strong exclamation giving emphasis to what follows.

1.3 *Enter* LORD CHAMBERLAIN *and* LORD SANDS

CHAMBERLAIN  Is't possible the spells of France should juggle
          Men into such strange mysteries?
SANDS                                    New customs
          Though they be never so ridiculous,
          Nay let 'em be unmanly, yet are followed.
CHAMBERLAIN  As far as I see, all the good our English          5
          Have got by the late voyage is but merely
          A fit or two o'th'face – but they are shrewd ones,
          For when they hold 'em, you would swear directly
          Their very noses had been counsellors
          To Pepin or Clotharius, they keep state so.            10
SANDS  They have all new legs, and lame ones; one would take it,
          That never see 'em pace before, the spavin,
          A springhalt reigned among 'em.
CHAMBERLAIN                          Death, my lord,
          Their clothes are after such a pagan cut to't,
          That sure th'have worn out Christendom.

          *Enter* SIR THOMAS LOVELL

                                    How now?                     15
          What news, Sir Thomas Lovell?
LOVELL                               Faith, my lord,
          I hear of none but the new proclamation

Act 1, Scene 3    1.3] *Scæna Tertia* F    0 SD SANDS] *Rowe; Sandys* F    11] *Pope; They…legs, / And…it* F
13 A] F; *And Pope; Or Dyce*    14 to't] too't F; *too Rowe*

Act 1, Scene 3
  0 SD  In this scene, a room at court, the atmosphere is much more relaxed and informal than in
the two previous scenes. It demonstrates Shakespeare's compression of time for dramatic effect,
as Buckingham's trial was in 1521 and Henry first
met Anne in 1526.
  1 **juggle** conjure, beguile.
  2 **mysteries** fantastic modes of behaviour (as
if they were held by spells); hence 'juggle'.
  4 **unmanly** effeminate.
  6 **late** recent.
  7 **fit…face** paroxysm of the face; hence, a
strained and peculiar expression.
  7 **shrewd** artful (*OED* sv *a* 13a, b).
  8 **hold 'em** hold their expressions.
  10 **Pepin or Clotharius** Early kings of the
Franks.

  10 **keep…state** maintain their dignity.
  11 **new legs** new ways of 'making a leg' (bow-
ing), and new ways of walking.
  12 **see** saw; an old past tense.
  12 **pace** walk; used particularly of the gait of
a trained horse.
  12 **spavin** tumour on a horse's leg.
  13 **A** Often corrected to 'And' or 'Or' since
spavin and springhalt are different diseases, but
the uncorrected 'A' suggests they may have both.
  13 **springhalt** A disease causing sudden contractions of the leg muscles.
  14 **to't** moreover, in addition.
  15 **worn out Christendom** i.e. they have tried
out all the fashions of Christendom and have
now gone on to pagan fashions.

That's clapped upon the court gate.
CHAMBERLAIN                                           What is't for?
LOVELL The reformation of our travelled gallants
That fill the court with quarrels, talk, and tailors.                    20
CHAMBERLAIN I'm glad 'tis there; now I would pray our monsieurs
To think an English courtier may be wise,
And never see the Louvre.
LOVELL                                         They must either,
For so run the conditions, leave those remnants
Of fool and feather that they got in France,                             25
With all their honourable points of ignorance
Pertaining thereunto, as fights and fireworks,
Abusing better men than they can be
Out of a foreign wisdom, renouncing clean
The faith they have in tennis and tall stockings,                        30
Short blistered breeches, and those types of travel,
And understand again like honest men,
Or pack to their old playfellows; there, I take it,

21] *Pope; I'm...there; / Now...monsieurs* F

18 **court gate** One of the gates of the royal precincts, probably facing a public area or street. In Elizabethan and Jacobean times, one of the gates of Whitehall facing Charing Cross was so called (Wright).

19 **our travelled gallants** Holinshed mentions the effect of France on the 'young gentlemen of England' who sojourned at the French court after a treaty was signed in 1520 (p. 850). The treatment in this scene is light and mocking, in comparison with the severe moral strictures of earlier humanists like Roger Ascham and later Puritan preachers. *Woodstock* (1591–4) gives a vivid portrayal of the adoption of exaggerated continental fashions by Richard II and his courtiers (2.3.87–100). There are similar references in John of Gaunt's speech in *Richard II*, in *Edward II* with reference to Gaveston, and in Chapman's *Bussy D'Ambois* (1.2.42–50).

23 **Louvre** Palace of the French king.

25 **fool and feather** Folly and feathers in hats are often linked in contemporary portrayals of gallants. Dekker in *The Gull's Hornbook* (1609), 'How a gallant should behave himself in a play house', notes that the 'rabble' may cry out 'Away with the fool' to the gallant sitting on the stage, and that the writer of the play may mock 'either your feather, or your red beard or your little legs' (ch. 6).

26 **honourable...ignorance** i.e. in their ignorance they think that all these fashionable attributes are signs of honour. 'Points' may also suggest laces.

27 **fights and fireworks** duelling and whoring. Maxwell notes that 'fireworks' is often used of whores 'considered as transmitters of venereal disease', quoting Marlowe's Faustus who complains 'a hot whore' at the sight of the 'diuell drest like a woman, with fier workes' (A 595–6 SD; B 539). See also *Err.* 4.3.56–7: 'light wenches will burn. Come not near her.' There may be a secondary allusion to the mock battles and fireworks devised for Princess Elizabeth's wedding in February 1613.

30 **tennis** Popular in Henry VIII's time, as it was at court under James I.

31 **blistered** ornamented with puffs (*OED* has this ref. and one earlier from Nashe's *Pierce Penilesse*: sv *ppl a* 2).

31 **types** marks, badges.

32 **understand** Perhaps a reference (and a gesture) to the groundlings who 'stood under' the courtiers in the theatre, as well as the literal meaning.

33 **pack** go off.

They may *cum privilegio* 'oui' away
The lag end of their lewdness, and be laughed at.                    35
SANDS 'Tis time to give 'em physic, their diseases
Are grown so catching.
CHAMBERLAIN                    What a loss our ladies
Will have of these trim vanities!
LOVELL                              Ay, marry,
There will be woe indeed, lords; the sly whoresons
Have got a speeding trick to lay down ladies.                        40
A French song and a fiddle has no fellow.
SANDS The devil fiddle 'em, I am glad they are going,
For sure there's no converting of 'em. Now
An honest country lord, as I am, beaten
A long time out of play, may bring his plain-song              45
And have an hour of hearing, and by'r lady
Held current music too.
CHAMBERLAIN              Well said, Lord Sands,
Your colt's tooth is not cast yet?
SANDS                              No, my lord,
Nor shall not while I have a stump.
CHAMBERLAIN                          Sir Thomas,
Whither were you a-going?
LOVELL                        To the cardinal's;                     50
Your lordship is a guest too.
CHAMBERLAIN                    O, 'tis true;
This night he makes a supper, and a great one,
To many lords and ladies; there will be
The beauty of this kingdom I'll assure you.
LOVELL That churchman bears a bounteous mind indeed,          55
A hand as fruitful as the land that feeds us;
His dews fall everywhere.
CHAMBERLAIN              No doubt he's noble;

34 oui] F (wee); wear F2      42] *Pope;* The…'em, / I…going F      55] *Pope;* That Churchman / Bears…indeed F

34 *cum privilegio* with immunity.
35 **lag end** remainder.
36 **physic** medicine.
38 **trim** neat, fine (used ironically).
40 **speeding** effective.
45 **play** playing music; also, 'love play'.
45 **plain-song** simple melody (contrasted with the elaborate French song of 41).

47 **current** accepted, with full value.
48 **colt's tooth** Proverbial expression for youthful desires, wantonness, often used about old men (Tilley C525).
49 **stump** of a tooth; but a bawdy reference as well.
52 **makes** gives.

He had a black mouth that said other of him.

SANDS He may, my lord; 'has wherewithal; in him
   Sparing would show a worse sin than ill doctrine;  60
   Men of his way should be most liberal,
   They are set here for examples.

CHAMBERLAIN        True, they are so;
   But few now give so great ones. My barge stays;
   Your lordship shall along. Come, good Sir Thomas,
   We shall be late else, which I would not be,  65
   For I was spoke to, with Sir Henry Guilford
   This night to be comptrollers.

SANDS          I am your lordship's.

                 *Exeunt*

**1.4** *Hautboys. A small table under a state for the Cardinal, a longer table*
*for the guests. Then enter* ANNE BULLEN *and divers other ladies and*
*gentlemen as guests at one door; at another door enter* SIR HENRY
GUILFORD

GUILFORD Ladies, a general welcome from his grace
   Salutes ye all; this night he dedicates
   To fair content, and you. None here, he hopes,
   In all this noble bevy, has brought with her
   One care abroad: he would have all as merry  5

---

59] *Rowe³*; He...Lord / Ha's...him F  63] *Rowe³*; But...ones: / My...stays F  Act 1, Scene 4  1.4]
*Scena Quarta* F  1] *Pope;* Ladyes, / A...Grace F

**58 black mouth** evil mouth.
**61 way** way of life, calling.
**63** Maxwell suggests that the unnecessary division of single lines into two at 55, 59, and 63 was introduced by the compositor so that the scene would end at the foot of the column.
**66 spoke to** asked.
**67 comptrollers** stewards.

**Act 1, Scene 4**
**0 SD** The scene is a banqueting hall or presence-chamber in York Place, the cardinal's palace. Holinshed mentions the banquet and masque as having taken place in 1527, but the full account used by the dramatist comes from

Holinshed's summing up of Wolsey's character and career after his death (pp. 921–2). As Maxwell reminds us, Holinshed got it from Stow who got it from Cavendish, who was an eye-witness. The initial meeting of Henry and Anne on this occasion is the dramatist's invention.
 **0 SD** *Hautboys* An early form of the oboe, often used with recorders and other instruments for festive occasions; see 34, 63 below. Trumpets and cornets were normally used for royal entries of a formal kind.
 **0 SD** *under a state* under a canopy of state.
 **4 bevy** company.

As first, good company, good wine, good welcome
Can make good people.

*Enter* LORD CHAMBERLAIN, LORD SANDS, *and* LOVELL

O my lord, y'are tardy;
The very thought of this fair company
Clapped wings to me.
CHAMBERLAIN                    You are young, Sir Harry Guilford.
SANDS Sir Thomas Lovell, had the cardinal                        10
But half my lay-thoughts in him, some of these
Should find a running banquet ere they rested,
I think would better please 'em; by my life,
They are a sweet society of fair ones.
LOVELL O that your lordship were but now confessor              15
To one or two of these.
SANDS                      I would I were,
They should find easy penance.
LOVELL                              Faith, how easy?
SANDS As easy as a down bed would afford it.
CHAMBERLAIN Sweet ladies, will it please you sit? Sir Harry,
Place you that side, I'll take the charge of this:              20
His grace is entering. Nay, you must not freeze,
Two women placed together makes cold weather.
My Lord Sands, you are one will keep 'em waking:
Pray sit between these ladies.
SANDS                          By my faith,
And thank your lordship: by your leave, sweet ladies,          25
If I chance to talk a little wild, forgive me;
I had it from my father.
ANNE                      Was he mad, sir?
SANDS O very mad, exceeding mad, in love too;
But he would bite none; just as I do now,
He would kiss you twenty with a breath.
CHAMBERLAIN                              Well said, my lord.    30

6 **first** Implies 'then' before 'good wine'.
11 **lay-thoughts** secular thoughts.
12 **running banquet** light refreshments (possibly hasty, suggesting stolen pleasures). See 5.3.58 n.

20 **Place** Assign places to the guests.
23 **waking** lively.

So now y'are fairly seated: gentlemen,
The penance lies on you if these fair ladies
Pass away frowning.

SANDS                              For my little cure
Let me alone.

*Hautboys. Enter* CARDINAL WOLSEY *and takes his state*

WOLSEY Y'are welcome, my fair guests; that noble lady    35
Or gentlemen that is not freely merry
Is not my friend. This to confirm my welcome,
And to you all good health. [*Drinks*]

SANDS                                    Your grace is noble;
Let me have such a bowl may hold my thanks,
And save me so much talking.

WOLSEY                                    My Lord Sands,    40
I am beholding to you; cheer your neighbours:
Ladies, you are not merry; gentlemen,
Whose fault is this?

SANDS                              The red wine first must rise
In their fair cheeks, my lord, then we shall have 'em
Talk us to silence.

ANNE                              You are a merry gamester,    45
My Lord Sands.

SANDS                              Yes, if I make my play:
Here's to your ladyship, and pledge it, madam,
For 'tis such a thing –

ANNE                              You cannot show me.

*Drum and trumpet; chambers discharged*

SANDS I told your grace they would talk anon.

WOLSEY                                    What's that?

CHAMBERLAIN Look out there, some of ye.

38 SD] *Theobald; not in* F

33 **Pass away** Move off.
33 **cure** charge, care of souls; as in the ecclesiastical images of 15–18; also, 'remedy'.
34 SD **takes his state** takes his chair of state under the canopy.
38 **noble** i.e. noble in your welcome.
41 **beholding** beholden, indebted.
45 **gamester** A gamester is a player at any sport or game, and Anne means a frolicsome

fellow, but two common meanings of the time are picked up in the following lines: 'one addicted to love-making', and 'gambler'.
46 **make my play** win my hand (in cards, or in love).
48 SD **chambers** Small cannon used to fire salutes. This discharge may have caused the fire in the thatch that burned down the Globe in 1613; see Wotton's letter, p. 1 above.

WOLSEY                                    What warlike voice,        50
  And to what end is this? Nay, ladies, fear not;
  By all the laws of war y'are privileged.

                   *Enter a* SERVANT

CHAMBERLAIN How now, what is't?
SERVANT                                    A noble troop of strangers,
  For so they seem; th'have left their barge and landed,
  And hither make, as great ambassadors               55
  From foreign princes.
WOLSEY                                    Good Lord Chamberlain,
  Go, give 'em welcome; you can speak the French tongue;
  And pray receive 'em nobly, and conduct 'em
  Into our presence, where this heaven of beauty
  Shall shine at full upon them. Some attend him.        60
       *All rise and tables removed. [Exit Chamberlain attended]*
  You have now a broken banquet, but we'll mend it.
  A good digestion to you all; and once more
  I shower a welcome on ye: welcome all.

     *Hautboys. Enter* KING *and others as masquers, habited like*
     *shepherds, ushered by the* LORD CHAMBERLAIN. *They pass*
       *directly before the Cardinal, and gracefully salute him*

  A noble company! What are their pleasures?
CHAMBERLAIN Because they speak no English, thus they prayed    65
  To tell your grace: that having heard by fame
  Of this so noble and so fair assembly
  This night to meet here, they could do no less,
  Out of the great respect they bear to beauty,
  But leave their flocks, and under your fair conduct     70

---

60 SD *Exit. . .attended*] Capell; *not in* F

---

50 **voice** noise; here, the speaking of the cannon as the voice of war.
52 **privileged** immune, secure from harm.
55 **make** make their way, come.
60 SD *tables removed* Tables were not removed in Holinshed's account; the dancers performed before the banqueting guests, then drew the ladies into the dance. On the Elizabethan stage, they would need to be removed to make room for the masque.
61 **broken** interrupted.

63 SD.1 **habited** dressed.
63 SD.2 **like shepherds** Holinshed's account scarcely suggests the fields and moors: 'all in garments like sheepheards, made of fine cloth of gold, and crimosin sattin paned, & caps of the same, with visards of good physnomie, their haires & beards either of fine gold-wire silke, or blacke silke. . .' (pp. 921–2).
66 **fame** rumour or report.
70 **conduct** direction, allowance.

Crave leave to view these ladies, and entreat
An hour of revels with 'em.

WOLSEY                          Say, Lord Chamberlain,
They have done my poor house grace; for which I pay
'em
A thousand thanks and pray 'em take their pleasures.
                *Choose ladies, King and Anne Bullen*
KING  The fairest hand I ever touched: O beauty,                   75
Till now I never knew thee.
                        *Music, dance*
WOLSEY  My lord.
CHAMBERLAIN    Your grace?
WOLSEY                          Pray tell 'em thus much from me:
There should be one amongst 'em by his person
More worthy this place than myself, to whom,
If I but knew him, with my love and duty                           80
I would surrender it.
CHAMBERLAIN             I will, my lord.  *Whisper*
WOLSEY  What say they?
CHAMBERLAIN      Such a one, they all confess,
There is indeed, which they would have your grace
Find out, and he will take it.
WOLSEY                          Let me see then,
By all your good leaves, gentlemen; here I'll make              85
My royal choice.
KING  [*Unmasking*]      Ye have found him, cardinal:
You hold a fair assembly; you do well, lord:
You are a churchman, or I'll tell you, cardinal,
I should judge now unhappily.
WOLSEY                     I am glad
Your grace is grown so pleasant.
KING                          My Lord Chamberlain,       90

73–4 They... / ...pleasures] *Pope; three lines, ending...grace:* / ...thankes, / ...pleasures F    81 SD
*Whisper*] *Foakes; follows* surrender it *in* F    86 SD] *Capell; not in* F

72 **revels** lively entertainment. The term
usually included dancing, masquing, games and
feasting.
79 **this place** the chair of state.
84 **it** the place of honour.
86 **found him** In Holinshed's account, Wolsey

made the wrong choice, though he chose 'a
comelie knight'; there was much laughter from
the king and the rest of the assembly.
89 **unhappily** unfavourably.
90 **pleasant** merry.

Prithee come hither; what fair lady's that?
CHAMBERLAIN An't please your grace, Sir Thomas Bullen's
    daughter,
    The Viscount Rochford, one of her highness' women.
KING By heaven she is a dainty one. Sweetheart,
    I were unmannerly to take you out                                   95
    And not to kiss you. A health, gentlemen!
    Let it go round.
WOLSEY Sir Thomas Lovell, is the banquet ready
    I'th'privy chamber?
LOVELL                              Yes, my lord.
WOLSEY                                              Your grace,
    I fear, with dancing is a little heated.                             100
KING I fear, too much.
WOLSEY                        There's fresher air, my lord,
    In the next chamber.
KING Lead in your ladies every one: sweet partner,
    I must not yet forsake you. Let's be merry,
    Good my lord cardinal: I have half a dozen healths                  105
    To drink to these fair ladies, and a measure
    To lead 'em once again, and then let's dream
    Who's best in favour. Let the music knock it.

                                         *Exeunt with trumpets*


**2.1** *Enter two* GENTLEMEN *at several doors*


1 GENTLEMAN Whither away so fast?
2 GENTLEMAN                                    O, God save ye:

92–3 An't.../... women] *Pope; three lines, ending...* Grace, / ...Rochford, / ...women F    Act 2, Scene 1
**2.1**] *Actus Secundus Scena Prima* F

**92–3** Pope's changes in lineation here, as at
73–4 above, give the correct line structure,
though the F arrangement reflects the natural
pauses of speech.
**95 take you out** lead you out into the dance.
**96 kiss you** A customary courtesy to one's
partner after a dance.
**101 I fear, too much** A hint, perhaps, that the
king is heated by more than the dancing.
**106 measure** stately dance.
**108 best in favour** highest in the ladies'
favour.

**108 knock it** strike up.

**Act 2, Scene 1**
  0 SD The neutral ground of the scene is presumably a street. The speakers as 'gentlemen'
have access to Westminster Hall where the trial
was held, as they have to Westminster Abbey
for the coronation in 4.1. In a wider sense, they
represent public opinion of the citizens (see
supplementary note).
  0 SD *several* different.

Even to the hall, to hear what shall become
Of the great Duke of Buckingham.

1 GENTLEMAN                                    I'll save you
That labour, sir. All's now done but the ceremony
Of bringing back the prisoner.

2 GENTLEMAN                        Were you there?          5

1 GENTLEMAN  Yes indeed was I.

2 GENTLEMAN                    Pray speak what has happened.

1 GENTLEMAN  You may guess quickly what.

2 GENTLEMAN                              Is he found guilty?

1 GENTLEMAN  Yes truly is he, and condemned upon't.

2 GENTLEMAN  I am sorry for't.

1 GENTLEMAN                      So are a number more.

2 GENTLEMAN  But pray, how passed it?                      10

1 GENTLEMAN  I'll tell you in a little. The great duke
Came to the bar; where to his accusations
He pleaded still not guilty, and alleged
Many sharp reasons to defeat the law.
The king's attorney on the contrary                        15
Urged on the examinations, proofs, confessions
Of divers witnesses, which the duke desired
To him brought viva voce to his face;
At which appeared against him his surveyor,
Sir Gilbert Perke his chancellor, and John Car,           20
Confessor to him, with that devil monk,
Hopkins, that made this mischief.

2 GENTLEMAN                              That was he
That fed him with his prophecies.

1 GENTLEMAN                            The same;
All these accused him strongly, which he fain

---

8] *Pope; Yes...he, / And...upon't* F    18 him] F; have F4 *and other editions*    20 Perke] *Foakes;* Pecke F

10 **how passed it** how did the trial proceed?
11 **in a little** briefly.
13 **alleged** advanced.
14 **sharp reasons** acute arguments.
14 **defeat** frustrate.
16 **proofs** written evidence.
18 **him brought** Most editors have followed F4,

emending 'him' to 'have', but, as Maxwell argues, the change is not essential.
18 **viva voce** in person (literally 'with a living voice').
20 **Sir Gilbert Perke** See 1.1.219 n. 'Sir' was a courtesy title for a priest.
24 **which** i.e. which accusations.

Would have flung from him; but indeed he could not;          25
And so his peers upon this evidence
Have found him guilty of high treason. Much
He spoke, and learnedly for life; but all
Was either pitied in him or forgotten.

2 GENTLEMAN After all this, how did he bear himself?          30
1 GENTLEMAN When he was brought again to th'bar, to hear
His knell rung out, his judgement, he was stirred
With such an agony he sweat extremely,
And something spoke in choler, ill and hasty;
But he fell to himself again, and sweetly                    35
In all the rest showed a most noble patience.

2 GENTLEMAN I do not think he fears death.
1 GENTLEMAN                              Sure he does not,
He never was so womanish; the cause
He may a little grieve at.

2 GENTLEMAN                    Certainly
The cardinal is the end of this.

1 GENTLEMAN                              'Tis likely,          40
By all conjectures: first Kildare's attendure,
Then deputy of Ireland, who removed,
Earl Surrey was sent thither, and in haste too,
Lest he should help his father.

2 GENTLEMAN                       That trick of state
Was a deep envious one.

1 GENTLEMAN                  At his return                     45
No doubt he will requite it; this is noted,
And generally, whoever the king favours,
The cardinal instantly will find employment,
And far enough from court too.

2 GENTLEMAN                       All the commons
Hate him perniciously, and o'my conscience                    50
Wish him ten fathom deep. This duke as much

---

32 **judgement** sentence.
35 **fell to himself** regained control of himself.
40 **the end of** at the bottom of.
41 **attendure** condemnation, with loss of
office and estate (a rare form of 'attainder').
42 **deputy** governor, viceroy.

44 **father** Often used for 'father-in-law'.
Buckingham was Surrey's father-in-law.
45 **deep envious** deeply malicious.
47 **generally** by everybody.
48 **employment** employment for.
50 **perniciously** to the death.

They love and dote on; call him bounteous Buckingham,
The mirror of all courtesy –

*Enter* BUCKINGHAM *from his arraignment, tipstaves before him,*
*the axe with the edge towards him, halberds on each side, accompanied*
*with* SIR THOMAS LOVELL, SIR NICHOLAS VAUX, SIR WALTER
SANDS, *and common people, etc.*

1 GENTLEMAN                  Stay there, sir,
And see the noble ruined man you speak of.
2 GENTLEMAN Let's stand close and behold him.
BUCKINGHAM                All good people,   55
You that thus far have come to pity me,
Hear what I say, and then go home and lose me.
I have this day received a traitor's judgement,
And by that name must die; yet heaven bear witness,
And if I have a conscience, let it sink me,   60
Even as the axe falls, if I be not faithful.
The law I bear no malice for my death,
'T has done upon the premises but justice:
But those that sought it, I could wish more Christians:
Be what they will, I heartily forgive 'em;   65
Yet let 'em look they glory not in mischief,
Nor build their evils on the graves of great men,
For then my guiltless blood must cry against 'em.
For further life in this world I ne'er hope,
Nor will I sue, although the king have mercies   70
More than I dare make faults. You few that loved me,
And dare be bold to weep for Buckingham,
His noble friends and fellows, whom to leave
Is only bitter to him, only dying,

71] *Rowe*³; More…faults. / You…me F

53 SD.1 **tipstaves** Officers of the court appointed to take the accused into custody or to execution; so called because they carried 'tipstaves' or staves with metal tips.

53 SD.2 **halberds** Guards carrying halberds, a combination of spear and battle-axe mounted on a handle 5 to 7 feet long (*OED*).

53 SD.4 SIR WALTER SANDS The Lord Sands of 1.3 and 1.4. He was a knight at the time of Buckingham's trial and was elevated to the peerage before the historical meeting of Henry and Anne (Foakes).

55 **close** to one side, silent.
57 **lose** forget.
58 **judgement** sentence.
60 **sink** destroy (*OED* sv v 21).
61 **faithful** loyal and true.
63 **premises** evidence.
66 **look** look to it.
67 **their…graves** their evil designs or ambitions on the downfalls.
71 **make faults** commit offences.
74 Alone is bitter to him, alone is dying.

Go with me like good angels to my end;                          75
And as the long divorce of steel falls on me,
Make of your prayers one sweet sacrifice
And lift my soul to heaven. Lead on a'God's name.
LOVELL  I do beseech your grace, for charity,
If ever any malice in your heart                               80
Were hid against me, now to forgive me frankly.
BUCKINGHAM  Sir Thomas Lovell, I as free forgive you
As I would be forgiven: I forgive all.
There cannot be those numberless offences
'Gainst me that I cannot take peace with: no black envy         85
Shall make my grave. Commend me to his grace;
And if he speak of Buckingham, pray tell him
You met him half in heaven: my vows and prayers
Yet are the king's, and till my soul forsake
Shall cry for blessings on him. May he live                    90
Longer than I have time to tell his years;
Ever beloved and loving may his rule be;
And when old time shall lead him to his end,
Goodness and he fill up one monument.
LOVELL  To th'water side I must conduct your grace,             95
Then give my charge up to Sir Nicholas Vaux,
Who undertakes you to your end.
VAUX                                Prepare there,
The duke is coming: see the barge be ready,
And fit it with such furniture as suits
The greatness of his person.
BUCKINGHAM                      Nay, Sir Nicholas,              100
Let it alone; my state now will but mock me.
When I came hither, I was Lord High Constable

---

78] *Pope;* And...Heaven. / Lead...name F    85–6 'Gainst... / ...grace] *Pope; three lines, ending...*with:
/...Grave. / ...Grace F    85 that I cannot] F; I can't *Pope, Capell;* that I can't *Var. 1773*    86 make] F; mark
*Hanmer*    89 forsake] F; forsake me F4

76 **divorce** i.e. the divorce between body and
soul.
77 **sacrifice** offering.
79–81 **I do...frankly** See 1.2.185–6.
85 **take peace** make peace.
85 **envy** malice.
86 **make my grave** accompany me to my
grave. The emendation to 'mark' by some editors
is unnecessary.

89 **forsake** leave the body. 'Forsake' is not
used intransitively elsewhere in Shakespeare
(Wright).
91 **tell** count.
97 **undertakes you** takes you in charge.
99 **furniture** equipment, fittings.

And Duke of Buckingham: now, poor Edward Bohun.
Yet I am richer than my base accusers
That never knew what truth meant: I now seal it,                    105
And with that blood will make 'em one day groan for't.
My noble father, Henry of Buckingham,
Who first raised head against usurping Richard,
Flying for succour to his servant Banister,
Being distressed, was by that wretch betrayed,                     110
And without trial fell; God's peace be with him.
Henry the Seventh succeeding, truly pitying
My father's loss, like a most royal prince
Restored me to my honours, and out of ruins
Made my name once more noble. Now his son,                         115
Henry the Eighth, life, honour, name and all
That made me happy, at one stroke has taken
For ever from the world. I had my trial,
And must needs say a noble one; which makes me
A little happier than my wretched father;                          120
Yet thus far we are one in fortunes: both
Fell by our servants, by those men we loved most:
A most unnatural and faithless service.
Heaven has an end in all. Yet you that hear me,
This from a dying man receive as certain:                          125
Where you are liberal of your loves and counsels,
Be sure you be not loose; for those you make friends
And give your hearts to, when they once perceive
The least rub in your fortunes, fall away
Like water from ye, never found again                              130
But where they mean to sink ye. All good people,
Pray for me; I must now forsake ye; the last hour
Of my long weary life is come upon me.

103 **Bohun** So Holinshed (p. 865). The family
name was Stafford, but Buckingham inherited
the title of Lord High Constable through the
female line from the Bohuns, Earls of Hereford
(Pooler).

  105 **seal** ratify, authenticate as by a seal.
  108 **raised head** rebelled, raised forces.
  124 **end** purpose.

  125 **as certain** as truth.
  127 **loose** without restraint.
  129 **rub** obstacle. The metaphor came originally from the game of bowls; see *Ham.* 3.1.64.
  131 **sink** ruin (as at 60 above).
  133 **long…life** Buckingham was 43 when
executed. Note that Katherine calls herself old
at the same age in 3.1.120.

Farewell; and when you would say something that is
    sad,
Speak how I fell. I have done, and God forgive me.      135
                        *Exeunt Duke and train*

1 GENTLEMAN  O, this is full of pity! Sir, it calls,
I fear, too many curses on their heads
That were the authors.

2 GENTLEMAN             If the duke be guiltless,
'Tis full of woe: yet I can give you inkling
Of an ensuing evil, if it fall,                140
Greater than this.

1 GENTLEMAN        Good angels keep it from us.
What may it be? you do not doubt my faith, sir?

2 GENTLEMAN  This secret is so weighty, 'twill require
A strong faith to conceal it.

1 GENTLEMAN            Let me have it;
I do not talk much.

2 GENTLEMAN        I am confident;         145
You shall, sir: did you not of late days hear
A buzzing of a separation
Between the king and Katherine?

1 GENTLEMAN          Yes, but it held not;
For when the king once heard it, out of anger
He sent command to the lord mayor straight     150
To stop the rumour, and allay those tongues
That durst disperse it.

2 GENTLEMAN        But that slander, sir,
Is found a truth now; for it grows again
Fresher than e'er it was, and held for certain
The king will venture at it. Either the cardinal,   155
Or some about him near, have out of malice

134] F; Farewell; / And...sad *Capell*    135] *Pope;* Speak...fell. / I...me F

134 Editors since Capell have usually given 'Farewell' a line to itself since the F line is strictly a hexameter, but it need not be spoken as such.

  139 **inkling** hint.
  140 **fall** befall.
  142 **faith** trustworthiness.
  145 **am confident** have trust in you.
  146 The two Gentlemen provide a link

between Buckingham's disaster and the next major episode, the downfall of Katherine.
  147 **buzzing** rumour.
  148 **held not** did not continue.
  151 **allay** restrain.
  154 **held** believed.
  156 **about him near** i.e. his intimates.

To the good queen possessed him with a scruple
That will undo her. To confirm this too,
Cardinal Campeius is arrived, and lately,
As all think for this business.

1 GENTLEMAN                              'Tis the cardinal;                    160
And merely to revenge him on the emperor,
For not bestowing on him at his asking
The archbishopric of Toledo, this is purposed.

2 GENTLEMAN  I think you have hit the mark; but is't not cruel
That she should feel the smart of this? The cardinal              165
Will have his will, and she must fall.

1 GENTLEMAN                              'Tis woeful.
We are too open here to argue this:
Let's think in private more.

                                                    *Exeunt*


2.2  *Enter* LORD CHAMBERLAIN, *reading this letter*


CHAMBERLAIN  'My lord, the horses your lordship sent for, with
all the care I had, I saw well chosen, ridden and furnished.
They were young and handsome, and of the best breed in the
north. When they were ready to set out for London, a man of
my lord cardinal's, by commission and main power took 'em          5
from me, with this reason: his master would be served before
a subject, if not before the king, which stopped our mouths,
sir.'

164] *Pope;* I thinke / You...cruel F    **Act 2, Scene 2**    2.2] *Scena Secunda* F

**157 scruple** doubt.
**158 undo** ruin.
**159 Cardinal Campeius** Laurence Campeius
(Campeggio) came as the pope's legate in 1528,
seven years after Buckingham's death; another
example of the compression of historical events.
**161 emperor** Charles V, the Holy Roman
Emperor, Katherine's nephew.
**164 hit...mark** Already in common speech,
the metaphor is from archery.
**167 open** in the open, exposed to public view.
**167 argue** discuss.

**Act 2, Scene 2**
   **0 SD** This scene, in a room at court adjacent
to the king's private apartments, owes little to
Holinshed or other sources, beyond a few hints.
It is important for showing that the rumours of
the previous scene have more than a little substance and for revealing further machinations of
Wolsey, and the king's continued dependence
upon him.
   **2 ridden** broken in.
   **2 furnished** equipped.
   **5 commission...power** warrant and sheer
force.

I fear he will indeed; well, let him have them;
He will have all, I think.                                                    10

*Enter to the* LORD CHAMBERLAIN, *the* DUKES OF NORFOLK *and*
SUFFOLK

NORFOLK Well met, my Lord Chamberlain.
CHAMBERLAIN Good day to both your graces.
SUFFOLK How is the king employed?
CHAMBERLAIN                                    I left him private,
Full of sad thoughts and troubles.
NORFOLK                                           What's the cause?
CHAMBERLAIN It seems the marriage with his brother's wife          15
Has crept too near his conscience.
SUFFOLK [*Aside*]                              No, his conscience
Has crept too near another lady.
NORFOLK                                              'Tis so;
This is the cardinal's doing: the king-cardinal,
That blind priest, like the eldest son of fortune,
Turns what he list. The king will know him one day.               20
SUFFOLK Pray God he do, he'll never know himself else.
NORFOLK How holily he works in all his business,
And with what zeal! For now he has cracked the league
Between us and the emperor (the queen's great-nephew),
He dives into the king's soul, and there scatters                 25
Dangers, doubts, wringing of the conscience,
Fears and despairs, and all these for his marriage.
And out of all these, to restore the king,
He counsels a divorce, a loss of her

---

16 SD] *Vaughan; not in* F    21] *Pope;* Pray...doe, / He'll...else F

---

14 **sad** serious.
16 SD *Aside* Suffolk's words must form an
aside since the others do not seem to hear him
and Norfolk's speech obviously refers back to
what the Lord Chamberlain has said. Suffolk's
observation remains in the minds of the audience
as the king confers with the two cardinals.
19–20 **blind...list** Fortune was pictured in
the Middle Ages and Renaissance as blind, turning her wheel arbitrarily; see *H5* 3.6.28–40.
Wolsey as her eldest son inherits her blindness
and turns the wheel as he chooses (list).

21 **know himself** This may be a hint of the
way Henry's character will develop during the
course of the play.
23 **cracked** broken. Buckingham in 1.1.176
had described how Wolsey had earlier engineered
the breaking of the peace with France because of
the emperor's gold and promises.
26 **wringing...conscience** distress of conscience.

That like a jewel has hung twenty years                30
About his neck, yet never lost her lustre;
Of her that loves him with that excellence
That angels love good men with; even of her
That when the greatest stroke of fortune falls
Will bless the king: and is not this course pious?       35
CHAMBERLAIN  Heaven keep me from such counsel; 'tis most true
These news are everywhere, every tongue speaks 'em,
And every true heart weeps for't. All that dare
Look into these affairs see this main end,
The French king's sister. Heaven will one day open       40
The king's eyes, that so long have slept upon
This bold bad man.
SUFFOLK                    And free us from his slavery.
NORFOLK  We had need pray,
And heartily, for our deliverance,
Or this imperious man will work us all                   45
From princes into pages. All men's honours
Lie like one lump before him, to be fashioned
Into what pitch he please.
SUFFOLK                          For me, my lords,
I love him not, nor fear him, there's my creed:
As I am made without him, so I'll stand,                 50
If the king please; his curses and his blessings
Touch me alike: th'are breath I not believe in.
I knew him and I know him: so I leave him
To him that made him proud, the pope.
NORFOLK                                      Let's in,
And with some other business put the king                55

30 **jewel** Costly ornament on a gold chain worn by gentlemen of the time.

32 **excellence** surpassing virtue.

36 **counsel** Advice which Wolsey is pressing upon the king (29). There may be a reference, following the sarcastic mention of piety at 35, to the theological concept of the counsels or precepts of Christ in the gospels which the churchman, Wolsey, seems to be denying in offering such advice.

37 **These news** 'News' was considered as the plural form of 'new', the new.

39 **end** object.

40 **French...sister** Duchess of Alençon; see 3.2.85.

41 **slept upon** been blind to.

47 **lump** i.e. of clay. Foakes suggests an allusion to Rom. 9.21: 'Hath not the potter power of the clay to make of the same lumpe one vessell to honour, and another unto dishonour?'

48 **pitch** level, status; usually means 'height' but can be used figuratively as 'status'; see *TN* 1.1.12 (Onions).

50 **made** i.e. a nobleman.

50 **stand** stand firm.

52 **breath** Unsubstantial and fleeting as breath; compare *MM* 3.1.8–9.

From these sad thoughts that work too much upon him:
My lord, you'll bear us company?
CHAMBERLAIN                              Excuse me,
        The king has sent me otherwise; besides
        You'll find a most unfit time to disturb him.
        Health to your lordships.                                    60

> *Exit Lord Chamberlain and the* KING *draws*
> *the curtain and sits reading pensively*

SUFFOLK  How sad he looks; sure he is much afflicted.
KING  Who's there? Ha?
NORFOLK                        Pray God he be not angry.
KING  Who's there, I say? How dare you thrust yourselves
        Into my private meditations?
        Who am I? Ha?                                              65
NORFOLK  A gracious king that pardons all offences
        Malice ne'er meant. Our breach of duty this way
        Is business of estate, in which we come
        To know your royal pleasure.
KING                          Ye are too bold:
        Go to; I'll make ye know your times of business.             70
        Is this an hour for temporal affairs? Ha?

> *Enter* WOLSEY *and* CAMPEIUS *with a commission*

        Who's there? my good lord cardinal? O my Wolsey,
        The quiet of my wounded conscience;
        Thou art a cure fit for a king. [*To Campeius*] You're
            welcome,
        Most learned reverend sir, into our kingdom;                 75
        Use us, and it. [*To Wolsey*] My good lord, have great care
        I be not found a talker.
WOLSEY                      Sir, you cannot.
        I would your grace would give us but an hour
        Of private conference.

74 SD] *Theobald; not in* F    76 SD] *Johnson; not in* F

60 SD There is an obvious allusion to the curtain concealing the discovery space at the back
of the stage where the king is revealed reading.
Probably he did not draw the curtain himself but
had it done by an attendant.
  61 **afflicted** troubled.
  67 **this way** in this respect.

68 **estate** state.
70 **Go to** An expression of displeasure.
73 **quiet** ease.
  77 **a talker** i.e. ready to talk about welcome
but do nothing about it; a proverbial expression,
as Foakes points out. See Tilley T64, W820.

KING [*To Norfolk and Suffolk*] We are busy; go.

NORFOLK [*Aside to Suffolk*] This priest has no pride in him?

SUFFOLK [*Aside to Norfolk*]                                    Not to
    speak of:                                                          80
    I would not be so sick though for his place:
    But this cannot continue.

NORFOLK [*Aside to Suffolk*]          If it do
    I'll venture one; have at him!

SUFFOLK [*Aside to Norfolk*]             I another.

                        *Exeunt Norfolk and Suffolk*

WOLSEY Your grace has given a precedent of wisdom
    Above all princes, in committing freely                           85
    Your scruple to the voice of Christendom.
    Who can be angry now? what envy reach you?
    The Spaniard, tied by blood and favour to her,
    Must now confess, if they have any goodness,
    The trial just and noble. All the clerks,                         90
    I mean the learned ones in Christian kingdoms,
    Have their free voices. Rome, the nurse of judgement,
    Invited by your noble self, hath sent
    One general tongue unto us: this good man,
    This just and learned priest, Cardinal Campeius,                   95
    Whom once more I present unto your highness.

KING And once more in mine arms I bid him welcome,
    And thank the holy conclave for their loves;
    They have sent me such a man I would have wished for.

CAMPEIUS Your grace must needs deserve all strangers' loves,           100
    You are so noble. To your highness' hand
    I tender my commission; by whose virtue,

---

79 SD] *Theobald; not in* F      80 SD.1, 80 SD.2, 82 SD, 83 SD.1] *Capell; not in* F

**79–83** The asides of Norfolk and Suffolk represent their conversation as they walk towards the exit door; the king is engaged with the cardinals at the back of centre stage, though no doubt they move forward in the following exchanges.

**81 so sick...place** sick with such pride even for his high position.

**83 have at him!** A challenge.

**86 voice** vote; note 90–2 below. Holinshed tells us that Henry had sent letters and delegates to 'the great clearkes off all christendome',

especially in the universities of France and Italy, asking for their learned opinion (p. 906). See also 3.2.64–7 n.

**90 clerks** scholars.

**92 Have...voices** May vote freely or express their opinions on this matter freely.

**94 One...tongue** One to speak for all.

**98 conclave** assembly of cardinals.

**100 strangers** foreigners, those who come from another land.

**102 virtue** authority.

The court of Rome commanding, you, my Lord
Cardinal of York, are joined with me their servant
In the unpartial judging of this business.                          105
KING  Two equal men: the queen shall be acquainted
Forthwith for what you come. Where's Gardiner?
WOLSEY  I know your majesty has always loved her
So dear in heart, not to deny her that
A woman of less place might ask by law:                             110
Scholars allowed freely to argue for her.
KING  Ay, and the best she shall have; and my favour
To him that does best, God forbid else. Cardinal,
Prithee call Gardiner to me, my new secretary.
I find him a fit fellow.                                            115

*Enter* GARDINER

WOLSEY  [*Aside to Gardiner*]  Give me your hand: much joy and
          favour to you;
     You are the king's now.
GARDINER  [*Aside to Wolsey*]       But to be commanded
     For ever by your grace, whose hand has raised me.
KING  Come hither, Gardiner.
                         *Walks and whispers*
CAMPEIUS  My Lord of York, was not one Doctor Pace       120
     In this man's place before him?
WOLSEY                                Yes, he was.
CAMPEIUS  Was he not held a learned man?
WOLSEY                                Yes, surely.
CAMPEIUS  Believe me, there's an ill opinion spread then,
     Even of yourself, lord cardinal.
WOLSEY                                How? of me?
CAMPEIUS  They will not stick to say you envied him,       125
     And fearing he would rise, he was so virtuous,

---

103 commanding, you] F4; commanding. You F   116 SD] *Capell; not in* F   117 SD] *Capell; not in* F

105 **unpartial** impartial.
106 **equal** fair, just.
110 **less place** lower rank.
114 **Gardiner** Stephen Gardiner was appointed in July 1529 and became Bishop of Winchester in 1531. As Bishop of Winchester, he appears in Act 5.
120 **Doctor Pace** Holinshed speaks of Pace as being 'continuallie abroad in ambassages, and the same often times not much necessarie, by the cardinals appointment, at length he tooke such greefe therewith, that he fell out of his right wits' (p. 907). He died in 1536, six years after Wolsey's death.
125 **stick** scruple.

Kept him a foreign man still, which so grieved him
That he ran mad and died.
WOLSEY                                    Heaven's peace be with him!
That's Christian care enough; for living murmurers
There's places of rebuke. He was a fool,                          130
For he would needs be virtuous. That good fellow,
If I command him, follows my appointment,
I will have none so near else. Learn this, brother,
We live not to be griped by meaner persons.
KING Deliver this with modesty to th'queen.                       135

                                        *Exit Gardiner*
The most convenient place that I can think of
For such receipt of learning is Black-Friars:
There ye shall meet about this weighty business.
My Wolsey, see it furnished. O my lord,
Would it not grieve an able man to leave                          140
So sweet a bedfellow? But conscience, conscience;
O 'tis a tender place, and I must leave her.

                                        *Exeunt*


**2.3** *Enter* ANNE BULLEN *and an* OLD LADY

ANNE Not for that neither; here's the pang that pinches.
His highness, having lived so long with her, and she
So good a lady that no tongue could ever
Pronounce dishonour of her – by my life,

Act 2, Scene 3     2.3] *Scena Tertia* F

127 **foreign…still** employed continuously
abroad.
129 **murmurers** grumblers.
132 **appointment** bidding.
133 **near** familiar, close to the king.
134 **griped** seized, caught. The verb 'gripe'
can also mean 'grip by the hand'. Wolsey reveals
himself as a Machiavellian politician (in the
popular Elizabethan sense). It may seem
surprising that he would betray so much to
another churchman except on the assumption
that the papal court was like Henry's or any other
royal court.
135 **Deliver** Make known.
135 **with modesty** mildly.
137 **such…learning** (1) the hearing of such

learned opinions, (2) the reception of such learned
men (probably the former). For the placing of
'such' see Abbott 423.
139 **furnished** properly fitted out for the
purpose.

**Act 2, Scene 3**
0 SD This scene, in one of the queen's apartments, has no known source apart from the bare
statement in Holinshed (p. 928) that the king in
September 1532 gave Anne Bullen such a title
and pension. Anne is humanised through her pity
for the queen and in her reactions to the teasing
of the Old Lady.
1 **pinches** torments, hurts.

She never knew harm-doing – O, now, after                    5
So many courses of the sun enthroned,
Still growing in a majesty and pomp, the which
To leave, a thousand-fold more bitter than
'Tis sweet at first t'acquire: after this process
To give her the avaunt, it is a pity                         10
Would move a monster!
OLD LADY                          Hearts of most hard temper
Melt and lament for her.
ANNE                              O God's will, much better
She ne'er had known pomp; though't be temporal,
Yet if that quarrel, fortune, do divorce
It from the bearer, 'tis a sufferance panging               15
As soul and body's severing.
OLD LADY                          Alas, poor lady,
She's a stranger now again.
ANNE                              So much the more
Must pity drop upon her: verily
I swear, 'tis better to be lowly born,
And range with humble livers in content,                    20
Than to be perked up in a glistering grief
And wear a golden sorrow.
OLD LADY                              Our content
Is our best having.
ANNE                              By my troth and maidenhead,
I would not be a queen.
OLD LADY                              Beshrew me, I would,
And venture maidenhead for't, and so would you,             25

14 quarrel, fortune, do] F2; quarrell. Fortune, do F; quarr'ler Fortune do *Hanmer*

6 **courses. . . sun** years.
**8–9 more. . . sweet** An audience which knew
Anne's subsequent history would recognise the
irony of this statement. Note also 12–16 below
and other sentiments expressed by Anne.
9 **process** long course of events.
10 **avaunt** order to leave, rejection.
10 **pity** calamity.
11 **temper** disposition.
13 **temporal** worldly.
14 **quarrel** quarreller; one who constantly
finds occasion for contention and quarrels. Most
critics accept this meaning, but as Foakes points
out, F's full stop after 'quarrell' may represent the

compositor's misreading of an ampersand, giving
'quarrel and fortune', i.e. the quarrel between
Katherine and the king and the baleful influence
of fortune.
20 **range** occupy a place.
20 **humble livers** those who live humble lives.
21 **perked up** made fine (as with splendid
clothes). Also the sense of 'lifted up' may be
intended.
23 **having** possession.
23 **troth** faith.
24 **Beshrew me** Devil take me, evil befall me.
A mild oath.

For all this spice of your hypocrisy:
You that have so fair parts of woman on you,
Have too a woman's heart, which ever yet
Affected eminence, wealth, sovereignty;
Which, to say sooth, are blessings; and which gifts,                    30
Saving your mincing, the capacity
Of your soft cheveril conscience would receive,
If you might please to stretch it.

ANNE                                              Nay, good troth.

OLD LADY  Yes troth, and troth; you would not be a queen?

ANNE  No, not for all the riches under heaven.                          35

OLD LADY  'Tis strange; a threepence bowed would hire me,
Old as I am, to queen it: but I pray you,
What think you of a duchess? Have you limbs
To bear that load of title?

ANNE                                         No in truth.

OLD LADY  Then you are weakly made; pluck off a little,                 40
I would not be a young count in your way
For more than blushing comes to: if your back
Cannot vouchsafe this burthen, 'tis too weak
Ever to get a boy.

ANNE                                    How you do talk!
I swear again, I would not be a queen                                   45
For all the world.

OLD LADY                          In faith, for little England
You'd venture an emballing: I myself

---

26 **spice** taste, dash.

27 **fair parts** (1) fine qualities, (2) beauty.

29 **Affected** Desired, aspired to.

31 **Saving**...**mincing** With all respect to your affectation.

32 **cheveril** easily stretched, like kid-leather; proverbially applied to conscience, so Tilley c608.

36 **bowed** bent, hence worthless. There is a quibble with 'bawd'.

36 **hire** Disyllabic.

37 **queen** Suggests 'quean' or strumpet, with the preceding phrase.

40 **pluck off** come lower.

41 **count** earl; one rank below a duke.

41 **way** (1) path, (2) condition (i.e. virginity).

42 **For**...**to** The sense is obscure; the Old Lady may be suggesting that if Anne could not bear to be a duchess, she would get no further with a count than a mere blush.

46 **little England** Probably she means the whole of England (as compared with barren Caernarvonshire (48)), often called 'little' in comparison with larger countries. Caratach speaks of 'little Britain' in *Bonduca* (3.1.70). Foakes thinks it is a reference to Pembrokeshire, called 'Little England beyond Wales' by John Speed in *Theatre of the Empire of Great Britain* (1611): note 63 below.

47 **emballing** The sexual sense is plain; there is probably also a reference to investing with the ball (and sceptre) as an emblem of royalty.

Would for Caernarvonshire, although there longed
No more to the crown but that. Lo, who comes here?

*Enter* LORD CHAMBERLAIN

CHAMBERLAIN Good morrow, ladies; what were't worth to know        50
    The secret of your conference?
ANNE                                   My good lord,
    Not your demand; it values not your asking:
    Our mistress' sorrows we were pitying.
CHAMBERLAIN It was a gentle business, and becoming
    The action of good women; there is hope        55
    All will be well.
ANNE                         Now I pray God, amen.
CHAMBERLAIN You bear a gentle mind, and heavenly blessings
    Follow such creatures. That you may, fair lady,
    Perceive I speak sincerely, and high note's
    Ta'en of your many virtues, the king's majesty        60
    Commends his good opinion of you, and
    Does purpose honour to you no less flowing
    Than Marchioness of Pembroke; to which title
    A thousand pound a year, annual support,
    Out of his grace he adds.
ANNE                               I do not know        65
    What kind of my obedience I should tender;
    More than my all is nothing: nor my prayers
    Are not words duly hallowed, nor my wishes
    More worth than empty vanities; yet prayers and wishes
    Are all I can return. Beseech your lordship,        70
    Vouchsafe to speak my thanks and my obedience,
    As from a blushing handmaid, to his highness,
    Whose health and royalty I pray for.

**59** note's] *Theobald;* notes F     **61** of you, and] *Capell;* of you, to you; and F

**48 Caernarvonshire** A county in Wales, often considered to be barren and poor.
**48 longed** belonged.
**51 conference** conferring together.
**52 values not** is not worth.
**61 Commends...you** Presents his compliments (Pooler).
**61 of you** The F reading suggests that the compositor took the extra 'to you' from the next line.
**62 flowing** brimming, full to overflowing (*OED* Flowing *vbl sb* 6).
**66 kind** manner, fashion.
**67–8 nor...not** The double negative gives emphasis.
**71 Vouchsafe** Be so good.

CHAMBERLAIN                                    Lady,
    I shall not fail t'approve the fair conceit
    The king hath of you. [*Aside*] I have perused her well;   75
    Beauty and honour in her are so mingled
    That they have caught the king: and who knows yet
    But from this lady may proceed a gem
    To lighten all this isle. – I'll to the king,
    And say I spoke with you.     *Exit Lord Chamberlain*
ANNE                                   My honoured lord.    80
OLD LADY Why this it is: see, see,
    I have been begging sixteen years in court,
    Am yet a courtier beggarly, nor could
    Come pat betwixt too early and too late
    For any suit of pounds: and you, O fate!    85
    A very fresh fish here – fie, fie, fie upon
    This compelled fortune! – have your mouth filled up
    Before you open it.
ANNE                             This is strange to me.
OLD LADY How tastes it? Is it bitter? Forty pence, no.
    There was a lady once ('tis an old story)    90
    That would not be a queen, that would she not
    For all the mud in Egypt: have you heard it?
ANNE Come, you are pleasant.
OLD LADY                             With your theme, I could
    O'ermount the lark. The Marchioness of Pembroke?
    A thousand pounds a year, for pure respect?    95
    No other obligation? by my life,
    That promises moe thousands: honour's train
    Is longer than his foreskirt. By this time

75 SD] *Pope; not in* F

74 **approve…conceit** confirm the good opinion.

79 **lighten** give light to; gems were thought to give off light. The Lord Chamberlain's aside foreshadows Cranmer's prophecy in 5.4.

83 **beggarly** very poor, still begging.

84 **pat** at the right moment.

85 **suit of pounds** petition involving money. Also 'pounds' = 'ponds', hence the reference to fish at 86 (Foakes).

87 **compelled** forced upon her.

89 **Forty pence** A small sum (worth one-sixth of a pound), commonly used for a small bet or the fee paid to an attorney; see *AWW* 2.2.22.

92 **mud in Egypt** Source of Egypt's wealth, but also a somewhat derisive reference to wealth as mud.

93 **pleasant** merry.

97 **moe** more.

97–8 **honour's…foreskirt** More rewards and honours will follow, like the train of an elaborate dress becoming longer with increasing rank, the foreskirt remaining necessarily much shorter. Pooler notes that attempts had been made by Henry VII's mother to regulate the length of trains according to rank.

I know your back will bear a duchess. Say,
Are you not stronger than you were?
ANNE                                    Good lady,                    100
Make yourself mirth with your particular fancy,
And leave me out on't. Would I had no being
If this salute my blood a jot; it faints me
To think what follows.
The queen is comfortless, and we forgetful              105
In our long absence: pray do not deliver
What here y'have heard to her.
OLD LADY                      What do you think me? –
                                          *Exeunt*

**2.4** *Trumpets, sennet, and cornets. Enter two Vergers with short silver
wands; next them two* SCRIBES *in the habit of doctors; after them the*
ARCHBISHOP OF CANTERBURY *alone; after him, the* BISHOPS OF
LINCOLN, ELY, ROCHESTER, *and* ST ASAPH: *next them, with some
small distance, follows a Gentleman bearing the purse, with the great seal,
and a cardinal's hat: then two Priests, bearing each a silver cross: then a*
GENTLEMAN USHER *bareheaded, accompanied with a Sergeant-at-Arms,
bearing a silver mace: then two Gentlemen bearing two great silver pillars:
after them, side by side, the two* CARDINALS, *two Noblemen with the sword
and mace. The* KING *takes place under the cloth of state. The two Cardinals
sit under him as judges. The* QUEEN *takes place some distance from the
King. The Bishops place themselves on each side the court in manner of a
consistory: below them the Scribes. The Lords sit next the Bishops. The rest
of the attendants stand in convenient order about the stage*

Act 2, Scene 4    2.4] *Scena Quarta* F    0 SD.3 ARCHBISHOP] *Johnson;* Bishop F

101 **particular** private.
103 **salute...jot** arouses any kind of physical
response in me.
103 **faints me** makes me faint.
106 **deliver** make known.

**Act 2, Scene 4**
0 SD The trial scene is set at Black-Friars
according to the king's direction (2.2.137). Much
of it is closely dependent upon Holinshed,
who describes the place and its furnishings and
gives an account of the proceedings (pp. 907–8).
Shakespeare has made the entry into a splendid
procession. Details of insignia and ornaments
come from passages elsewhere in Holinshed
which describe Wolsey's love of show on public
occasions.

0 SD.1 **sennet** A ceremonial fanfare played
on trumpets or cornets, here on both.
0 SD.2 **habit of doctors** Costumes worn by
doctors of law, i.e. flat caps and black gowns
bordered with fur.
0 SD.8 **silver pillars** Portable columns of
silver-gilt, a symbol of dignity and high office.
They were, according to the chroniclers, carried
before Cardinal Wolsey, and later Cardinal Pole.
0 SD.10 **takes place** seats himself.
0 SD.10 **cloth of state** canopy above the royal
chair.
0 SD.13 **consistory** tribunal, court of judgement. The term is also used of a bishop's court
trying offences against ecclesiastical law.

WOLSEY Whilst our commission from Rome is read,
　　Let silence be commanded.
KING 　　　　　　　　　　　What's the need?
　　It hath already publicly been read,
　　And on all sides th'authority allowed;
　　You may then spare that time.
WOLSEY 　　　　　　　　　　Be't so, proceed. 　5
SCRIBE Say, Henry, King of England, come into the court.
CRIER Henry, King of England, etc.
KING Here.
SCRIBE Say, Katherine, Queen of England, come into the court.
CRIER Katherine, Queen of England, etc. 　10
　　*The Queen makes no answer, rises out of her chair, goes about the*
　　*court, comes to the King, and kneels at his feet: then speaks*
KATHERINE Sir, I desire you do me right and justice,
　　And to bestow your pity on me, for
　　I am a most poor woman, and a stranger
　　Born out of your dominions: having here
　　No judge indifferent, nor no more assurance 　15
　　Of equal friendship and proceeding. Alas, sir,
　　In what have I offended you? What cause
　　Hath my behaviour given to your displeasure,
　　That thus you should proceed to put me off
　　And take your good grace from me. Heaven witness, 　20
　　I have been to you a true and humble wife,
　　At all times to your will conformable,
　　Ever in fear to kindle your dislike,
　　Yea, subject to your countenance, glad or sorry,
　　As I saw it inclined. When was the hour 　25
　　I ever contradicted your desire,
　　Or made it not mine too? Or which of your friends
　　Have I not strove to love, although I knew
　　He were mine enemy? What friend of mine,

25 inclined.] *Rowe³; inclin'd?* F

1 **commission** See 2.2.102.
10 SD The queen has been placed at some distance from the king, no doubt to emphasise their separate identities during the proceedings. She now upsets the arrangement by moving through the court to the very feet of the king.
13 **stranger** foreigner.

15 **indifferent** impartial.
16 **equal** fair, just.
16 **proceeding** legal process.
19 **put me off** dismiss me (through annulment of the marriage).
20 **grace** Henry's favour, also referring to his person.

That had to him derived your anger, did I                     30
Continue in my liking? nay, gave notice
He was from thence discharged? Sir, call to mind
That I have been your wife, in this obedience,
Upward of twenty years, and have been blest
With many children by you. If in the course          35
And process of this time, you can report,
And prove it too, against mine honour aught,
My bond to wedlock, or my love and duty
Against your sacred person; in God's name
Turn me away, and let the foul'st contempt           40
Shut door upon me, and so give me up
To the sharp'st kind of justice. Please you, sir,
The king your father was reputed for
A prince most prudent, of an excellent
And unmatched wit and judgement. Ferdinand           45
My father, King of Spain, was reckoned one
The wisest prince that there had reigned by many
A year before. It is not to be questioned
That they had gathered a wise council to them
Of every realm, that did debate this business,      50
Who deemed our marriage lawful. Wherefore I humbly
Beseech you, sir, to spare me till I may
Be by my friends in Spain advised, whose counsel
I will implore. If not, i'th'name of God
Your pleasure be fulfilled.

WOLSEY                               You have here, lady,    55
And of your choice, these reverend fathers, men
Of singular integrity and learning,
Yea, the elect o'th'land, who are assembled
To plead your cause. It shall be therefore bootless
That longer you desire the court, as well            60
For your own quiet, as to rectify
What is unsettled in the king.

---

30 **derived** drawn.

35 **many children** Katherine bore six children to Henry between 1510 and 1518, but apart from Mary they were stillborn or died in infancy. See 184–91 below.

39 **Against** Towards (*OED* sv 3).

45 **wit** wisdom.

46 **one** one of (the wisest princes). Shakespeare draws this statement from Holinshed's account.

59 **bootless** useless, without profit.

60 **longer...desire** you entreat any longer (for a delay in the trial). For 'desire' in this sense see *Cor.* 2.3.55.

CAMPEIUS                                    His grace
Hath spoken well and justly; therefore, madam,
It's fit this royal session do proceed,
And that without delay their arguments                          65
Be now produced and heard.
KATHERINE                              Lord cardinal,
To you I speak.
WOLSEY                      Your pleasure, madam.
KATHERINE                                        Sir,
I am about to weep; but thinking that
We are a queen, or long have dreamed so, certain
The daughter of a king, my drops of tears                       70
I'll turn to sparks of fire.
WOLSEY                          Be patient yet.
KATHERINE I will, when you are humble; nay before,
Or God will punish me. I do believe,
Induced by potent circumstances, that
You are mine enemy, and make my challenge                       75
You shall not be my judge. For it is you
Have blown this coal betwixt my lord and me –
Which God's dew quench! Therefore I say again,
I utterly abhor, yea, from my soul
Refuse you for my judge, whom yet once more                     80
I hold my most malicious foe, and think not
At all a friend to truth.
WOLSEY                            I do profess
You speak not like yourself; who ever yet
Have stood to charity and displayed th'effects
Of disposition gentle, and of wisdom                            85
O'ertopping woman's power. Madam, you do me wrong:
I have no spleen against you, nor injustice

66 **produced** brought forward, exhibited.
69 **certain** certainly.
74 **Induced** Persuaded.
74 **potent** convincing.
75 **challenge** A legal protest or objection.
78 **dew** Foakes quotes *Cym.* 5.5.351: 'The benediction of these covering heavens / Fall on their heads like dew.' The coal image is not in Holinshed but may come from Foxe (or Halle, whom Foxe quotes): 'therefore of malice you have kindled this fire, and set this matter abroach' (*Acts*, p. 958).

79 **abhor** loathe, hate utterly. Onions suggests 'protest against', referring to this passage and *Err.* 3.2.165. The relevant passage in Holinshed may justify this interpretation: 'the queene...openlie protested, that she did utterlie abhorre, refuse, and forsake such a judge...' (p. 908).
82 **profess** affirm.
84 **stood to** upheld.
84 **charity** Christian love.
87 **spleen** anger, spite.

For you or any; how far I have proceeded,
Or how far further shall, is warranted
By a commission from the consistory,                              90
Yea, the whole consistory of Rome. You charge me
That I have blown this coal: I do deny it;
The king is present; if it be known to him
That I gainsay my deed, how may he wound,
And worthily, my falsehood, yea, as much                          95
As you have done my truth. If he know
That I am free of your report, he knows
I am not of your wrong. Therefore in him
It lies to cure me, and the cure is to
Remove these thoughts from you. The which before                 100
His highness shall speak in, I do beseech
You, gracious madam, to unthink your speaking
And to say so no more.

KATHERINE                           My lord, my lord,
I am a simple woman, much too weak
T'oppose your cunning. Y'are meek and humble-mouthed,            105
You sign your place and calling, in full seeming,
With meekness and humility; but your heart
Is crammed with arrogancy, spleen and pride.
You have by fortune, and his highness' favours,
Gone slightly o'er low steps, and now are mounted                110
Where powers are your retainers, and your words,
Domestics to you, serve your will as't please
Yourself pronounce their office. I must tell you,
You tender more your person's honour than
Your high profession spiritual; that again                        115
I do refuse you for my judge, and here
Before you all, appeal unto the pope,

90 **consistory** council or ecclesiastical senate of the pope and cardinals.
94 **gainsay my deed** deny what I have done.
95 **worthily** justly.
97 **free** innocent.
97 **report** account.
98 **I . . . wrong** I am not free of the wrong you have done me, i.e. the accusation you have brought.
101 **in** with reference to.
106 **sign your place** mark your office.

106 **in full seeming** in all outward appearance.
108 **spleen** malice.
110 **slightly** easily, lightly.
111 **powers** men of authority.
111 **retainers** followers, servants.
111–13 **your words . . . office** your words are like domestic servants, serving your will as you declare their function.
114 **tender** cherish.

To bring my whole cause 'fore his holiness,
And to be judged by him.

*She curtsies to the King and offers to depart*

CAMPEIUS                              The queen is obstinate,
Stubborn to justice, apt to accuse it, and                       120
Disdainful to be tried by't; 'tis not well.
She's going away.

KING   Call her again.

CRIER   Katherine, Queen of England, come into the court.

GENTLEMAN USHER   Madam, you are called back.                    125

KATHERINE   What need you note it? pray you keep your way,
When you are called, return. Now the Lord help,
They vex me past my patience. Pray you pass on;
I will not tarry: no, nor ever more
Upon this business my appearance make                            130
In any of their courts.

*Exit Queen and her attendants*

KING                            Go thy ways, Kate;
That man i'th'world who shall report he has
A better wife, let him in nought be trusted,
For speaking false in that; thou art alone –
If thy rare qualities, sweet gentleness,                         135
Thy meekness saint-like, wife-like government,
Obeying in commanding, and thy parts
Sovereign and pious else, could speak thee out –
The queen of earthly queens. She's noble born,
And like her true nobility, she has                              140
Carried herself towards me.

WOLSEY                              Most gracious sir,
In humblest manner I require your highness

120 **Stubborn to justice** Unyielding to justice.
120 **accuse** find fault with.
126 **note it** take notice of it.
126 **keep your way** keep going.
127 **When…return** Katherine tells the gentleman usher that when he is called back, he may return but she will not. A gentleman usher is a gentleman acting as an usher or attendant for a person of high rank. Holinshed names the usher as Griffith (p. 907); he appears later in the play (4.2).
135 **rare** excelling.

136 **government** demeanour, conduct.
137 **Obeying in commanding** Following 'wife-like', the phrase may mean that she is obedient to her husband in giving commands, or possibly that she obeys the need for restraint and control in giving commands.
137 **parts** qualities.
138 **Sovereign** Excellent.
138 **else** besides.
138 **speak thee out** describe you.
141 **Carried herself** Behaved.
142 **require** beg, request.

That it shall please you to declare in hearing
Of all these ears – for where I am robbed and bound,
There must I be unloosed, although not there                    145
At once and fully satisfied – whether ever I
Did broach this business to your highness, or
Laid any scruple in your way which might
Induce you to the question on't; or ever
Have to you, but with thanks to God for such                    150
A royal lady, spake one the least word that might
Be to the prejudice of her present state
Or touch of her good person?

KING                                        My lord cardinal,
I do excuse you; yea, upon mine honour,
I free you from't. You are not to be taught                     155
That you have many enemies that know not
Why they are so, but like to village curs
Bark when their fellows do. By some of these
The queen is put in anger. Y'are excused:
But will you be more justified? you ever                        160
Have wished the sleeping of this business, never desired
It to be stirred, but oft have hindered, oft
The passages made toward it; on my honour,
I speak my good lord cardinal to this point,
And thus far clear him. Now, what moved me to't,               165
I will be bold with time and your attention.
Then mark th'inducement. Thus it came; give heed to't:
My conscience first received a tenderness,
Scruple and prick, on certain speeches uttered
By th'Bishop of Bayonne, then French ambassador,              170
Who had been hither sent on the debating
A marriage 'twixt the Duke of Orleans and
Our daughter Mary. I'th'progress of this business,

165] *Pope;* And...him. / Now...to't F    172 A] *Rome*³; And F

146 **satisfied** given satisfaction or recompense.
149 **on't** of it.
151 **one the least** the very least.
153 **touch** reproach.
157–8 **curs...do** Proverbial; Tilley D539.
163–5 **on...him** The king turns here to speak to the whole court, noting that he has cleared the cardinal with respect to 'this point', the question raised by Wolsey.
167 **inducement** i.e. what persuaded (me).
168 **tenderness** sensitivity.
172 **Duke of Orleans** Second son of Francis I, later Henry II of France (Foakes).

Ere a determinate resolution, he
(I mean the bishop) did require a respite,                          175
Wherein he might the king his lord advertise
Whether our daughter were legitimate
Respecting this our marriage with the dowager,
Sometimes our brother's wife. This respite shook
The bosom of my conscience, entered me,                            180
Yea, with a spitting power, and made to tremble
The region of my breast, which forced such way
That many mazed considerings did throng
And pressed in with this caution. First, methought
I stood not in the smile of heaven, who had                        185
Commanded nature, that my lady's womb,
If it conceived a male child by me, should
Do no more offices of life to't than
The grave does to th'dead: for her male issue
Or died where they were made, or shortly after                     190
This world had aired them. Hence I took a thought
This was a judgement on me, that my kingdom,
Well worthy the best heir o'th'world, should not
Be gladded in't by me. Then follows that
I weighed the danger which my realms stood in                      195
By this my issue's fail, and that gave to me
Many a groaning throe. Thus hulling in
The wild sea of my conscience, I did steer
Toward this remedy, whereupon we are

181 spitting] F; splitting F2

174 **determinate resolution** final settlement.
175 **require** request.
176 **advertise** inform, i.e. call the attention
of the king to this matter (accented on second
syllable as usual in Shakespeare).
179 **Sometimes** Formerly.
180 **bosom** seat. The heart was thought of as
the seat of the conscience: see *Temp.* 2.1.278.
181 **spitting** piercing, as with a spit.
183 **mazed** confused as if in a maze.
183–4 **throng...pressed in** i.e. like a crowd
of people. Maxwell cites *The Rape of Lucrece*
1301–2.
184 **caution** taking heed, admonition.
185 **heaven** Perhaps a substitution in F for

'God' after the Act of Abuses in 1606 (Foakes).
Henry's fears, described in the following lines,
were in A. F. Pollard's view a major reason for
his seeking a divorce (*Thomas Cranmer*, 1906,
p. 34).
188 **offices** services.
191 **aired** exposed to view.
194 **gladded** made happy.
196 **issue's fail** failure of issue; possibly 'death
of issue'. Compare 1.2.145.
197 **throe** pang; often used of the pain of
childbirth.
197 **hulling** Drifting in a ship with sails furled,
wind or current acting on the hull alone (*OED*
Hull $v^2$ 1).

Now present here together: that's to say,                     200
I meant to rectify my conscience, which
I then did feel full sick, and yet not well,
By all the reverend fathers of the land
And doctors learned. First I began in private
With you, my Lord of Lincoln; you remember          205
How under my oppression I did reek
When I first moved you.

LINCOLN                            Very well, my liege.

KING I have spoke long, be pleased yourself to say
How far you satisfied me.

LINCOLN                               So please your highness,
The question did at first so stagger me,                      210
Bearing a state of mighty moment in't,
And consequence of dread, that I committed
The daring'st counsel which I had to doubt,
And did entreat your highness to this course
Which you are running here.

KING                                        I then moved you,          215
My Lord of Canterbury, and got your leave
To make this present summons: unsolicited
I left no reverend person in this court,
But by particular consent proceeded
Under your hands and seals; therefore, go on,           220
For no dislike i'th'world against the person
Of the good queen, but the sharp thorny points
Of my allegèd reasons drives this forward:
Prove but our marriage lawful, by my life

217 summons: unsolicited] *Theobald;* Summons unsolicited. F

201 **rectify** set right.
202 **yet** which is still.
205 **Lincoln** Holinshed describes the Bishop of Lincoln as the king's confessor (p. 906).
206 **oppression** distress.
206 **reek** sweat.
207 **moved** appealed to.
211 **Bearing...moment** Containing a matter of great importance.

212 **consequence of dread** fearful outcome.
212–13 **committed...doubt** i.e. distrusted the most daring advice I could give. Pooler interprets 'distrusted the advice which I should have ventured on most boldly (or with most confidence)'.
220 **Under...seals** With your written consent.
223 **allegèd** i.e. that I have brought forward.

And kingly dignity, we are contented                               225
To wear our mortal state to come with her,
Katherine our queen, before the primest creature
That's paragoned o'th'world.

CAMPEIUS                                    So please your highness,
The queen being absent, 'tis a needful fitness
That we adjourn this court till further day;                        230
Meanwhile must be an earnest motion
Made to the queen to call back her appeal
She intends unto his holiness.

KING [*Aside*]                              I may perceive
These cardinals trifle with me: I abhor
This dilatory sloth and tricks of Rome.                             235
My learn'd and well belovèd servant, Cranmer,
Prithee return; with thy approach, I know,
My comfort comes along. – Break up the court;
I say, set on.

                        *Exeunt in manner as they entered*


3.1 *Enter* QUEEN *and her women as at work*


KATHERINE Take thy lute, wench, my soul grows sad with
          troubles;
    Sing, and disperse 'em if thou canst: leave working.

233 SD] *Capell; not in* F    **Act 3, Scene 1**    3.1] *Actus Tertius Scena Prima* F    1] *Pope;* Take...wench, /
My...troubles F

226 **state** condition.
227 **primest** most excellent.
228 **paragoned** made a paragon or perfect
model (a unique example of the verb used in this
sense).
229 **fitness** propriety, i.e. what is proper to
the circumstances.
230 **further** a future.
231 **motion** appeal.
236 **Cranmer** Cranmer had not yet been appointed Archbishop of Canterbury and was travel-
ling on the continent gathering learned opinions
on the divorce question; see 3.2.64–7 n.

**Act 3, Scene 1**
0 SD This domestic scene in the queen's
apartments presents Katherine as the good
queen, not averse to taking part in housewifely
duties with her women, just as she fulfilled public
duties in 1.2. The quiet opening of the scene is in
striking contrast to the angry confrontation with
Wolsey in 2.4. The visit of the cardinals and the
substance of their conversation with Katherine
are recounted by Holinshed (p. 908), though the
dramatist has sharpened many of the exchanges
and enlarged Katherine's speeches.
2 **leave** cease.

*Song*

Orpheus with his lute made trees,
And the mountain tops that freeze,
    Bow themselves when he did sing.                    5
To his music plants and flowers
Ever sprung, as sun and showers
    There had made a lasting spring.

Every thing that heard him play,
Even the billows of the sea,                            10
    Hung their heads and then lay by.
In sweet music is such art,
Killing care and grief of heart
    Fall asleep, or hearing die.

*Enter a* GENTLEMAN

KATHERINE  How now?                                     15
GENTLEMAN  And't please your grace, the two great cardinals
    Wait in the presence.
KATHERINE                    Would they speak with me?
GENTLEMAN  They willed me say so, madam.
KATHERINE                              Pray their graces
    To come near:

                              [*Exit Gentleman*]
            What can be their business
With me, a poor weak woman, fall'n from favour?        20
I do not like their coming; now I think on't,
They should be good men, their affairs as righteous:
But all hoods make not monks.

*Enter the two Cardinals,* WOLSEY *and* CAMPEIUS

WOLSEY                              Peace to your highness!

---

**19** SD] *Capell; not in* F    **23** SD CAMPEIUS] F4; *Campian* F

---

**3 Orpheus** The power of Orpheus's music over nature was a well-known tradition in Renaissance poetry, deriving from Ovid's *Metamorphoses* X–XI, and other classical sources. Pooler and W. J. Craig refer to Beaumont and Fletcher's *The Captain* (1610) where there is a similar passage in 3.1 describing the power of Orpheus, but in blank verse.

**7 sprung** issued forth.

**7 as** as if.

**10 sea** Rhyming with 'play'.

**11 lay by** came to a standstill; a nautical metaphor usually referring to a ship (*OED* By *adv* 2b).

**17 presence** presence-chamber.

**23 all...monks** Proverbial: Tilley H586. As Pooler notes, Shakespeare uses the Latin form *cucullus non facit monachum* in *TN* (1.5.62) and *MM* (5.1.263).

KATHERINE Your graces find me here part of a housewife;
    I would be all, against the worst may happen:     25
    What are your pleasures with me, reverent lords?
WOLSEY May it please you, noble madam, to withdraw
    Into your private chamber; we shall give you
    The full cause of our coming.
KATHERINE          Speak it here.
    There's nothing I have done yet o'my conscience    30
    Deserves a corner; would all other women
    Could speak this with as free a soul as I do.
    My lords, I care not – so much I am happy
    Above a number – if my actions
    Were tried by every tongue, every eye saw 'em,    35
    Envy and base opinion set against 'em,
    I know my life so even. If your business
    Seek me out, and that way I am wife in,
    Out with it boldly: truth loves open dealing.
WOLSEY *Tanta est erga te mentis integritas, regina serenissima* –   40
KATHERINE O good my lord, no Latin;
    I am not such a truant since my coming
    As not to know the language I have lived in;
    A strange tongue makes my cause more strange,
      suspicious;
    Pray speak in English; here are some will thank you,   45
    If you speak truth, for their poor mistress' sake;
    Believe me, she has had much wrong. Lord cardinal,
    The willing'st sin I ever yet committed
    May be absolved in English.
WOLSEY         Noble lady,
    I am sorry my integrity should breed,       50

26 reverent] F; reverend F2   40, 49 SH WOLSEY] *Card.* F

25 **would be all** would be a complete housewife.
 25 **against...happen** if the worst should
happen.
 26 **reverent** reverend; frequently spelt so at
the time.
 31 **a corner** i.e. secrecy.
 32 **free** innocent.
 34 **a number** many.
 36 **Envy** Malice.
 36 **opinion** gossip, rumour.
 37 **even** constant, unwavering (in justice and
truth).

 38 **that...wife in** what concerns me as a wife.
 40 ***Tanta...serenissima*** Such is the integrity
of (my) mind towards you, most serene queen –
Holinshed mentions that the cardinal began to
speak to her in Latin.
 42 **truant** idler.
 44 **strange** The first 'strange' means 'foreign';
the second also, since Katherine is a foreigner,
but it has in addition the sense of what is very
unusual, hence 'suspicious'.
 48 **willing'st** most deliberate, intentional.

And service to his majesty and you,
So deep suspicion where all faith was meant.
We come not by the way of accusation,
To taint that honour every good tongue blesses,
Nor to betray you any way to sorrow –                                        55
You have too much, good lady – but to know
How you stand minded in the weighty difference
Between the king and you, and to deliver,
Like free and honest men, our just opinions
And comforts to your cause.

CAMPEIUS                                    Most honoured madam,              60
My Lord of York, out of his noble nature,
Zeal and obedience he still bore your grace,
Forgetting, like a good man, your late censure
Both of his truth and him, which was too far,
Offers, as I do, in a sign of peace                                          65
His service and his counsel.

KATHERINE [*Aside*]                         To betray me. –
My lords, I thank you both for your good wills;
Ye speak like honest men, pray God ye prove so;
But how to make ye suddenly an answer
In such a point of weight, so near mine honour                               70
(More near my life I fear), with my weak wit,
And to such men of gravity and learning,
In truth I know not. I was set at work
Among my maids, full little, God knows, looking
Either for such men or such business.                                        75
For her sake that I have been, for I feel
The last fit of my greatness, good your graces,
Let me have time and counsel for my cause.
Alas, I am a woman, friendless, hopeless.

WOLSEY Madam, you wrong the king's love with these fears;                    80
Your hopes and friends are infinite.

KATHERINE                                   In England

---

60 your] F2; our F    66 SD] *Capell; not in* F

51 The line sounds like Wolsey's afterthought.
52 **faith** loyalty.
55 **any way** in any fashion.
58 **deliver** declare, put forward.
59 **free** honourable.
62 **still bore** has always borne.

64 **was** went.
69 **suddenly** without preparation.
70 **near** close to and affecting.
73 **set** seated.
77 **fit** short spell.

But little for my profit; can you think, lords,
That any Englishman dare give me counsel?
Or be a known friend 'gainst his highness' pleasure
(Though he be grown so desperate to be honest)                85
And live a subject? Nay forsooth, my friends,
They that must weigh out my afflictions,
They that my trust must grow to, live not here;
They are, as all my other comforts, far hence
In mine own country, lords.

CAMPEIUS                               I would your grace        90
Would leave your griefs, and take my counsel.

KATHERINE                                        How, sir?

CAMPEIUS Put your main cause into the king's protection;
He's loving and most gracious. 'Twill be much
Both for your honour better and your cause:
For if the trial of the law o'ertake ye,                          95
You'll part away disgraced.

WOLSEY                               He tells you rightly.

KATHERINE Ye tell me what ye wish for both, my ruin.
Is this your Christian counsel? Out upon ye!
Heaven is above all yet; there sits a judge
That no king can corrupt.

CAMPEIUS                       Your rage mistakes us.           100

KATHERINE The more shame for ye; holy men I thought ye,
Upon my soul, two reverend cardinal virtues;
But cardinal sins and hollow hearts I fear ye:
Mend 'em for shame, my lords. Is this your comfort?
The cordial that ye bring a wretched lady,                      105
A woman lost among ye, laughed at, scorned?
I will not wish ye half my miseries,
I have more charity. But say I warned ye;
Take heed, for heaven's sake take heed, lest at once
The burthen of my sorrows fall upon ye.                        110

82 profit; can] F2; profit can F

85 desperate...honest reckless of con-
sequences as to speak what he thinks.
86 live a subject remain a loyal subject.
86 forsooth in truth.
87 weigh out measure and assess. So
Maxwell, but Onions interprets as 'outweigh,
compensate for'.
96 part away leave.
100 mistakes misjudges; note 1.1.195 above.

102 two...virtues two personifications of the
cardinal virtues (justice, prudence, temperance
and fortitude). The cardinal virtues were linked
with the theological virtues, faith, hope and
charity, as the seven virtues, to match the seven
deadly sins. The pun on 'cardinal' is carried on in
the next line.
106 lost brought to ruin.
109 at once all at once.

WOLSEY Madam, this is a mere distraction;
 You turn the good we offer into envy.
KATHERINE Ye turn me into nothing. Woe upon ye,
 And all such false professors. Would you have me,
 If you have any justice, any pity,                                    115
 If ye be anything but churchmen's habits,
 Put my sick cause into his hands that hates me?
 Alas, 'has banished me his bed already,
 His love, too, long ago. I am old, my lords,
 And all the fellowship I hold now with him                            120
 Is only my obedience. What can happen
 To me above this wretchedness? All your studies
 Make me a curse, like this.
CAMPEIUS                              Your fears are worse.
KATHERINE Have I lived thus long (let me speak myself,
 Since virtue finds no friends) a wife, a true one?                    125
 A woman, I dare say without vainglory,
 Never yet branded with suspicion?
 Have I with all my full affections
 Still met the king? loved him next heaven? obeyed him?
 Been, out of fondness, superstitious to him?                          130
 Almost forgot my prayers to content him?
 And am I thus rewarded? 'Tis not well, lords.
 Bring me a constant woman to her husband,
 One that ne'er dreamed a joy beyond his pleasure,
 And to that woman, when she has done most,                            135

111 SH WOLSEY] *Car.* F    118 'has] *Dyce;* ha's F

111 **mere distraction** absolute frenzy.
112 **envy** malice.
114 **false professors** hypocritical persons pro-
fessing such qualities as faith and justice; see 166
below.
116 **habits** robes. There may be a reference
to the proverb at 23.
118 **'has** he has. The F abbreviations 'Ha's'
and 'h'as' are both used, the latter more commonly
(Foakes).
119 **old** Historically, Katherine was 43 at this
time (1529).
122 **above** beyond.
122 **studies** endeavours (to help); possibly she
refers also to the learned enquiries being conducted on both sides of the question.
123 **Make...this** (All your efforts) make for

me only a great affliction, as in this present case.
'Curse' can also mean a cursed person (*OED* sv *sb*
4); Foakes suggests the possibility of a final *d* or *t*
being misread in the MS. as *e*, and Hoeniger
accepts this, reading 'accursed'. Pooler and Maxwell read 'make' as imperative – a defiance.
123 **worse** i.e. than this wretchedness.
124 **speak myself** commend, speak for myself
(*OED* sv *v* 27a); see 4.2.32.
130 **fondness** tenderness; often with the sense
of a foolish affection.
130 **superstitious** excessively devoted.
133 **constant...to** woman constant to (Abbott
comments on such transpositions, 419a). The
emphasis on constancy and patience (136) may
reflect the portrait of patient Griselde in
Chaucer's *The Clerk's Tale*.

Yet will I add an honour, a great patience.
WOLSEY Madam, you wander from the good we aim at.
KATHERINE My lord, I dare not make myself so guilty
　　　　　To give up willingly that noble title
　　　　　Your master wed me to: nothing but death　　　　　　　140
　　　　　Shall e'er divorce my dignities.
WOLSEY　　　　　　　　　　　　　Pray hear me.
KATHERINE Would I had never trod this English earth,
　　　　　Or felt the flatteries that grow upon it!
　　　　　Ye have angels' faces, but heaven knows your hearts.
　　　　　What will become of me now, wretched lady?　　　　　145
　　　　　I am the most unhappy woman living.
　　　　　Alas, poor wenches, where are now your fortunes?
　　　　　Shipwracked upon a kingdom where no pity,
　　　　　No friends, no hope, no kindred weep for me,
　　　　　Almost no grave allowed me: like the lily　　　　　　　150
　　　　　That once was mistress of the field and flourished,
　　　　　I'll hang my head and perish.
WOLSEY　　　　　　　　　　　　　If your grace
　　　　　Could but be brought to know our ends are honest,
　　　　　You'd feel more comfort. Why should we, good lady,
　　　　　Upon what cause, wrong you? Alas, our places,　　　　155
　　　　　The way of our profession is against it;
　　　　　We are to cure such sorrows, not to sow 'em.
　　　　　For goodness' sake, consider what you do,
　　　　　How you may hurt yourself, ay, utterly
　　　　　Grow from the king's acquaintance by this carriage.　　160
　　　　　The hearts of princes kiss obedience,
　　　　　So much they love it; but to stubborn spirits

---

**137, 141, 152** SH WOLSEY] *Car.* F　　　**137–8** Madam…guilty] *Rowe*³; *four lines, ending*…good / …aim at. / …Lord, / …guilty F

**144** Foakes and Maxwell see an allusion to the proverb 'Fair face, foul heart' (Tilley F3); also an allusion to the story about St Gregory and the beautiful boys sold as slaves in Rome. Being told that they were 'Angles', he said that they had 'angels' faces' but lamented that 'the foul fiend should be Lord of such faire folkes' (Foakes, quoting Camden's *Remains*, 1605).

**147 poor wenches** Katherine turns to her waiting-women.

**150–1 lily…field** Compare Spenser, *Faerie Queene*, II, vi, 16: 'The lilly, Ladie of the flowring field'. Perhaps also a hint of Christ's admonition: 'Learn how the lilies of the field do growe' (Matt. 6.28).

**153 honest** honourable.

**155 places** official positions.

**158 For goodness' sake** i.e. for the sake of the goodness that is in you.

**160 Grow…acquaintance** Become estranged from the king.

**160 carriage** behaviour.

They swell and grow as terrible as storms.
I know you have a gentle, noble temper,
A soul as even as a calm; pray think us                          165
Those we profess, peacemakers, friends and servants.
CAMPEIUS Madam, you'll find it so: you wrong your virtues
With these weak women's fears. A noble spirit,
As yours was put into you, ever casts
Such doubts as false coins from it. The king loves you,    170
Beware you lose it not. For us, if you please
To trust us in your business, we are ready
To use our utmost studies in your service.
KATHERINE Do what ye will, my lords, and pray forgive me;
If I have used myself unmannerly,                              175
You know I am a woman, lacking wit
To make a seemly answer to such persons.
Pray do my service to his majesty;
He has my heart yet, and shall have my prayers
While I shall have my life. Come, reverend fathers,           180
Bestow your counsels on me. She now begs
That little thought, when she set footing here,
She should have bought her dignities so dear.

*Exeunt*

3.2 *Enter the* DUKE OF NORFOLK, DUKE OF SUFFOLK, LORD
SURREY *and* LORD CHAMBERLAIN

NORFOLK If you will now unite in your complaints

---

**167]** *Pope;* Madam...so: / You...Vertues F    **174]** *Rowe;* Do...Lords: / And...me F    Act 3, Scene 2
**3.2]** *Scena Secunda* F

**164 temper** disposition.
**169 As...you** Such as the one you were
endowed with.
**173 studies** endeavours.
**175 used myself** behaved.
**176 wit** understanding.
**178 do my service** pay my respects.
**180–1** This quiet acceptance of advice marks
the end of Katherine's struggle and is in striking
contrast with the earlier spirited confrontation
with the cardinals. She seems to realise she has
no chance of carrying on her fight alone. The
following scene moves immediately to the revela-
tion to the king of Wolsey's secret dealings. Hence
the play moves swiftly from Katherine's fall to
Wolsey's (as it does in Holinshed). Subsequent
events involving Katherine are not represented,
but Cromwell tells Wolsey at the end of 3.2 about

Henry's secret marriage to Anne Bullen, and
early in 4.1 while waiting for Anne's coronation
procession, the Gentlemen talk of the final divorce
hearings and of Katherine's removal to Kimbolton. The last link between Wolsey and Katherine
occurs in 4.2 where Katherine hears of Wolsey's
death and attempts to reach a balanced conclusion about his character and conduct.

**Act 3, Scene 2**
**0 SD** The action of this scene, which takes
place in a room at court, is far more public in its
nature than 3.1, up to the point where Wolsey is
left alone. The opening section returns to the
bitter opposition to Wolsey among the nobles, last
made evident in 2.2. Much use is made of widely
separated passages in both Holinshed and Foxe,
and possibly in Halle and Speed.

And force them with a constancy, the cardinal
Cannot stand under them. If you omit
The offer of this time, I cannot promise
But that you shall sustain more new disgraces 5
With these you bear already.

SURREY            I am joyful
To meet the least occasion that may give me
Remembrance of my father-in-law, the duke,
To be revenged on him.

SUFFOLK          Which of the peers
Have uncontemned gone by him, or at least 10
Strangely neglected? When did he regard
The stamp of nobleness in any person
Out of himself?

CHAMBERLAIN      My lords, you speak your pleasures:
What he deserves of you and me I know;
What we can do to him, though now the time 15
Gives way to us, I much fear. If you cannot
Bar his access to th'king, never attempt
Any thing on him; for he hath a witchcraft
Over the king in's tongue.

NORFOLK           O fear him not,
His spell in that is out: the king hath found 20
Matter against him that for ever mars
The honey of his language. No, he's settled,
Not to come off, in his displeasure.

SURREY            Sir,
I should be glad to hear such news as this
Once every hour.

NORFOLK        Believe it, this is true. 25
In the divorce, his contrary proceedings

---

2 **force** press home.
2 **a constancy** perseverance.
3 **omit** neglect.
8 **duke** i.e. of Buckingham; see 2.1.44.
10 **uncontemned** not despised. *OED* cites this as the first use of the word.
11 **neglected** passed over, snubbed.
13 **Out of** Beyond.
16 **Gives way to** Favours.
20 **out** finished.
22–3 **No...displeasure** i.e. Wolsey is fixed,

without possibility of escape, in the king's displeasure. There is much dispute as to the reference of 'he' and 'his'; another possible interpretation takes 'he' as the king who is fixed or settled in his mind (see *Mac.* 1.7.79); 'come off' then has the sense of 'desist', though this meaning does not appear in *OED* before 1711 (Come *v* 61c).
26 **contrary** i.e. adverse to the divorce; suggests also the contradictory double-dealing of his tactics as outlined by Suffolk at 30–6.

Are all unfolded; wherein he appears
As I would wish mine enemy.
SURREY                                    How came
His practices to light?
SUFFOLK                    Most strangely.
SURREY                                    O how? how?
SUFFOLK The cardinal's letters to the pope miscarried,                    30
And came to th'eye o'th'king, wherein was read
How that the cardinal did entreat his holiness
To stay the judgement o'th'divorce; for if
It did take place, 'I do', quoth he, 'perceive
My king is tangled in affection to                    35
A creature of the queen's, Lady Anne Bullen.'
SURREY Has the king this?
SUFFOLK                    Believe it.
SURREY                                    Will this work?
CHAMBERLAIN The king in this perceives him, how he coasts
And hedges his own way. But in this point
All his tricks founder, and he brings his physic                    40
After his patient's death; the king already
Hath married the fair lady.
SURREY                                    Would he had!
SUFFOLK May you be happy in your wish, my lord,
For I profess you have it.
SURREY                                    Now all my joy
Trace the conjunction.
SUFFOLK                    My amen to't.
NORFOLK                                    All men's.                    45
SUFFOLK There's order given for her coronation;

---

**29 practices** intrigues.

**30 miscarried** Holinshed is less precise about
the details: 'Howbeit he went about nothing so
secretlie, but that the same came to the kings
knowledge, who tooke so high displeasure with
such his cloked dissimulation, that he determined
to abase his degree' (p. 909). Foxe describes how
an agent of Wolsey's named Clarentius got to
England and managed to see the king without
Wolsey's knowledge, after which 'the King neuer
put anymore confidence or trust in the Cardinall'
(*Acts*, p. 901).

**33 stay** delay.

**36 creature** servant or favourite.

**38 coasts** moves circuitously (*OED* Coast *v*
2d).

**39 hedges** shuffles, dodges. Pooler notes the
passage in *Tro.*: 'hedge aside from the direct
forthright' (3.3.158).

**40 physic** medicine.

**42 married** Henry married Anne in January
1533 though Holinshed dates it 14 November
1532. Shakespeare has brought the marriage
forward so as to occur before Wolsey's downfall
in 1529.

**45 Trace** Follow.

**45 conjunction** union. There may be an astrological reference to the coming together of two
planets in the heavens.

Marry, this is yet but young, and may be left
To some ears unrecounted. But my lords,
She is a gallant creature, and complete
In mind and feature. I persuade me, from her                    50
Will fall some blessing to this land, which shall
In it be memorised.

SURREY                            But will the king
Digest this letter of the cardinal's?
The Lord forbid!

NORFOLK                           Marry amen.

SUFFOLK                               No, no;
There be moe wasps that buzz about his nose                    55
Will make this sting the sooner. Cardinal Campeius
Is stolen away to Rome, hath ta'en no leave,
Has left the cause o'th'king unhandled, and
Is posted as the agent of our cardinal
To second all his plot. I do assure you                        60
The king cried 'Ha!' at this.

CHAMBERLAIN                       Now God incense him
And let him cry 'Ha' louder.

NORFOLK                               But my lord,
When returns Cranmer?

SUFFOLK He is returned in his opinions, which
Have satisfied the king for his divorce,                       65
Together with all famous colleges

---

47 **young** fresh, new.

49 **gallant** splendid.

49 **complete** perfect. Suffolk's praise of Anne is in line with the general tenor of the play in its portrait of Elizabeth's mother. The strong hope for a 'blessing' on the land echoes the words of the Lord Chamberlain (2.3.77–9) and looks forward to Cranmer's prophecy in 5.4.

51 **fall** befall, come to pass.

52 **memorised** made memorable.

53 **Digest** Put up with, swallow.

56–7 **Cardinal…leave** Holinshed states merely that Campeius 'took his leave of the king and nobilitie, and returned towards Rome' (p. 908). As Foakes suggests, Shakespeare probably went to Foxe or Halle for Suffolk's account. Foxe reports: 'Cardinal Campeius dissembling the matter, conueied himselfe home to Rome againe …The king seeing himselfe thus to be deferred and deluded by the Cardinalls, tooke it to no little griefe: whereupon the fall of the Cardinall of

Yorke followed not long after' (*Acts*, p. 959).

58 **unhandled** not dealt with.

59 **posted** dispatched as by post horses, as swiftly as possible.

61 **Ha!** This exclamation of annoyance is part of the legend of Henry VIII; Rowley uses it often in *When You See Me*.

64–7 **returned…Christendom** returned with the opinions concerning the divorce which have satisfied the king as well as all the colleges of Christendom. Another interpretation is that 'in his opinions' implies that Cranmer has not yet returned in person but has sent in advance the opinions collected abroad (Maxwell, quoting Tyrwhitt). However, later in this scene, Cromwell tells Wolsey that Cranmer is back. Holinshed mentions a mission abroad but does not include Cranmer; Shakespeare may have used Foxe, who describes Cranmer's role in the mission (*Acts*, pp. 1689–90).

Almost in Christendom. Shortly, I believe,
His second marriage shall be published, and
Her coronation. Katherine no more
Shall be called queen, but princess dowager                           70
And widow to Prince Arthur.
NORFOLK                                This same Cranmer's
A worthy fellow, and hath ta'en much pain
In the king's business.
SUFFOLK                                He has, and we shall see him
For it an archbishop.
NORFOLK                        So I hear.
SUFFOLK                                        'Tis so.

*Enter* WOLSEY *and* CROMWELL

The cardinal!
NORFOLK                Observe, observe, he's moody.                75
WOLSEY The packet, Cromwell, gave't you the king?
CROMWELL To his own hand, in's bedchamber.
WOLSEY                                        Looked he
O'th'inside of the paper?
CROMWELL                        Presently
He did unseal them, and the first he viewed,
He did it with a serious mind; a heed                                 80
Was in his countenance. You he bade
Attend him here this morning.
WOLSEY                                Is he ready
To come abroad?
CROMWELL                I think by this he is.
WOLSEY Leave me awhile.

*Exit Cromwell*

76 SH WOLSEY] *Car.* F *(Car., Card. / or / Wol. / throughout scene)*    76–8 The...Presently] *Foakes; five lines,
ending...Cromwell / ...King? / ...Bed-chamber / ...Paper / Presently* F    82–3 Attend...is] *Hanmer; three
lines, ending...Morning / ...abroad? / ...is* F

68 **published** publicly proclaimed.
72 **pain** pains, trouble.
74 **archbishop** Cranmer was appointed Archbishop of Canterbury in 1533 after the death of
Warham in 1532; Foxe gives his account of the
consecration following his mention of Cranmer's
mission to the German universities (*Acts*, p.
1690) (Maxwell).

76 **packet** A small parcel of letters, usually
of official or state papers in early usage (*OED sv
sb* 1).
78 **paper** wrapper.
78 **Presently** At once.
80 **heed** careful attention.

> [*Aside*] It shall be to the Duchess of Alençon,                    85
> The French king's sister; he shall marry her.
> Anne Bullen? No; I'll no Anne Bullens for him;
> There's more in't than fair visage. Bullen?
> No, we'll no Bullens: speedily I wish
> To hear from Rome. The Marchioness of Pembroke?        90

NORFOLK  He's discontented.

SUFFOLK                         May be he hears the king
> Does whet his anger to him.

SURREY                                    Sharp enough,
> Lord, for thy justice.

WOLSEY  [*Aside*]  The late queen's gentlewoman? a knight's
>                    daughter
> To be her mistress' mistress? the queen's queen?          95
> This candle burns not clear, 'tis I must snuff it,
> Then out it goes. What though I know her virtuous
> And well-deserving? yet I know her for
> A spleeny Lutheran, and not wholesome to
> Our cause, that she should lie i'th'bosom of              100
> Our hard-ruled king. Again, there is sprung up
> An heretic, an arch-one, Cranmer, one
> Hath crawled into the favour of the king
> And is his oracle.

NORFOLK                         He is vexed at something.

*Enter* KING *reading of a schedule* [*and* LOVELL]

85 SD] *Rowe; not in* F    94 SD] *Rowe; not in* F    94 The...daughter] *Pope;* The...Gentlewoman? /
A...Daughter F    104 SD *and* LOVELL] *Theobald; not in* F

85 **Duchess of Alençon** Holinshed speaks of
this scheme of Wolsey's when describing Wolsey's hatred for the Emperor Charles V after
Charles refused him the archbishopric of Toledo
(p. 906). See 2.1.160–3.
  92 **to** against.
  96 **clear** bright.
  96 **snuff it** As Maxwell notes, this means 'cut
the burnt wick from it' so that it will burn bright-
ly, not 'extinguish', which is a late-seventeenth-
century and modern sense. The question of
Henry's marriage to Anne Bullen is surrounded
with difficulties ('burns not clear'); Wolsey is the
one expected to solve these problems ('snuff it'),
and that will give him the chance to stop it completely. *OED* quotes Thomas Heywood (1637):
'To cleare the taper, if you snuffe too deepe, Out
goes the light' (Snuff *v*[1]).

  99 **spleeny** passionate.
  99 **Lutheran** It is Foxe rather than Holinshed
who bases Wolsey's hatred of Anne on the fact
that she is a Lutheran (*Acts*, p. 959).
  99 **wholesome** beneficial, giving health.
  100 **lie i'th'bosom** There is a double sense
of sharing the bed of the king and sharing his
secrets.
  101 **hard-ruled** managed with difficulty.
  102 **an arch-one** a chief one.
  103 **Hath** Who has. The omission of the rela-
tive pronoun is frequent; see Abbott 244.
  104 **oracle** adviser he listens to above all
others.
  104 SD *schedule* A paper or scroll containing
writing (Onions).

SURREY I would 'twere something that would fret the string,      105
    The master-cord on's heart.

SUFFOLK                 The king, the king!

KING What piles of wealth hath he accumulated
    To his own portion! and what expense by th'hour
    Seems to flow from him! How i'th'name of thrift
    Does he rake this together? Now, my lords,      110
    Saw you the cardinal?

NORFOLK            My lord, we have
    Stood here observing him. Some strange commotion
    Is in his brain; he bites his lip, and starts,
    Stops on a sudden, looks upon the ground,
    Then lays his finger on his temple; straight      115
    Springs out into fast gait, then stops again,
    Strikes his breast hard, and anon he casts
    His eye against the moon: in most strange postures
    We have seen him set himself.

KING              It may well be
    There is a mutiny in's mind. This morning      120
    Papers of state he sent me, to peruse
    As I required: and wot you what I found
    There, on my conscience put unwittingly?
    Forsooth an inventory, thus importing
    The several parcels of his plate, his treasure,      125

---

123 There, on...unwittingly?] *Pope;* There (on...unwittingly) F

---

**105 fret** devour, consume, torment (*OED* sv *v*¹ 3b). *OED* quotes Holland's *Livy* (1609): 'Their hearts alreadie fretted and cankered at the very roote, for the last disgrace received'.

**105–6 string...heart** Heart strings were thought to be the nerves or tendons that supported the heart. 'Fret', 'string' and 'cord' (chord) suggest a musical analogy since 'to fret' means to furnish a stringed instrument with frets (*OED* sv *v*⁵), to enable the string to be stopped with the finger. Thus *Ham.* 3.2.370–2: 'Call me what instrument you will, though you can fret me, you cannot play upon me.'

**106 on's** of his. Surrey might well wish Wolsey's death. Holinshed stresses the 'great enimitie betwixt the cardinall and the earle, for that on a time, when the cardinall tooke upon him to checke the earle, he had like to have thrust his

dagger into the cardinall' (p. 855). Note 6–9 above.

**108 portion** share.

**108 expense** Wolsey was famed for the magnificence of his social and public life, as earlier scenes suggest. See Holinshed, pp. 920–1.

**112 commotion** agitation, rebellion of one faculty against another ('mutiny' at 120).

**122 wot** know.

**124 inventory** Shakespeare has used a much earlier incident in Holinshed about Thomas Ruthall, Bishop of Durham: see 213–16 n. below.

**124 importing** signifying.

**125 several parcels** various items.

**125 plate** Utensils for table and domestic use; in a great house, usually of gold or silver for purposes of display as well as use.

Rich stuffs and ornaments of household, which
I find at such proud rate, that it outspeaks
Possession of a subject.

NORFOLK                              It's heaven's will;
Some spirit put this paper in the packet
To bless your eye withal.

KING                              If we did think                          130
His contemplation were above the earth
And fixed on spiritual object, he should still
Dwell in his musings, but I am afraid
His thinkings are below the moon, not worth
His serious considering.

*King takes his seat, whispers Lovell, who goes to the Cardinal*

WOLSEY                              Heaven forgive me.                     135
Ever God bless your highness!

KING                              Good my lord,
You are full of heavenly stuff, and bear the inventory
Of your best graces in your mind, the which
You were now running o'er; you have scarce time
To steal from spiritual leisure a brief span                              140
To keep your earthly audit; sure in that
I deem you an ill husband, and am glad
To have you therein my companion.

WOLSEY                                            Sir,
For holy offices I have a time; a time
To think upon the part of business which                                  145
I bear i'th'state; and nature does require
Her times of preservation, which perforce

142 glad] F2; gald F

126 **stuffs and ornaments** household
furnishings and trappings.
127 **rate** (1) value, (2) quantity (see *2H4* 4.1.22
for this possible meaning).
127–8 **outspeaks...subject** expresses more
than a subject should possess.
130 **withal** with that.
134 **below the moon** worldly, sublunary.
137 **stuff** substance, material of which a thing
is formed (*OED* sv *sb* 3a). There is also in 'stuff'
and 'inventory' an ironic reference to what the
king has read in Wolsey's papers.

138 **graces** virtues; in a theological sense,
virtues that are divine in origin.
141 **earthly audit** i.e. in contrast with the
heavenly audit of the Last Judgement.
142 **ill husband** bad manager.
143 **my companion** my fellow. Henry may be
speaking literally of his own failings as a husband
to Katherine.
144 **time...time** As Maxwell notes, a reference to Eccles. 3.1–8 and to the proverb 'There
is a time for all things' (Tilley T314).
147 **preservation** keeping from injury.

I her frail son, amongst my brethren mortal,
Must give my tendance to.
KING                                   You have said well.
WOLSEY And ever may your highness yoke together,          150
As I will lend you cause, my doing well
With my well saying.
KING                                   'Tis well said again,
And 'tis a kind of good deed to say well,
And yet words are no deeds. My father loved you,
He said he did, and with his deed did crown            155
His word upon you. Since I had my office
I have kept you next my heart, have not alone
Employed you where high profits might come home,
But pared my present havings to bestow
My bounties upon you.
WOLSEY [*Aside*]                What should this mean?     160
SURREY [*Aside*] The Lord increase this business.
KING                                   Have I not
      made you
The prime man of the state? I pray you tell me
If what I now pronounce you have found true:
And if you may confess it, say withal
If you are bound to us, or no. What say you?            165
WOLSEY My sovereign, I confess your royal graces,
Showered on me daily, have been more than could
My studied purposes requite, which went
Beyond all man's endeavours. My endeavours
Have ever come too short of my desires,                170
Yet filed with my abilities; mine own ends
Have been mine so that evermore they pointed

171 filed] *Hanmer;* fill'd F

149 **tendance** attention.
151–2 **doing...saying** Foakes points out
further proverbs: 'Saying is one thing, doing
another', 'From words to deeds is a great space',
etc. (Tilley s121, s123, w802).
155 **crown** nobly complete.
159 **havings** possessions.
162 **prime** chief, principal.
163 **pronounce** declare.
164 **withal** in addition.

166 **graces** favours.
168 **studied purposes** deliberate efforts.
171 **filed** matched, kept pace with. Some editors have kept the F 'fill'd' meaning 'fulfilled (to
the best of my abilities)', but most have accepted
Hanmer's emendation, pointing to other examples
of confusion in F between 'filed' and 'filled', e.g.
*WT* 4.4.611–12: 'I would have fill'd Keyes of that
hung in Chaynes'.
172 **so** to this extent.

To th'good of your most sacred person, and
The profit of the state. For your great graces
Heaped upon me, poor undeserver, I                                175
Can nothing render but allegiant thanks,
My prayers to heaven for you, my loyalty
Which ever has and ever shall be growing,
Till death, that winter, kill it.

KING                                         Fairly answered;
A loyal and obedient subject is                                   180
Therein illustrated; the honour of it
Does pay the act of it, as i'th'contrary
The foulness is the punishment. I presume
That as my hand has opened bounty to you,
My heart dropped love, my power rained honour, more      185
On you than any; so your hand and heart,
Your brain and every function of your power,
Should, notwithstanding that your bond of duty,
As 'twere in love's particular, be more
To me, your friend, than any.

WOLSEY                                         I do profess          190
That for your highness' good I ever laboured
More than mine own; that am, have, and will be –
Though all the world should crack their duty to you
And throw it from their soul, though perils did
Abound as thick as thought could make 'em, and        195
Appear in forms more horrid – yet my duty,
As doth a rock against the chiding flood,
Should the approach of this wild river break
And stand unshaken yours.

KING                                         'Tis nobly spoken:

---

**176 allegiant** loyal (*OED* cites this as the earliest example).

**181–2 honour . . . act of it** Proverbial: honour is the reward of virtue (Tilley H571). Maxwell comments that honour in this context is the intrinsic quality, not reputation. In this conversation, which he no doubt finds very puzzling and embarrassing, Wolsey makes considerable use of proverbial expressions, and the king replies in kind.

**183 foulness** impurity, corruption.

**184 opened** freely given.

**188 notwithstanding . . . duty** in spite of that

duty you owe (to the church and the pope). Foakes and Hoeniger read thus, but Maxwell suggests that 'duty' and 'love' are contrasted, and reads 'though duty is normally the prime motive, yet here the special force of love should have even more effect'.

**189 particular** special intimacy.

**192 have** i.e. have been (see 'has' at 178). The construction is left unfinished, as often in impassioned speech.

**197 chiding** brawling.

**198 break** dash in pieces. 'Break' and 'stand' follow the auxiliary 'should'.

Take notice, lords, he has a loyal breast,                    200
For you have seen him open't. [*Gives him papers*] Read
    o'er this,
And after, this, and then to breakfast with
What appetite you have.

                *Exit King, frowning upon the Cardinal, the Nobles*
                        *throng after him smiling and whispering*
WOLSEY                              What should this mean?
What sudden anger's this? How have I reaped it?
He parted frowning from me, as if ruin              205
Leaped from his eyes. So looks the chafèd lion
Upon the daring huntsman that has galled him;
Then makes him nothing. I must read this paper;
I fear, the story of his anger. 'Tis so;
This paper has undone me: 'tis th'accompt          210
Of all that world of wealth I have drawn together
For mine own ends – indeed to gain the popedom
And fee my friends in Rome. O negligence!
Fit for a fool to fall by: what cross devil
Made me put this main secret in the packet        215
I sent the king? Is there no way to cure this?
No new device to beat this from his brains?
I know 'twill stir him strongly; yet I know
A way, if it take right, in spite of fortune
Will bring me off again. What's this? 'To th'Pope'?  220
The letter, as I live, with all the business
I writ to's holiness. Nay then, farewell!
I have touched the highest point of all my greatness,

---

**201 SD**] *Pope; not in* F

**206 chafèd** angered, raging.
**207 galled** wounded.
**208 makes him nothing** annihilates him.
**210 accompt** account, reckoning.

**213 fee...Rome** Foxe describes the letters
written by Wolsey to Gardiner in Rome about
the bribes he is to use in order to advance Wolsey's ambitious plans, setting a limit at seven
thousand pounds. Gardiner and the other English
'orators' in Rome were to strive to have Wolsey
elected pope, 'if pope Clement were dead' (*Acts*,
p. 903).
**213–16 O negligence...king** As often noted,
the playwright at this point uses Holinshed's story

of the mistake made in 1508 by Thomas Ruthall,
Bishop of Durham, in including a private account
of all his wealth in a packet to the king via Wolsey,
which Wolsey then used to bring about his downfall. Wolsey's speech echoes Holinshed's comment: 'But see the mishap! that a man in all other
things so provident, should now be so negligent:
and at that time most forget himselfe, when (as it
so fell out) he had most need to have remembered
himselfe' (pp. 796–7).
**214 cross** perverse, thwarting.
**215 main** chief.
**219 take right** succeed.
**220 bring me off** rescue me.

And from that full meridian of my glory
I haste now to my setting. I shall fall                                    225
Like a bright exhalation in the evening,
And no man see me more.

*Enter to* WOLSEY, *the* DUKES OF NORFOLK *and* SUFFOLK, *the*
EARL OF SURREY, *and the* LORD CHAMBERLAIN

NORFOLK Hear the king's pleasure, cardinal, who commands you
To render up the great seal presently
Into our hands, and to confine yourself                                    230
To Asher-house, my Lord of Winchester's,
Till you hear further from his highness.

WOLSEY                                                Stay:
Where's your commission, lords? words cannot carry
Authority so weighty.

SUFFOLK                                Who dare cross 'em,
Bearing the king's will from his mouth expressly?                          235

WOLSEY Till I find more than will or words to do it
(I mean your malice) know, officious lords,
I dare, and must deny it. Now I feel
Of what coarse metal ye are moulded, envy;
How eagerly ye follow my disgraces                                         240
As if it fed ye, and how sleek and wanton
Ye appear in every thing may bring my ruin!
Follow your envious courses, men of malice;
You have Christian warrant for 'em, and no doubt

228] *Pope;* Hear...Cardinall / Who...you F    233 commission, lords] *Rowe;* Commission? Lords, F

**224 meridian** Literally, 'the point at which
the sun or a star reaches its highest altitude';
figuratively, 'splendour'. Foakes suggests that
the lines are based on Speed, *History of Great
Britain* (1611).

**226 exhalation** meteor; often thought of as a
fiery vapour 'exhaled' by the sun or one of the
stars. See *Rom.* 3.5.13: 'It is some meteor that
the sun exhal'd', and also Chapman's *Tragedy
of Byron* (1608): 'Farewell for ever! So have I dis-
cerned / An exhalation that would be a star / Fall,
when the sun forsook it, in a sink' (4.2.291–3).

**227 SD** Holinshed states simply that the two
dukes visited Wolsey to demand the great seal
(p. 909). However, Shakespeare has combined
with this epsiode details from another episode
in which the nobles collected a long list of griev-

ances against Wolsey and submitted the 'book' to
the king.

**229 presently** immediately.

**231 Asher-house** Esher House. Since Wolsey
at this point was still Bishop of Winchester (among
other titles), the house technically belonged to
him. Stephen Gardiner who later became Bishop
of Winchester, as in Act 5, is no doubt 'my Lord
of Winchester' here.

**233 commission** written warrant.

**234 cross** oppose.

**236 to do it** i.e. to render up the great seal.

**239 envy** malice, hatred.

**241 it** following his disgraces.

**244 Christian warrant** An ironic comment on
the justification that other Christians act similarly.

In time will find their fit rewards. That seal             245
You ask with such a violence, the king,
Mine and your master, with his own hand gave me;
Bade me enjoy it, with the place and honours
During my life; and to confirm his goodness,
Tied it by letters patents. Now who'll take it?           250
SURREY  The king that gave it.
WOLSEY                              It must be himself then.
SURREY  Thou art a proud traitor, priest.
WOLSEY                                Proud lord, thou liest:
Within these forty hours Surrey durst better
Have burnt that tongue than said so.
SURREY                                     Thy ambition,
Thou scarlet sin, robbed this bewailing land              255
Of noble Buckingham, my father-in-law;
The heads of all thy brother cardinals,
With thee and all thy best parts bound together,
Weighed not a hair of his. Plague of your policy;
You sent me deputy for Ireland                            260
Far from his succour, from the king, from all
That might have mercy on the fault thou gav'st him;
Whilst your great goodness, out of holy pity,
Absolved him with an axe.
WOLSEY                              This, and all else
This talking lord can lay upon my credit,                 265
I answer, is most false. The duke by law
Found his deserts. How innocent I was
From any private malice in his end,
His noble jury and foul cause can witness.
If I loved many words, lord, I should tell you            270

**245 fit rewards** i.e. punishment for wrongs. Foakes links the whole passage with the proverb 'Wrong has no warrant' (Tilley w947).

**250 letters patents** An open letter or document conferring a right or privilege on a particular person. The expression in this form is a translation of the French *lettres patentes* (*OED* Patent *a* 1).

**253 forty** Often used as a round number.

**255 scarlet sin** 'Scarlet' is both a rich cloth, usually bright red (*OED* sv *sb* 1), and also the colour of the cardinal's robe. 'Scarlet sin' alludes to the passage in Isa. 1.18: 'Though your sins

were as crimson, they shall bee made white as snow: though they were redde like scarlet, they shall be as wool' (Foakes).

**258 parts** qualities.

**259 Weighed** Equalled in weight (and value, as with precious metals).

**259 Plague of** A plague on.

**259 policy** crafty scheming.

**260 Ireland** Trisyllabic.

**263–4 goodness…Absolved** The religious terms are sarcastically at odds with what actually happened, summed up in the word 'axe'.

**265 credit** good name.

You have as little honesty as honour,
That in the way of loyalty and truth
Toward the king, my ever royal master,
Dare mate a sounder man than Surrey can be,
And all that love his follies.

SURREY                                    By my soul,                    275
Your long coat, priest, protects you; thou shouldst feel
My sword i'th'life blood of thee else. My lords,
Can ye endure to hear this arrogance?
And from this fellow? If we live thus tamely,
To be thus jaded by a piece of scarlet,                              280
Farewell nobility; let his grace go forward
And dare us with his cap, like larks.

WOLSEY                                                All goodness
Is poison to thy stomach.

SURREY                                        Yes, that goodness
Of gleaning all the land's wealth into one,
Into your own hands, cardinal, by extortion;                        285
The goodness of your intercepted packets
You writ to th'pope against the king: your goodness,
Since you provoke me, shall be most notorious.
My Lord of Norfolk, as you are truly noble,
As you respect the common good, the state                          290
Of our despised nobility, our issues,
Who, if he live, will scarce be gentlemen,
Produce the grand sum of his sins, the articles
Collected from his life. I'll startle you
Worse than the sacring bell, when the brown wench                   295

---

276] *Rowe;* Your...you / Thou...feele F    292 Who] F2; Whom F

272 **That** Conjunction following 'I should tell' and introducing '[I] Dare mate'.

272 **in the way of** in respect of.

274 **mate** match with. 'Mate' in this sense is not used elsewhere in Shakespeare.

279 **fellow** A term of contempt when used of someone who is not a servant.

280 **jaded** befooled (*OED v* 3, quoting *TN* 2.5.178); or possibly 'cowed' (*OED v* 1).

282 **dare** dazzle, render helpless (*OED v²* 5). The reference is to larks being caught by the use of a mirror or a piece of red cloth (the cardinal's cap) to take their attention, dazzle them, while a net is thrown over them.

287 **writ** Shakespeare's usual form of the past tense.

291 **issues** sons.

293 **articles** charges, items in an indictment.

295 **sacring bell** Small bell rung at the elevation of the host during the mass.

295 **brown wench** A country girl, dark in complexion or tanned by sun and weather. *OED* quotes William Warner's *Albion's England* (1592): 'That browne Girle of mine' (v.xxvi.127).

Lay kissing in your arms, lord cardinal.
WOLSEY How much, methinks, I could despise this man,
But that I am bound in charity against it.
NORFOLK Those articles, my lord, are in the king's hand:
But thus much, they are foul ones.
WOLSEY                                    So much fairer                    300
And spotless shall mine innocence arise,
When the king knows my truth.
SURREY                                    This cannot save you:
I thank my memory I yet remember
Some of these articles, and out they shall.
Now, if you can blush, and cry 'guilty', cardinal,                         305
You'll show a little honesty.
WOLSEY                                    Speak on, sir,
I dare your worst objections; if I blush,
It is to see a nobleman want manners.
SURREY I had rather want those than my head. Have at you!
First, that without the king's assent or knowledge,                        310
You wrought to be a legate, by which power
You maimed the jurisdiction of all bishops.
NORFOLK Then, that in all you writ to Rome, or else
To foreign princes, *Ego et Rex meus*
Was still inscribed: in which you brought the king                         315
To be your servant.
SUFFOLK                                    Then, that without the knowledge
Either of king or council, when you went
Ambassador to the emperor, you made bold
To carry into Flanders the great seal.

309] *Rome³*; I...head; / Have...you F

300 **But...much** But I can say this much.
307 **objections** accusations. See *2H6* 1.3.155–
6: 'As for your spiteful false objections, / Prove
them, and I lie open to the law' (cited by Pooler
and Foakes).
308, 309 **want** lack.
309 **Have at you** A challenge for an attack.
310–32 The list of charges comes from Holinshed, where nine are given from the 'book' presented to Parliament in 1529 (p. 912). The
dramatist leaves out three as of lesser importance.
311 **legate** official representative of the pope.
314 *Ego...meus* My king and I. The original
articles against Wolsey had not used the Latin

phrase but had objected to his placing himself
on an equal level with the king in his forms of
address. The Latin originated with Halle and
was copied by Holinshed, together with the comment on 'servant', although, as Pooler notes, the
Latin follows normal word order and does not
imply subordination. Wolsey's offence was in
mentioning himself at all in letters to foreign
princes.
315 **inscribed** written conspicuously. The
verb does not occur elsewhere in Shakespeare
(Foakes).
318 **emperor** Charles V.

SURREY Item, you sent a large commission　　　　　　320
　　　　To Gregory de Cassado, to conclude
　　　　Without the king's will or the state's allowance,
　　　　A league between his highness and Ferrara.
SUFFOLK That out of mere ambition, you have caused
　　　　Your holy hat to be stamped on the king's coin.　　325
SURREY Then, that you have sent innumerable substance
　　　　(By what means got, I leave to your own conscience)
　　　　To furnish Rome and to prepare the ways
　　　　You have for dignities, to the mere undoing
　　　　Of all the kingdom. Many more there are,　　330
　　　　Which since they are of you, and odious,
　　　　I will not taint my mouth with.
CHAMBERLAIN　　　　　　　　O my lord,
　　　　Press not a falling man too far; 'tis virtue.
　　　　His faults lie open to the laws, let them,
　　　　Not you, correct him. My heart weeps to see him　　335
　　　　So little of his great self.
SURREY　　　　　　　I forgive him.
SUFFOLK Lord cardinal, the king's further pleasure is,
　　　　Because all those things you have done of late
　　　　By your power legative within this kingdom
　　　　Fall into th'compass of a praemunire;　　340
　　　　That therefore such a writ be sued against you,
　　　　To forfeit all your goods, lands, tenements,

339 legative] F; legantine F4; legatine *Rowe*³

320 **commission** group of persons charged with a specific task.

322 **allowance** permission, acceptance.

325 **holy hat** cardinal's hat. As Foakes notes, quoting G. C. Brooke, *English Coins* (1950), Wolsey had usurped the king's prerogative by coining a silver groat with his insignia on it, although he did have the right to coin half-groats and half-pennies at York.

326 **innumerable substance** countless wealth. Holinshed's phrase; *OED* has many examples of the use of 'innumerable' with a singular noun.

328 **furnish** supply.

329 **mere undoing** complete ruin. 'Mere' in the sense of 'absolute, entire' (*OED a*² 4) is com-mon in the sixteenth and seventeenth centuries; see *Oth.* 2.2.3: 'mere perdition'.

333 **'tis virtue** i.e. not to do so.

334 **lie open** are exposed. See *2H6* 1.3.156 (cited at 307 n. above).

339 **legative** as a legate. Holinshed uses the phrase 'power legantine' and many editors correct to 'legatine' following Rowe. However, 'legative' is the common earlier form of the word (*OED*).

340 **praemunire** A writ (including the phrase *praemunire facias*) for summoning an individual before the king's court on a charge of asserting papal supremacy in England and hence denying the sovereign's power. The penalties included confiscation of the individual's property and loss of liberty (*OED* gives various examples).

Chattels and whatsoever, and to be
Out of the king's protection. This is my charge.
NORFOLK And so we'll leave you to your meditation                    345
How to live better. For your stubborn answer
About the giving back the great seal to us,
The king shall know it and, no doubt, shall thank you.
So fare you well, my little good lord cardinal.
                                    *Exeunt all but Wolsey*
WOLSEY So farewell, to the little good you bear me.               350
Farewell, a long farewell to all my greatness!
This is the state of man; today he puts forth
The tender leaves of hopes, tomorrow blossoms,
And bears his blushing honours thick upon him:
The third day comes a frost, a killing frost,               355
And when he thinks, good easy man, full surely
His greatness is a-ripening, nips his root,
And then he falls as I do. I have ventured
Like little wanton boys that swim on bladders,
This many summers in a sea of glory,                    360
But far beyond my depth; my high-blown pride
At length broke under me, and now has left me,
Weary and old with service, to the mercy
Of a rude stream that must for ever hide me.
Vain pomp and glory of this world, I hate ye!               365
I feel my heart new opened. O how wretched

---

343 Chattels] *Theobald;* Castles F

**343 Chattels** F has 'Castles', probably a mis-reading of 'Cattels' in the MS., the common sixteenth-century form of 'chattels'. Holinshed writes: 'to forfeit all his lands, tenements, goods, and cattels' (p. 909).
**350 farewell...good** Wolsey's bitter play on Norfolk's words is directed to the lords as they walk off stage. But the word 'farewell' strikes another chord within him as he begins to reflect on what he is saying goodbye to.
**354 blushing honours** glowing adornment, distinctions.
**355 frost...frost** Sometimes quoted as an example of Fletcher's liking for phrases in apposition and the repetition of a noun with an intensifier. Baldwin Maxwell notes that such repetitions are much rarer in the 'Fletcher scenes' of *Henry VIII* than in Fletcher's own plays (p. 63).
**356 easy** at his ease.
**358–64 I...hide me** Foakes suggests that these lines (like 222–7 earlier in the scene) were

drawn from Speed's *History of Great Britain* (1611): 'Formerly wee have spoken of the rising of this man [Wolsey], who now being swolne so bigge by the blasts of promotion, as the bladder not able to conteine more greatnesse, suddenly burst, and vented foorth the winde of all former favours' (p. 769). Note also Spenser, *Colin Clout*: 'highest looks...are like bladders blowen up with wynd, / That being prick't do vanish into noughts. / Even such is all their vaunted vanities' (715–19).
**359 bladders** Membranous bags from an animal's body, blown up as floats (*OED* sv *sb* 3).
**361–2 high-blown...broke** Carries on the figure of inflated bladders.
**364 rude** turbulent.
**365 Vain...world** Echoes the language of the baptismal service in the Book of Common Prayer: 'Dost thou...renounce...the vain pomp, and glory of the world...?'

Is that poor man that hangs on princes' favours!
There is betwixt that smile we would aspire to,
That sweet aspect of princes, and their ruin,
More pangs and fears than wars or women have;                    370
And when he falls, he falls like Lucifer,
Never to hope again.

*Enter* CROMWELL, *standing amazed*

                              Why how now, Cromwell?
CROMWELL I have no power to speak, sir.
WOLSEY                                       What, amazed
At my misfortunes? Can thy spirit wonder
A great man should decline? Nay, and you weep                    375
I am fall'n indeed.
CROMWELL                     How does your grace?
WOLSEY                                              Why, well;
Never so truly happy, my good Cromwell;
I know myself now, and I feel within me
A peace above all earthly dignities,
A still and quiet conscience. The king has cured me,            380
I humbly thank his grace; and from these shoulders,
These ruined pillars, out of pity, taken
A load would sink a navy, too much honour.
Ó 'tis a burden, Cromwell, 'tis a burden
Too heavy for a man that hopes for heaven.                      385
CROMWELL I am glad your grace has made that right use of it.
WOLSEY I hope I have: I am able now, methinks,
Out of a fortitude of soul I feel
To endure more miseries, and greater far
Than my weak-hearted enemies dare offer.                        390
What news abroad?
CROMWELL                     The heaviest and the worst

386–7 I am...methinks] *Pope; four lines, ending*...Grace / ...it / ...have / ...(me thinks) F

369 **aspect** expression of the face, appearance;
also in an astrological sense, 'the position of a
heavenly body in relation to the earth', hence in a
good or bad aspect.
369 **their ruin** the ruin they bring about.
371 **like Lucifer** i.e. from heaven to hell; see
Isa. 14.12.
375 **decline** descend, sink.
375 **and** if.
378 **know myself** 'Know thyself', or *nosce*

*teipsum*, was a well-known proverb given cur-
rency by Erasmus in the *Adages* (1.6.95), where
its classical background in Plato, Socrates and
many others is explored. In Sir John Davies's
*Nosce Teipsum* (1599) it is Affliction that leads the
poet to a true understanding in religious terms of
mind and soul (149–80). See also Tilley K175.
382 **pillars** There may be a secondary reference to the pillars as insignia of office, carried
before him in procession as at 2.4.0 SD.8

Is your displeasure with the king.
WOLSEY                                        God bless him.
CROMWELL The next is that Sir Thomas More is chosen
　　　　Lord Chancellor in your place.
WOLSEY                                That's somewhat sudden,
　　　　But he's a learned man. May he continue            395
　　　　Long in his highness' favour, and do justice
　　　　For truth's sake, and his conscience; that his bones,
　　　　When he has run his course and sleeps in blessings,
　　　　May have a tomb of orphans' tears wept on him.
　　　　What more?
CROMWELL          That Cranmer is returned with welcome,    400
　　　　Installèd Lord Archbishop of Canterbury.
WOLSEY That's news indeed.
CROMWELL                    Last, that the Lady Anne,
　　　　Whom the king hath in secrecy long married,
　　　　This day was viewed in open as his queen,
　　　　Going to chapel; and the voice is now              405
　　　　Only about her coronation.
WOLSEY There was the weight that pulled me down. O Cromwell,
　　　　The king has gone beyond me: all my glories
　　　　In that one woman I have lost for ever.
　　　　No sun shall ever usher forth mine honours,        410
　　　　Or gild again the noble troops that waited
　　　　Upon my smiles. Go get thee from me, Cromwell,
　　　　I am a poor fall'n man, unworthy now
　　　　To be thy lord and master. Seek the king –

407] *Pope;* There...downe / O Cromwell / F

**392 your...king** the king's displeasure toward you.

**393 More** In this and the following lines, there is considerable concentration of events to show the full extent in dramatic terms of Wolsey's fall, like the series of messengers bringing bad news to Richard II (3.2) and Richard III (4.4). More was made chancellor in 1529, Cranmer consecrated as archbishop in 1533, Henry and Anne's secret marriage took place in November 1532 (Holinshed: see 42 n. above), and the coronation was in 1533.

**399 tomb...tears** The lord chancellor was by his office guardian of all children under 21, as well as of the mentally unfit. Orphans would be a special case, where the guardianship might

have a more direct application.

**400 returned** i.e. from his tour of German centres of learning: see 64–7 n. above.

**404 in open** in public.

**406 coronation** Five syllables.

**408 gone beyond** overreached.

**410 mine honours** adornments of my high offices.

**411 gild...troops** Shakespeare may be thinking of Holinshed's colourful description: 'he proceeded foorth furnished like a cardinall: his gentlemen being verie manie in number, were clothed in liuerie coats of crimson veluet of the best, with chaines of gold about their necks...' (p. 921).

That sun, I pray, may never set – I have told him                    415
What, and how true thou art; he will advance thee:
Some little memory of me will stir him,
I know his noble nature, not to let
Thy hopeful service perish too. Good Cromwell,
Neglect him not; make use now, and provide                          420
For thine own future safety.
CROMWELL                                  O my lord,
Must I then leave you? Must I needs forgo
So good, so noble, and so true a master?
Bear witness, all that have not hearts of iron,
With what a sorrow Cromwell leaves his lord.                         425
The king shall have my service, but my prayers
For ever and for ever shall be yours.
WOLSEY  Cromwell, I did not think to shed a tear
In all my miseries; but thou hast forced me,
Out of thy honest truth, to play the woman.                         430
Let's dry our eyes; and thus far hear me, Cromwell,
And when I am forgotten, as I shall be,
And sleep in dull cold marble, where no mention
Of me more must be heard of, say I taught thee;
Say Wolsey, that once trod the ways of glory,                       435
And sounded all the depths and shoals of honour,
Found thee a way, out of his wrack, to rise in,
A sure and safe one, though thy master missed it.
Mark but my fall, and that that ruined me:
Cromwell, I charge thee, fling away ambition,                       440
By that sin fell the angels; how can man then,
The image of his maker, hope to win by it?

420 **make use now** take advantage of the present moment.

424 **hearts of iron** hard hearts. See *Tim.* 3.4.82–3: 'The place which I have feasted, does it now, / Like all mankind, show me an iron heart?'

430 **play the woman** A frequent expression at the time for shedding tears (Pooler).

433 **dull** inert. The sense of 'gloomy, melancholy' may also be included; see *2H4* 1.1.71: 'So dull, so dead in look, so woe-begone', and *Ado* 2.3.71: 'dumps so dull and heavy'.

436–7 **sounded…shoals…wrack** Sea images that culminate in a shipwreck and look back to Katherine's 'Shipwracked upon a kingdom' in the previous scene (3.1.148).

440 **fling…ambition** In the chronicle play *The Life and Death of Thomas Lord Cromwell* (1609–11), Cromwell just before his execution advises his son: 'Ambition, like the plague, see thou eschew it' (5.5.97).

441 **By…angels** Pride is traditionally the sin of Lucifer and his fellow angels. However, Maxwell points to a passage in Raleigh's *History of the World* (1614) which names ambition as 'the first sinne that the world had, and beganne in *Angels*' (2.13.7, p. 432).

442 **image…maker** See Gen. 1.27.

442 **win** profit.

Love thyself last, cherish thou hearts that hate thee;
Corruption wins not more than honesty.
Still in thy right hand carry gentle peace                          445
To silence envious tongues. Be just, and fear not;
Let all the ends thou aim'st at be thy country's,
Thy God's and truth's; then if thou fall'st, O Cromwell,
Thou fall'st a blessed martyr.
Serve the king; and prithee lead me in:                            450
There take an inventory of all I have,
To the last penny; 'tis the king's. My robe,
And my integrity to heaven, is all
I dare now call mine own. O Cromwell, Cromwell,
Had I but served my God with half the zeal                          455
I served my king, he would not in mine age
Have left me naked to mine enemies.

CROMWELL Good sir, have patience.

WOLSEY                              So I have. Farewell
The hopes of court; my hopes in heaven do dwell.

                                        *Exeunt*


**4.1** *Enter two* GENTLEMEN, *meeting one another*

1 GENTLEMAN Y'are well met once again.
2 GENTLEMAN                          So are you.
1 GENTLEMAN You come to take your stand here, and behold
The Lady Anne pass from her coronation?

**449–50** Thou...in] F; Thou...martyr. Serve...king; / And...in *Rome*³     **Act 4, Scene 1**     **4.1**] *Actus Quartus Scena Prima* F

**443** Paraphrase of Matt. 5.44: 'Love your enemies...doe good to them that hate you' (Foakes).

**445** carry...peace offer olive-branch rather than sword; see *3H6* 4.6.34.

**448** if thou fall'st See 440 n. above. Cromwell with his Lutheran sympathies (see 5.2.114–15 below) was not to be a 'blessed martyr' for the church in quite the terms Wolsey envisages.

**455–7** Had...enemies Holinshed attributes this statement to Wolsey on his deathbed at the 'abbeie of Leicester' (p. 917). Similar expressions are often reported in the literature of tragic falls from prosperity to wretchedness.

**457** naked defenceless. See *Oth.* 5.2.258.

**458** patience Cromwell's plea for patience

obviously points to some intensity of passion in Wolsey's speech.

**Act 4, Scene 1**

**0** SD The scene is a street in London where the procession from Westminster Abbey will pass. Shakespeare's use of the same Gentlemen as in 2.1 for his choral figures and commentators gives a degree of continuity to the play which is stressed in the pattern of 'sorrow...joy' in 6–7. A third gentleman enters at 55 as a messenger or *nuntius* to describe off-stage action. The material comes from Holinshed pp. 929–30 and 933. As noted by Foakes, these events took place in 1533, three years after Wolsey's death.

2 GENTLEMAN  'Tis all my business. At our last encounter,
    The Duke of Buckingham came from his trial.      5
1 GENTLEMAN  'Tis very true. But that time offered sorrow,
    This general joy.
2 GENTLEMAN             'Tis well: the citizens
    I am sure have shown at full their royal minds –
    As, let 'em have their rights, they are ever forward –
    In celebration of this day with shows,      10
    Pageants, and sights of honour.
1 GENTLEMAN               Never greater,
    Nor, I'll assure you, better taken, sir.
2 GENTLEMAN  May I be bold to ask what that contains,
    That paper in your hand?
1 GENTLEMAN            Yes, 'tis the list
    Of those that claim their offices this day,      15
    By custom of the coronation.
    The Duke of Suffolk is the first, and claims
    To be high steward; next the Duke of Norfolk,
    He to be earl marshal: you may read the rest.
2 GENTLEMAN  I thank you, sir: had I not known those customs  20
    I should have been beholding to your paper.
    But I beseech you, what's become of Katherine,
    The princess dowager? how goes her business?
1 GENTLEMAN  That I can tell you too. The Archbishop
    Of Canterbury, accompanied with other      25
    Learned and reverend fathers of his order,
    Held a late court at Dunstable, six miles off
    From Ampthill where the princess lay, to which
    She was often cited by them, but appeared not;
    And to be short, for not appearance, and      30
    The king's late scruple, by the main assent

---

20 SH 2 GENTLEMAN] F4; 1 F

**8 royal minds** devotion to royalty.
**9 let...rights** to give them their due.
**9 forward** eager.
**10–11 shows, Pageants** Holinshed (drawing upon Halle) describes in detail the elaborate pageants prepared by the city crafts and guilds on barges on the Thames and along decorated streets in London through which Anne journeyed to her coronation (pp. 929–34). The audience in 1613 would have remembered the similar great

shows for the wedding of the Princess Elizabeth.
**12 taken** received.
**21 beholding** indebted; a common variation on 'beholden'.
**26 order** rank or status.
**27 late** recent (as at 31).
**28 lay** resided.
**31 main assent** general agreement; compare *Tro.* 1.3.372: 'our main opinion'.

Of all these learned men, she was divorced
And the late marriage made of none effect:
Since which she was removed to Kimmalton,
Where she remains now sick.

2 GENTLEMAN                    Alas, good lady.                    35
    The trumpets sound: stand close, the queen is coming.
                        *Hautboys*

THE ORDER OF THE CORONATION

1. *A lively flourish of trumpets.*
2. *Then two judges.*
3. LORD CHANCELLOR, *with purse and mace before
    him.*
4. *Choristers singing. Music.*
5. MAYOR OF LONDON, *bearing the mace. Then*
    GARTER, *in his coat of arms, and on his head he
    wore a gilt copper crown.*
6. MARQUESS DORSET, *bearing a sceptre of gold, on
    his head a demi-coronal of gold. With him the* EARL
    OF SURREY, *bearing the rod of silver with the dove,
    crowned with an earl's coronet. Collars of esses.*
7. DUKE OF SUFFOLK, *in his robe of estate, his
    coronet on his head, bearing a long white wand, as
    High Steward. With him the* DUKE OF NORFOLK,
    *with the rod of marshalship, a coronet on his head.
    Collars of esses.*
8. *A canopy, borne by four of the Cinque-ports; under it*

---

34 Kimmalton] Kymmalton F; Kimbolton F3    36 The...coming] *Pope;* The...close / The...comming F

33 **late** former.
33 **of none effect** null.
34 **Kimmalton** modern Kimbolton; perhaps
a phonetic spelling.
36 **close** silent and aside, out of sight.
36 SD.2 THE ORDER An abbreviated list drawn
from Holinshed's paragraphs describing the
coronation procession (p. 933).
36 SD.7 *Music* Musicians.
36 SD.9 GARTER The Garter King-at-Arms
or chief herald of the court; see 5.4.1–2.
36 SD.10 *gilt copper* i.e. made of gilded
copper, hence not a crown of gold. For an
interesting comment, see *Tro.* 4.4.105.

36 SD.14 *Collars of esses* Ornamental chains
'consisting of a series of S's either joined together
side by side or fastened in a row upon a band or
ribbon' (*OED* Collar *sb* 3c). Originally a badge
associated with John of Gaunt and Henry of
Lancaster and his followers, they were often
linked with the family insignia of the swan, as on
the tomb of John Gower in St Mary Overy,
Southwark (John Cherry, 'The Dunstable swan
jewel', *Journal of the British Archeological Associa-
tion* 3rd ser. 32 (1969), 47–8).
36 SD.15 *estate* state.
36 SD.20 *four of the Cinque-ports* four of

*the* QUEEN *in her robe, in her hair, richly adorned*
*with pearl, crowned. On each side her, the* BISHOPS
OF LONDON *and* WINCHESTER.
9. *The old* DUCHESS OF NORFOLK, *in a coronal of*
*gold, wrought with flowers, bearing the queen's train.*
10. *Certain ladies or countesses, with plain circlets of*
*gold, without flowers.*

          *Exeunt, first passing over the stage in order*
          *and state, and then, a great flourish of trumpets*

2 GENTLEMAN A royal train, believe me: these I know.
Who's that that bears the sceptre?
1 GENTLEMAN                Marquess Dorset;
And that the Earl of Surrey, with the rod.
2 GENTLEMAN A bold brave gentleman. That should be      40
The Duke of Suffolk.
1 GENTLEMAN           'Tis the same: high steward.
2 GENTLEMAN And that my Lord of Norfolk?
1 GENTLEMAN               Yes.
2 GENTLEMAN [*Looking on the Queen*]      Heaven bless thee!
Thou hast the sweetest face I ever looked on.
Sir, as I have a soul, she is an angel;
Our king has all the Indies in his arms,      45
And more, and richer, when he strains that lady;
I cannot blame his conscience.
1 GENTLEMAN           They that bear

---

**42** SD] *Johnson; not in* F

the barons of the Cinque-ports; see 48–9 below.
Hastings, Sandwich, Dover, Romney and Hythe
were the original five ports, to which Rye and
Winchelsea were added. An ancient right of the
barons was to carry a canopy over the sovereign
on state occasions (*OED*).

**36** SD.21 **in her hair** with hair hanging loosely
(customary for brides). Foakes quotes John
Chamberlain, *Letters*, ed. N. E. McClure, 2 vols.,
1939, describing the Princess Elizabeth at her
marriage in February 1613: 'in her haire that
hung downe long, with an exceeding rich coronet
on her head' (I, 424).

**36** SD.28–9 *Exeunt...trumpets* The true
exeunt occurs at 55. The 'Order of the Coronation'
is a lengthy stage direction detailing the partic-

ipants in the procession. Presumably it would
move from one doorway, cross the stage well
forward and then move away through the other
doorway. The Gentlemen who comment from 37
would stand at one side of the forestage so as
to be heard by the audience. Directors of major
eighteenth- and nineteenth-century productions
added extensively to the numbers of those taking
part and to the magnificence and colour of the
pageantry (see pp. 49–52 above) but omitted
the Gentlemen and their commentary.

**37** **train** retinue.

**39** **rod** wand or staff, symbol of office.

**45** **all the Indies** The West Indies and the
East Indies, bywords for wealth.

**46** **strains** embraces.

The cloth of honour over her are four barons
Of the Cinque-ports.

2 GENTLEMAN Those men are happy, and so are all are near her.    50
I take it, she that carries up the train
Is that old noble lady, Duchess of Norfolk.

1 GENTLEMAN It is, and all the rest are countesses.

2 GENTLEMAN Their coronets say so. These are stars indeed –

1 GENTLEMAN And sometimes falling ones.

2 GENTLEMAN                          No more of that.    55

                              [*Exit procession*]

*Enter a* THIRD GENTLEMAN

1 GENTLEMAN God save you, sir. Where have you been broiling?

3 GENTLEMAN Among the crowd i'th'abbey, where a finger
Could not be wedged in more: I am stifled
With the mere rankness of their joy.

2 GENTLEMAN                              You saw
The ceremony?

3 GENTLEMAN              That I did.

1 GENTLEMAN                  How was it?    60

3 GENTLEMAN Well worth the seeing.

2 GENTLEMAN                          Good sir, speak it to us.

3 GENTLEMAN As well as I am able. The rich stream
Of lords and ladies, having brought the queen
To a prepared place in the choir, fell off
A distance from her; while her grace sat down    65
To rest a while, some half an hour or so,
In a rich chair of state, opposing freely
The beauty of her person to the people.
Believe me, sir, she is the goodliest woman
That ever lay by man: which when the people    70

---

50 Those...her] *Pope*; Those...happy / And...her F    54–6] *Conj. W. S. Walker;* 2 Their... / And.... 2 No... / 1 God... F; 2. Their... / And... 1. No... / God... F3 *and other editors*    55 SD.1] *Capell; not in* F

54–6 It appears that a speech heading for *1 Gent.* has dropped out before 55 (as at 20 above) since immediately succeeding speeches are given to *2 Gent.*: 'Their coronets...falling ones' and 'No...that'.

55 **falling ones** meteors; but also suggesting the surrender of chastity.

59 **mere rankness** sheer exuberance; with a strong hint also of foul breath in 'stifled'.

64 **fell off** stepped back; quoted by *OED* as the first example of this usage.

67 **opposing** exposing (by being opposite the people).

70 **That...man** The joy in sexual union and fruitfulness runs throughout the scene. Note 45 above and 76–81 below.

Had the full view of, such a noise arose
As the shrouds make at sea in a stiff tempest,
As loud, and to as many tunes. Hats, cloaks,
Doublets I think, flew up, and had their faces
Been loose, this day they had been lost. Such joy          75
I never saw before. Great-bellied women,
That had not half a week to go, like rams
In the old time of war, would shake the press
And make 'em reel before 'em. No man living
Could say 'This is my wife' there, all were woven          80
So strangely in one piece.

2 GENTLEMAN                           But what followed?

3 GENTLEMAN At length her grace rose, and with modest paces
Came to the altar, where she kneeled, and saint-like
Cast her fair eyes to heaven and prayed devoutly;
Then rose again and bowed her to the people;              85
When by the Archbishop of Canterbury
She had all the royal makings of a queen,
As holy oil, Edward Confessor's crown,
The rod, and bird of peace, and all such emblems
Laid nobly on her; which performed, the choir            90
With all the choicest music of the kingdom
Together sung *Te Deum*. So she parted,
And with the same full state paced back again
To York Place, where the feast is held.

1 GENTLEMAN                                          Sir,
You must no more call it York Place, that's past;        95
For since the cardinal's fall, that title's lost,
'Tis now the king's, and called Whitehall.

3 GENTLEMAN                                    I know it;

---

72 **shrouds** rigging of a ship, sail-ropes.
77 **rams** battering rams.
78 **press** crowd.
81 **piece** i.e. of cloth.
82 **modest** moderate; hence 'decorous'.
87 **makings** additions; i.e. the symbolic tokens and symbols that make her a queen; perhaps a coinage in this sense. *OED* has no other example before 1837 (sv *sb* 8).
88 **As** Such as.
91 **music** musicians. See Order of the Coronation, 36 SD.7 above.
92 **parted** departed.
94 **York Place** Holinshed tells us (p. 933) that

the queen was brought first to Westminster Hall, which is next to the Abbey. Shakespeare introduces York Place to be able to keep Wolsey and his fall in the audience's mind. Holinshed reports (p. 928): 'The king having purchased of the cardinall after his attendure ...his house at Westminster, called Yorke place...he bestowed great cost in going forward with the building thereof, and changed the name, so that it was after called the kings palace of Westminster.' The new palace was also called Whitehall.

101 **the one of Winchester** Reversed order: it is Gardiner who is now Bishop of Winchester and had been the king's secretary. See 2.2.114.

But 'tis so lately altered that the old name
Is fresh about me.

2 GENTLEMAN                      What two reverend bishops
Were those that went on each side of the queen?          100

3 GENTLEMAN Stokesley and Gardiner, the one of Winchester,
Newly preferred from the king's secretary;
The other, London.

2 GENTLEMAN                      He of Winchester
Is held no great lover of the archbishop's,
The virtuous Cranmer.

3 GENTLEMAN                      All the land knows that:          105
However, yet there is no great breach; when it comes
Cranmer will find a friend will not shrink from him.

2 GENTLEMAN Who may that be, I pray you?

3 GENTLEMAN                            Thomas Cromwell,
A man in much esteem with th'king, and truly
A worthy friend. The king has made him          110
Master o'th'jewel house,
And one already of the privy council.

2 GENTLEMAN He will deserve more.

3 GENTLEMAN                      Yes, without all doubt.
Come, gentlemen, ye shall go my way,
Which is to th'court, and there ye shall be my guests:          115
Something I can command. As I walk thither,
I'll tell ye more.

BOTH                      You may command us, sir.

*Exeunt*

**4.2** *Enter* KATHERINE DOWAGER, *sick, led between* GRIFFITH, *her
Gentleman Usher, and* PATIENCE, *her woman*

GRIFFITH How does your grace?

Act 4, Scene 2    4.2] *Scena Secunda* F

**104 no great lover** Another example of the
linking of scenes forward and backward. The
events of 5.1 and 5.2 are foreshadowed; we have
already heard a number of references to Cranmer,
though not to Cromwell's friendship with him.
**116 Something** A little influence.

**Act 4, Scene 2**
**0 SD** Katherine's private apartments at Kimbolton. Katherine is supported in her isolation
and sorrow by two faithful servants, as Wolsey

was by Cromwell after his downfall. The character Patience is fictional but may suggest
through her name, as Foakes urges, a quality
which the major characters must come to
understand in the crises of their lives. The scene
makes a dramatic link between the death of
Wolsey and that of Katherine, even though
Wolsey died in 1530 and Katherine in 1536.
There is also a notable contrast between this
scene and the splendour of Anne's coronation.

KATHERINE                              O Griffith, sick to death:
My legs like loaden branches bow to th'earth,
Willing to leave their burthen. Reach a chair;
So now, methinks, I feel a little ease.
Did'st thou not tell me, Griffith, as thou led'st me,                    5
That the great child of honour, Cardinal Wolsey,
Was dead?
GRIFFITH              Yes, madam; but I think your grace,
Out of the pain you suffered, gave no ear to't.
KATHERINE Prithee, good Griffith, tell me how he died.
If well, he stepped before me happily                                    10
For my example.
GRIFFITH                      Well, the voice goes, madam;
For after the stout Earl Northumberland
Arrested him at York, and brought him forward
As a man sorely tainted, to his answer,
He fell sick suddenly, and grew so ill                                   15
He could not sit his mule.
KATHERINE                              Alas, poor man.
GRIFFITH At last, with easy roads, he came to Leicester,
Lodged in the abbey, where the reverend abbot
With all his covent honourably received him;
To whom he gave these words: 'O father abbot,                           20
An old man, broken with the storms of state,
Is come to lay his weary bones among ye;
Give him a little earth for charity.'
So went to bed, where eagerly his sickness
Pursued him still, and three nights after this,                         25
About the hour of eight, which he himself
Foretold should be his last, full of repentance,

---

7 think] F2; thanke F    19 covent] F; convent *Rowe*

6 **child of honour** A phrase used of a youth of
noble birth promising honour in his future life.
Prince Hal speaks thus of Hotspur in *1H4* 3.2.139,
but Katherine's use may be more than a little
qualified.

10 **happily** haply, perhaps: see *Shr.* 4.4.54:
'happily we might be interrupted'. It may mean
'appropriately' or 'fortunately', but since the
spelling 'happily' for 'haply' occurs often in
Shakespeare, the first interpretation seems more
likely.

11 **voice** general opinion or talk.
14 **sorely tainted** stained with guilt.
14 **answer** defence against the charges.
17 **roads** spells of riding, stages.
19 **covent** convent; an old form of the word
common until the seventeenth century (*OED*).
23 **a little earth** i.e. for burial in consecrated
ground. The begging for this 'charity' from the
monks is in strong contrast with Wolsey's earlier
pride.
24 **eagerly** harshly, severely.

Continual meditations, tears and sorrows,
He gave his honours to the world again,
His blessed part to heaven, and slept in peace.                    30
KATHERINE So may he rest, his faults lie gently on him.
　　Yet thus far, Griffith, give me leave to speak him,
　　And yet with charity. He was a man
　　Of an unbounded stomach, ever ranking
　　Himself with princes; one that by suggestion                   35
　　Tied all the kingdom; simony was fair play;
　　His own opinion was his law. I'th'presence
　　He would say untruths, and be ever double
　　Both in his words and meaning. He was never,
　　But where he meant to ruin, pitiful.                           40
　　His promises were, as he then was, mighty;
　　But his performance, as he is now, nothing.
　　Of his own body he was ill, and gave
　　The clergy ill example.
GRIFFITH　　　　　　　　　　　Noble madam,
　　Men's evil manners live in brass, their virtues                45
　　We write in water. May it please your highness
　　To hear me speak his good now?
KATHERINE　　　　　　　　　　　Yes, good Griffith,
　　I were malicious else.
GRIFFITH　　　　　　　　　This cardinal,
　　Though from an humble stock, undoubtedly
　　Was fashioned to much honour. From his cradle                  50

31] *Pope;* So...rest / His...him F    50 honour. From...cradle] F; honour, from...cradle; *Theobald*

28 **sorrows** sighs, laments.
32 **speak him** give testimony about him.
34 **stomach** proud or arrogant spirit (Onions).
35 **suggestion** underhand means. Shakespeare uses Holinshed's word from the source passage: 'by craftie suggestion gat into his hands innumerable treasure'. One of the primary meanings of the word is 'incitement to evil, temptation' (*OED* sv *sb* 1) so that it may imply Wolsey's manipulation of the king. Note *R3* 3.2.101: 'By the suggestion of the queen's allies'.
36 **Tied** Enslaved.
36 **simony** The buying or selling of ecclesiastical preferments.
36 **fair play** Foakes notes the phrase as a coinage of Shakespeare's, as in *John* 5.1.67 and *Temp.* 5.1.175.
37 **presence** presence-chamber.

38 **double** deceitfully ambiguous.
39 **words...meaning** The phrase distinguishes form or style from content.
41 **mighty** large and splendid.
43 **his...body** i.e. in sexual morality.
43 **ill** depraved.
45–6 **Men's...water** Proverbial: long-lasting memories of evil are contrasted with short-lived memories of good. Tilley 171: 'Injuries are written in brass.'
47 **speak his good** testify to his good qualities.
50 **honour...cradle** Theobald's emendation of F punctuation ('honour from his cradle;') is followed by Maxwell and others, but Foakes and Hoeniger are probably right to make no change, since Holinshed stresses Wolsey's extraordinary aptitude for learning as a boy (p. 917).

He was a scholar, and a ripe and good one,
Exceeding wise, fair-spoken, and persuading;
Lofty and sour to them that loved him not,
But to those men that sought him, sweet as summer.
And though he were unsatisfied in getting,                           55
Which was a sin, yet in bestowing, madam,
He was most princely: ever witness for him
Those twins of learning that he raised in you,
Ipswich and Oxford; one of which fell with him,
Unwilling to outlive the good that did it;                           60
The other, though unfinished, yet so famous,
So excellent in art, and still so rising
That Christendom shall ever speak his virtue.
His overthrow heaped happiness upon him,
For then, and not till then, he felt himself,                        65
And found the blessedness of being little;
And to add greater honours to his age
Than man could give him, he died fearing God.
KATHERINE  After my death I wish no other herald,
No other speaker of my living actions                                70
To keep mine honour from corruption,
But such an honest chronicler as Griffith.
Whom I most hated living, thou hast made me,
With thy religious truth and modesty,
Now in his ashes honour: peace be with him.                          75
Patience, be near me still, and set me lower;
I have not long to trouble thee. Good Griffith,
Cause the musicians play me that sad note
I named my knell, whilst I sit meditating
On that celestial harmony I go to.                                    80

52 **persuading** persuasive.
53 **Lofty** Haughty.
54 **sought him** sought him out, applied to him. Holinshed has 'sought his freendship' (Foakes).
55 **unsatisfied** never satisfied.
58 **raised** established, built.
59 **Ipswich and Oxford** The college that Wolsey founded at Ipswich, his original home, did not survive him, as Holinshed notes; the college at Oxford, after suffering some difficulties, was refounded by Henry as Christ Church.
60 **good** goodness, virtue (of Wolsey).
60 **did it** created it.
62 **art** the learning of the schools, scholarship.

62 **still so rising** still famous for its learning and influence as it grows.
65 **felt himself** perceived, recognised himself. See 3.2.378: 'I know myself now.'
70 **living** while alive. See *R2* 5.1.39: 'thy last living leave'.
74 **religious** conscientious.
74 **modesty** moderation.
78 **note** strain of music.
80 **celestial harmony** A reference to the music of the spheres which the poetic tradition claimed the liberated soul could hear (*Per.* 5.1.229–34), and which signified also the harmonious beauty of heaven itself.

*Sad and solemn music*

GRIFFITH  She is asleep; good wench, let's sit down quiet
For fear we wake her. Softly, gentle Patience.

### THE VISION

*Enter solemnly tripping one after another, six personages,
clad in white robes, wearing on their heads garlands of
bays, and golden vizards on their faces, branches of bays or
palms in their hands. They first congee unto her, then
dance; and at certain changes, the first two hold a spare
garland over her head, at which the other four make
reverend curtsies. Then the two that held the garland
deliver the same to the other next two, who observe the
same order in their changes, and holding the garland over
her head. Which done, they deliver the same garland to the
last two, who likewise observe the same order. At which, as
it were by inspiration, she makes in her sleep signs of
rejoicing, and holdeth up her hands to heaven. And so, in
their dancing vanish, carrying the garland with them. The
music continues*

KATHERINE  Spirits of peace, where are ye? Are ye all gone,
And leave me here in wretchedness behind ye?
GRIFFITH  Madam, we are here.
KATHERINE                                It is not you I call for.          85
Saw ye none enter since I slept?
GRIFFITH                                None, madam.
KATHERINE  No? Saw you not even now a blessed troop
Invite me to a banquet, whose bright faces
Cast thousand beams upon me, like the sun?
They promised me eternal happiness,                                90
And brought me garlands, Griffith, which I feel

82 SD There is no source for the vision in the chronicles. For possible sources, see p. 19 above.
82 SD.2 **personages** Perhaps denoting sex-lessness, as spirits: see A. Brissenden, *Shakespeare and the Dance*, p. 105.
82 SD.3 **white robes** White represents virtue and purity.
82 SD.3–4 **garlands of bays** The bays or bay leaves signify triumph.
82 SD.4 **golden vizards** Foakes notes that 'golded vizards' were worn in Dekker's *Old*

*Fortunatus* (1600) to represent spirits, albeit demonic ones. Gold is a Christian symbol for incorruptibility: 'gold tried in the fire' (Rev. 3.18).
82 SD.5 **palms** Palms are carried by the immortal souls praising God in Rev. 7.9 (Brissenden).
82 SD.5 **congee** curtsy.
82 SD.6 **changes** Figures in the dance where there are changes of pattern: see *LLL* 5.2.209. The order of the dance symbolises the eternal order of heaven.

I am not worthy yet to wear: I shall, assuredly.
GRIFFITH I am most joyful, madam, such good dreams
Possess your fancy.
KATHERINE                    Bid the music leave,
They are harsh and heavy to me.

*Music ceases*

PATIENCE                              Do you note                    95
How much her grace is altered on the sudden?
How long her face is drawn? how pale she looks,
And of an earthy cold? Mark her eyes!
GRIFFITH She is going, wench; pray, pray.
PATIENCE                              Heaven comfort her.

*Enter a* MESSENGER

MESSENGER And't like your grace –
KATHERINE                         You are a saucy fellow,        100
Deserve we no more reverence?
GRIFFITH                              You are to blame,
Knowing she will not lose her wonted greatness
To use so rude behaviour. Go to, kneel.
MESSENGER I humbly do entreat your highness' pardon,
My haste made me unmannerly. There is staying        105
A gentleman sent from the king to see you.
KATHERINE Admit him entrance, Griffith. But this fellow,
Let me ne'er see again.

*Exit Messenger*

*Enter* LORD CAPUCHIUS

If my sight fail not,
You should be lord ambassador from the emperor,
My royal nephew, and your name Capuchius.        110

100 And't] F; An't *Hanmer and others*

94 **fancy** imagination; the faculty that perceives or creates images not present to the senses.
There is no suggestion in Griffith's comment that
these are mere illusions.
94 **the music leave** the musicians leave off or
cease playing.
95 **heavy** wearisome.
98 **earthy** pale and lifeless as earth (Onions).
The body was thought to return to the element,
earth, at death.

100 **And't like** The F spelling is usually altered
to 'An't like' but both have the same meaning: 'If
it pleases'. However, the greeting, used by near
equals or by a servant to his master, is not
appropriate for a servant addressing a queen, and
103 suggests that the servant has not approached
with any suitable physical gesture.
102 **lose** forgo.
103 **use** deal with, accept.
105 **staying** waiting.

CAPUCHIUS Madam, the same: your servant.
KATHERINE                                    O my lord,
    The times and titles now are altered strangely
    With me, since first you knew me. But I pray you,
    What is your pleasure with me?
CAPUCHIUS                                    Noble lady,
    First mine own service to your grace, the next          115
    The king's request that I would visit you,
    Who grieves much for your weakness, and by me
    Sends you his princely commendations,
    And heartily entreats you take good comfort.
KATHERINE O my good lord, that comfort comes too late,          120
    'Tis like a pardon after execution;
    That gentle physic, given in time, had cured me;
    But now I am past all comforts here but prayers.
    How does his highness?
CAPUCHIUS                         Madam, in good health.
KATHERINE So may he ever do, and ever flourish,               125
    When I shall dwell with worms, and my poor name
    Banished the kingdom. Patience, is that letter
    I caused you write yet sent away?
PATIENCE                                    No, madam.
KATHERINE Sir, I most humbly pray you to deliver
    This to my lord the king.
CAPUCHIUS                         Most willing, madam.          130
KATHERINE In which I have commended to his goodness
    The model of our chaste loves, his young daughter –
    The dews of heaven fall thick in blessings on her! –
    Beseeching him to give her virtuous breeding;
    She is young, and of a noble, modest nature,          135
    I hope she will deserve well; and a little
    To love her for her mother's sake, that loved him,
    Heaven knows how dearly. My next poor petition
    Is that his noble grace would have some pity

113] *Rowe³;* With...knew me / But...you F     138] *Rowe³;* Heaven...dearly. / My...petition F

112 **titles...altered** Specifically from queen
to princess dowager (4.1.23).
112 **strangely** greatly, in an extraordinary
fashion.
118 **commendations** compliments.
123 **here** i.e. in this world.

130 **willing** willingly.
132 **model** image, symbol.
132 **daughter** Mary, who succeeded to the
throne in 1553 after the death of Edward VI.
134 **breeding** training and education.

Upon my wretched women, that so long                          140
Have followed both my fortunes faithfully,
Of which there is not one, I dare avow,
And now I should not lie, but will deserve
For virtue and true beauty of the soul,
For honesty and decent carriage,                              145
A right good husband, let him be a noble;
And sure those men are happy that shall have 'em.
The last is for my men; they are the poorest,
But poverty could never draw 'em from me;
That they may have their wages duly paid 'em,                 150
And something over to remember me by.
If heaven had pleased to have given me longer life
And able means, we had not parted thus.
These are the whole contents; and, good my lord,
By that you love the dearest in this world,                   155
As you wish Christian peace to souls departed,
Stand these poor people's friend, and urge the king
To do me this last right.

CAPUCHIUS                          By heaven I will,
Or let me lose the fashion of a man.

KATHERINE I thank you, honest lord. Remember me               160
In all humility unto his highness:
Say his long trouble now is passing
Out of this world. Tell him in death I blessed him,
For so I will; mine eyes grow dim. Farewell,
My lord. Griffith, farewell. Nay, Patience,                   165
You must not leave me yet. I must to bed,
Call in more women. When I am dead, good wench,
Let me be used with honour; strew me over
With maiden flowers, that all the world may know

141 **both my fortunes** my good fortune and my bad.

145 **honesty** chastity.

145 **decent carriage** proper conduct. 'Decent' does not occur elsewhere in Shakespeare.

146 **a noble** i.e. a noble husband, one honourable in character and high in rank, since the queen's waiting-women would have been gentlewomen.

153 **able means** sufficient means.

155 She asks him to swear by all that he holds dearest.

159 **Or** Else.

159 **fashion** likeness, outward form.

163 **blessed him** The idea of forgiveness and blessing is carried on from earlier parts of the play; thus Buckingham at 2.1.90 and Wolsey at 3.2.380–1.

169 **maiden flowers** flowers betokening chastity. Ophelia is allowed her 'maiden strewments' (*Ham.* 5.1.233), and Arviragus promises to strew 'fairest flowers' on Fidele's grave (*Cym.* 4.2.218–24).

I was a chaste wife to my grave. Embalm me,                    170
Then lay me forth, although unqueened, yet like
A queen and daughter to a king inter me.
I can no more.

*Exeunt leading Katherine*

**5.1** *Enter* GARDINER, BISHOP OF WINCHESTER, *a* PAGE *with a torch*
*before him, met by* SIR THOMAS LOVELL

GARDINER It's one a'clock, boy, is't not?
BOY                               It hath struck.
GARDINER These should be hours for necessities,
    Not for delights; times to repair our nature
    With comforting repose, and not for us
    To waste these times. Good hour of night, Sir Thomas:       5
    Whither so late?
LOVELL                    Came you from the king, my lord?
GARDINER I did, Sir Thomas, and left him at primero
    With the Duke of Suffolk.
LOVELL                              I must to him too
    Before he go to bed. I'll take my leave.
GARDINER Not yet, Sir Thomas Lovell: what's the matter?         10
    It seems you are in haste; and if there be
    No great offence belongs to't, give your friend
    Some touch of your late business. Affairs that walk,
    As they say spirits do, at midnight, have
    In them a wilder nature than the business                   15
    That seeks dispatch by day.

Act 5, Scene 1      5.1] *Actus Quintus Scena Prima* F

171 **lay me forth** lay me out for burial.
173 **can** can say or do. Foakes notes Shakespeare's use of the phrase in *Ham*. 5.2.320 and
*Ant*. 4.15.59.

**Act 5, Scene 1**
0 SD A gallery at court. Shakespeare once
again brings together separate events for dramatic
effect, the birth of Elizabeth in 1533, reported
briefly by Holinshed, and the attack on Cranmer,
which Foxe describes; though not dated, it seems
to have happened some ten years later. This
scene and the following are full of movement,

intrigue and confrontation as the plot is set in
motion again after the pageantry of 4.1 and the
quiet pathos of 4.2.
    3 **repair** restore.
    7 **primero** A card game fashionable at court
and among gentlemen and gamesters from about
1530 to 1640 (*OED*). It was usually played for
high stakes; see Sir John Harington, *Epigrams*
(1618), II, 99.
    12 **offence** impropriety.
    13 **touch** hint.
    13 **late** recent.

LOVELL                                    My lord, I love you,
And durst commend a secret to your ear
Much weightier than this work. The queen's in labour,
They say in great extremity, and feared
She'll with the labour end.

GARDINER                          The fruit she goes with          20
I pray for heartily, that it may find
Good time, and live: but for the stock, Sir Thomas,
I wish it grubbed up now.

LOVELL                                    Methinks I could
Cry the amen, and yet my conscience says
She's a good creature, and, sweet lady, does          25
Deserve our better wishes.

GARDINER                          But sir, sir,
Hear me, Sir Thomas, y'are a gentleman
Of mine own way. I know you wise, religious,
And let me tell you, it will ne'er be well,
'Twill not, Sir Thomas Lovell, take't of me,          30
Till Cranmer, Cromwell, her two hands, and she
Sleep in their graves.

LOVELL                              Now, sir, you speak of two
The most remarked i'th'kingdom. As for Cromwell,
Beside that of the jewel house, is made master
O'th'rolls, and the king's secretary; further, sir,          35
Stands in the gap and trade of moe preferments
With which the time will load him. Th'archbishop

37 time] F4; Lime F

17 **commend** entrust.
18 **work** the business I've been involved in.
19 **feared** it is feared that; or possibly, 'feared for, that...' (Pooler).
22 **Good time** i.e. for birth; possibly 'good fortune'. Foakes compares *WT* 2.1.19–20: 'She is spread of late / Into a goodly bulk. Good time encounter her!'
22 **stock** stem (of the family tree).
23 **grubbed up** uprooted. Gardiner hopes that Anne may die in childbirth.
24 **Cry the amen** Say amen to that, assent.
28 **way** i.e. of religious thinking; they are both against the heresies of the Lutherans. As editors have noted, 'way' is a biblical term (Acts 9.2).
31 **hands** the means by which she acts for the Lutheran cause.

33 **remarked** noted, conspicuous; quoted by *OED* as the earliest example.
34 **Beside** As well as.
34–5 **master...rolls** A judge of the Court of Appeal, in charge of rolls, patents, and grants, and keeper of the records of the Court of Chancery (*OED*). Cromwell's various appointments are mentioned by Holinshed as occurring over several years.
36 **gap and trade** opening (opportunity) and beaten path. A 'common trade' is a public thoroughfare (*OED* sv *sb* 1). See *R2* 3.3.156.
36 **moe** more.
37 **the time** this present age.

Is the king's hand and tongue, and who dare speak
One syllable against him?
GARDINER                             Yes, yes, Sir Thomas,
There are that dare, and I myself have ventured                  40
To speak my mind of him; and indeed this day,
Sir, I may tell it you, I think I have
Incensed the lords o'th'council, that he is
(For so I know he is, they know he is)
A most arch-heretic, a pestilence                               45
That does infect the land; with which they, moved,
Have broken with the king, who hath so far
Given ear to our complaint, of his great grace
And princely care foreseeing those fell mischiefs
Our reasons laid before him, hath commanded                     50
Tomorrow morning to the council board
He be convented. He's a rank weed, Sir Thomas,
And we must root him out. From your affairs
I hinder you too long: good night, Sir Thomas.
                              *Exeunt Gardiner and Page*
LOVELL Many good nights, my lord; I rest your servant.          55

                    *Enter* KING *and* SUFFOLK

KING Charles, I will play no more tonight,
     My mind's not on't, you are too hard for me.

---

43 Incensed] F; Insens'd *Rann*     50 hath] F; 'hath *Collier;* he hath *Pope*

---

**38 king's…tongue** A deliberate comparison between Cranmer's power with the king and Wolsey's similar power earlier in the play is pointed here and subsequently in action and speech, as at 5.2.139–41. Gardiner and Lovell talk about Cranmer just as Buckingham and other nobles spoke about Wolsey; note 2.2.18–20 and the Lord Chamberlain's comment 'for he hath a witchcraft / Over the king in's tongue' (3.2.18–19).

**43 Incensed** Roused or angered. Some editors have read 'insensed' meaning 'informed', following Rann's edition of 1791, because of the construction with 'that'. But Shakespeare does not use that word elsewhere, whereas 'incensed' occurs several times in this play alone.

**44 For…is** Some editors place a comma after 'For' and interpret 'so' as 'provided that', suggesting that the lords will believe what he knows

to be true. However, the change is not necessary.

**45 most** very great.

**46 moved** being moved, aroused to anger.

**47 broken with** revealed their views to.

**49 fell** cruel, dreadful.

**52 convented** summoned as for a trial or examination.

**52 rank** overgrown, gross; but also with the sense of 'virulent' or 'poisonous'.

**56 Charles** Charles Brandon, Duke of Suffolk, was an intimate of Henry's and a favourite at court. He was for long regarded as an upstart, a man of no family (like Wolsey). However, he married the king's sister secretly when Mary's first husband, Louis XII of France, died shortly after her marriage to him. Brandon eventually won Henry's approval for the match. The story forms part of the plot of Rowley's *When You See Me You Know Me*.

SUFFOLK Sir, I did never win of you before.
KING But little, Charles,
    Nor shall not when my fancy's on my play.                    60
    Now, Lovell, from the queen what is the news?
LOVELL I could not personally deliver to her
    What you commanded me, but by her woman
    I sent your message, who returned her thanks
    In the great'st humbleness, and desired your highness        65
    Most heartily to pray for her.
KING                       What say'st thou? Ha?
    To pray for her? what, is she crying out?
LOVELL So said her woman, and that her sufferance made
    Almost each pang a death.
KING                   Alas, good lady.
SUFFOLK God safely quit her of her burthen, and                     70
    With gentle travail, to the gladding of
    Your highness with an heir.
KING            'Tis midnight, Charles,
    Prithee to bed, and in thy prayers remember
    Th'estate of my poor queen. Leave me alone,
    For I must think of that which company                       75
    Would not be friendly to.
SUFFOLK             I wish your highness
    A quiet night, and my good mistress will
    Remember in my prayers.
KING                Charles, good night.

                          *Exit Suffolk*

         *Enter* SIR ANTHONY DENNY

    Well, sir, what follows?
DENNY Sir, I have brought my lord the archbishop,               80

78 SD.2] *Johnson; after* follows *in* F

60 **fancy** inclination, liking.
64 **who** i.e. the queen.
68 **sufferance** suffering. The scene stresses Anne's pains in childbirth.
70 **quit** release.
71 **gladding** making happy.
72 **midnight** the middle of the night (not a specific time). As Foakes points out, the term was more general than it is today.

74 **estate** state, condition.
75–6 **which company...to** i.e. which is more suitable for solitary meditation than for company.
79 **what follows** what comes next (after your entry and bow), what news do you bring?

As you commanded me.
KING                                    Ha? Canterbury?
DENNY Ay, my good lord.
KING                              'Tis true: where is he, Denny?
DENNY He attends your highness' pleasure.
KING                                    Bring him to us.

*[Exit Denny]*

LOVELL *[Aside]* This is about that which the bishop spake;
        I am happily come hither.                                    85

*Enter* CRANMER *and* DENNY

KING Avoid the gallery.
                        *(Lovell seems to stay)*
                        Ha? I have said. Be gone.
        What?

*Exeunt Lovell and Denny*

CRANMER *[Aside]* I am fearful: wherefore frowns he thus?
        'Tis his aspect of terror. All's not well.
KING How now, my lord? You do desire to know
        Wherefore I sent for you.
CRANMER *[Kneeling]*                    It is my duty                90
        T'attend your highness' pleasure.
KING                                    Pray you arise,
        My good and gracious Lord of Canterbury.
        Come, you and I must walk a turn together;
        I have news to tell you. Come, come, give me your hand.
        Ah my good lord, I grieve at what I speak,                   95
        And am right sorry to repeat what follows.
        I have, and most unwillingly, of late
        Heard many grievous, I do say my lord,
        Grievous complaints of you; which being considered,
        Have moved us and our council, that you shall               100

---

83 SD] *Rowe; not in* F      84 SD] *Rowe; not in* F      86] *Capell;* Avoid...Gallery / Ha?...gone F      87 SD] *Capell; not in* F      89–90 How...duty] *Rowe³; four lines, ending...*Lord? / ...wherefore / ...you. / ...dutie F      90 SD] *Johnson; not in* F      94] *Pope (without second* come); I...you. / Come...hand F

85 **happily** fortunately.
86 **gallery** A long room in a Tudor mansion or castle where one might take exercise; as Foxe says, the meeting took place in 'the Galerie where the king walked' (*Acts*, p. 1694).

88 **aspect** expression.
98 **grievous** serious.
100 **moved** prompted.

This morning come before us; where I know
You cannot with such freedom purge yourself,
But that, till further trial in those charges
Which will require your answer, you must take
Your patience to you, and be well contented                105
To make your house our Tower; you, a brother of us,
It fits we thus proceed, or else no witness
Would come against you.

CRANMER [*Kneeling*]                    I humbly thank your highness
And am right glad to catch this good occasion
Most throughly to be winnowed, where my chaff           110
And corn shall fly asunder. For I know
There's none stands under more calumnious tongues
Than I myself, poor man.

KING                                  Stand up, good Canterbury,
Thy truth and thy integrity is rooted
In us, thy friend. Give me thy hand, stand up,           115
Prithee let's walk. Now by my holidame,
What manner of man are you? My lord, I looked
You would have given me your petition, that
I should have ta'en some pains to bring together
Yourself and your accusers, and to have heard you        120
Without indurance further.

CRANMER                          Most dread liege,
The good I stand on is my truth and honesty;
If they shall fail, I with mine enemies
Will triumph o'er my person, which I weigh not,
Being of those virtues vacant. I fear nothing            125
What can be said against me.

KING                                  Know you not
How your state stands i'th'world, with the whole world?

102 **freedom** ease.
102 **purge** clear.
104–5 **take...you** Paulina uses the same words to Leontes in *WT* 3.2.231.
106 **you...us** i.e. you being a fellow councillor.
110 **throughly** thoroughly.
110–11 **winnowed...asunder** A biblical metaphor; see Matt. 3.12 and Luke 3.17.
112 **stands under** is subject to.
116 **holidame** An oath referring to holiness or

a sacred object, frequent in Shakespeare; originally 'haligdom' or 'halidom'. In popular etymology it was thought to be derived from Our Lady (dame).
121 **indurance** imprisonment, or the enduring of hardship (the latter more usual in Shakespeare). Foxe uses the word twice in the relevant passage.
124 **weigh not** value not.
125 **vacant** empty.
125 **nothing** not at all.

Your enemies are many, and not small; their practices
Must bear the same proportion, and not ever
The justice and the truth o'th'question carries                    130
The due o'th'verdict with it; at what ease
Might corrupt minds procure knaves as corrupt
To swear against you? Such things have been done.
You are potently opposed, and with a malice
Of as great size. Ween you of better luck,                        135
I mean in perjured witness, than your master,
Whose minister you are, whiles here he lived
Upon this naughty earth? Go to, go to,
You take a precipice for no leap of danger,
And woo your own destruction.

CRANMER                                    God and your majesty      140
Protect mine innocence, or I fall into
The trap is laid for me.

KING                                       Be of good cheer,
They shall no more prevail than we give way to.
Keep comfort to you, and this morning see
You do appear before them. If they shall chance                   145
In charging you with matters to commit you,
The best persuasions to the contrary
Fail not to use, and with what vehemency
Th'occasion shall instruct you. If entreaties
Will render you no remedy, this ring                              150
Deliver them, and your appeal to us
There make before them. Look, the good man weeps:

---

139 precipice] F2; Precepit F     152 good man] F3; goodman F

**128 not small** i.e. in rank or positions of power.
**128 practices** intrigues, plots.
**129 bear...proportion** be as great.
**129 ever** always.
**131 due...verdict** just verdict.
**131 at what ease** how easily.
**134 potently** powerfully.
**135 Ween you of** Do you imagine.
**136 witness** evidence, or the person giving such evidence.
**138 naughty** wicked.
**139 precipice** F2 correction is always follow-

ed, but *OED* accepts F's 'precepit' as a rare alternative form from French *precipite* (precipice) and Latin *praeceps, praecipitis*.
**140–2** The king gives Cranmer a lesson in the hard facts of political and religious rivalries at court and the dangers he faces in such an environment. Cranmer is at last ready to acknowledge the possibility of a trap; the scene also demonstrates the king's mature awareness of the realities of power.
**142 is** which is.
**143 give way to** give them scope.
**146 commit** to the Tower.

He's honest on mine honour. God's blest mother,
I swear he is true-hearted, and a soul
None better in my kingdom. Get you gone,                              155
And do as I have bid you.

                                                    *Exit Cranmer*
                                He has strangled
His language in his tears.

                        *Enter* OLD LADY

GENTLEMAN *within*                    Come back: what mean you?
OLD LADY I'll not come back; the tidings that I bring
    Will make my boldness manners. Now good angels
    Fly o'er thy royal head, and shade thy person              160
    Under their blessed wings.
KING                          Now by thy looks
    I guess thy message. Is the queen delivered?
    Say ay, and of a boy.
OLD LADY                    Ay, ay, my liege,
    And of a lovely boy: the God of heaven
    Both now and ever bless her! 'Tis a girl                    165
    Promises boys hereafter. Sir, your queen
    Desires your visitation, and to be
    Acquainted with this stranger; 'tis as like you
    As cherry is to cherry.
KING                          Lovell!

                        [*Enter* LOVELL]

LOVELL                            Sir?
KING Give her an hundred marks. I'll to the queen.    *Exit King*   170
OLD LADY An hundred marks? By this light, I'll ha' more.
    An ordinary groom is for such payment.
    I will have more, or scold it out of him.

---

156–7 And...strangled / His...tears] *Hanmer;* And...you. / He...teares F; And...you. / He'as strangled all
his language in his tears *Pope*    169 SD] *Var. 1773; not in* F    170] *Pope;* Give...Markes. / I'll...Queene F

---

157 SD OLD LADY This is probably the Old
Lady who appeared with Anne in 2.3 since she
talks in much the same way; hence, a linking
device with an earlier scene.

163–4 Ay...boy The Old Lady follows the
king's instructions on what to say but then has to
correct herself (J. D. Wilson in Maxwell).

170 hundred marks The mark was not a coin
but a sum of money. Originally it was the weight
of 8 ounces of silver, which represented 160
pennies at 20 pennies per ounce. Hence a mark
was the value of two-thirds of a pound.

Said I for this the girl was like to him?
I'll have more, or else unsay't; and now, while 'tis hot,          175
I'll put it to the issue.

*Exit Lady [with Lovell]*

**5.2** *Enter* CRANMER, *Archbishop of Canterbury,* [*pursuivants, pages,
and others about the door*]

CRANMER  I hope I am not too late, and yet the gentleman
That was sent to me from the council prayed me
To make great haste. All fast? What means this? Ho!
Who waits there? Sure you know me?

*Enter* KEEPER

KEEPER                                              Yes, my lord:
But yet I cannot help you.
CRANMER                          Why?
KEEPER                                        Your grace          5
Must wait till you be called for.

*Enter* DOCTOR BUTTS

CRANMER                                        So.
BUTTS [*Aside*] This is a piece of malice: I am glad
I came this way so happily. The king
Shall understand it presently.          *Exit Butts*
CRANMER [*Aside*]                          'Tis Butts,
The king's physician; as he passed along,          10
How earnestly he cast his eyes upon me:
Pray heaven he sound not my disgrace; for certain

---

176 SD *with Lovell*] *Var. 1773; Exit Ladie* F    **Act 5, Scene 2**    5.2] *Scena Secunda* F    0 SD.1–2
*pursuivants...door*] *Var. 1778 and other editions*    5–6 But yet...So] *Foakes; four lines, ending...help you / Why? /
...for / So* F    7 SD] *Dyce; not in* F    7 piece] F2; *Pecre* F    9 SD.2 *Aside*] *Johnson; not in* F

176 **put...issue** bring it to a head.

**Act 5, Scene 2**
0 SD The scene is at first an anteroom outside
the council chamber at court which then becomes
the council chamber. This edition follows F and
Foakes in not dividing 5.2 into two scenes at 34.
There are difficulties about staging, but nothing
inherently foreign to the Elizabethan tradition in
moving from 'outside' to 'inside' in a single scene.

The material comes from Foxe but is made much
more dramatic in the play (see supplementary
note).
3 **fast** closed up.
8 **happily** fortunately.
9 **presently** at once.
12 **sound** tell, proclaim; see *R2* 3.4.74: 'How
dares thy harsh rude tongue sound this unpleasing
news?' Sometimes interpreted 'measure the depth
of, fathom'.

This is of purpose laid by some that hate me
(God turn their hearts, I never sought their malice)
To quench mine honour. They would shame to make me        15
Wait else at door, a fellow councillor,
'Mong boys, grooms and lackeys. But their pleasures
Must be fulfilled, and I attend with patience.

*Enter the* KING *and* BUTTS *at a window above*

BUTTS  I'll show your grace the strangest sight –
KING                                      What's that, Butts?
BUTTS  I think your highness saw this many a day.          20
KING  Body a'me, where is it?
BUTTS                    There, my lord:
The high promotion of his grace of Canterbury
Who holds his state at door 'mongst pursuivants,
Pages and footboys.
KING                      Ha? 'tis he indeed.
Is this the honour they do one another?                    25
'Tis well there's one above 'em yet; I had thought
They had parted so much honesty among 'em,
At least good manners, as not thus to suffer
A man of his place, and so near our favour,
To dance attendance on their lordships' pleasures,        30
And at the door too, like a post with packets.
By holy Mary, Butts, there's knavery!
Let 'em alone, and draw the curtain close:

17] *Rowe*³; 'Mong...Lackeyes / But...pleasures F

13 **laid** planned.
18 SD *above* This F SD is a clear indication of the use of the upper stage, in conjunction with action on the main stage below. See *Oth.* 1.1.81 SD *Brabantio at a window*.
21 **Body a'me** Body of me. A mild oath.
23 **holds his state** maintains his dignity.
23 **pursuivants** Messengers engaged on state affairs, but often used (as here) of lesser messengers.
26 **one above 'em** i.e. in the hierarchy of this world, though a hint too of the providence above them all.
27 **parted** shared.
29 **place** rank and office (as archbishop).
31 **post** courier. Posts were stationed from the sixteenth century at regular intervals along the post-roads to carry the king's packets and later other letters to the next stage (*OED* sv *sb*² 1)
33 **draw...close** The upper-stage 'window' was apparently fitted with a curtain that could be drawn, as was usual for the music-room 'above' in private theatres, and in public theatres after 1609. Richard Hosley notes that such curtains permitted discoveries 'above' ('The Playhouses', *Revels History of Drama in English*, 1975, III, 231). The king's order suggests that the king will overhear without being seen. When the anteroom becomes the council chamber, the audience would expect the king still to be listening, even though there are no comments from above. The king must descend at some point to make his entrance at 147.

We shall hear more anon.

*A council-table brought in with chairs and stools, and placed under the state.*
*Enter* LORD CHANCELLOR, *places himself at the upper end of the table, on*
*the left hand: a seat being left void above him, as for Canterbury's seat.*
DUKE OF SUFFOLK, DUKE OF NORFOLK, SURREY, LORD
CHAMBERLAIN, GARDINER, *seat themselves in order on each side.*
CROMWELL *at lower end, as secretary*

CHANCELLOR Speak to the business, master secretary;                    35
Why are we met in council?
CROMWELL                                         Please your honours,
The chief cause concerns his grace of Canterbury.
GARDINER Has he had knowledge of it?
CROMWELL                                         Yes.
NORFOLK                                         Who waits there?
KEEPER Without, my noble lords?
GARDINER                              Yes.
KEEPER                                         My lord archbishop;
And has done half an hour to know your pleasures.                      40
CHANCELLOR Let him come in.
KEEPER                                    Your grace may enter now.
*Cranmer approaches the council-table*
CHANCELLOR My good lord archbishop, I'm very sorry
To sit here at this present and behold
That chair stand empty: but we all are men,
In our own natures frail, and capable                                  45
Of our flesh; few are angels; out of which frailty

---

34 SD] F; *Cam. adds / Exeunt / and / Scene III*    34 SD.1–2 *A council-table...state*] F; *omitted Var. 1773 and other*
*editions*    35 master] *Var. 1778;* M. F    45 frail, and capable] F; frail, incapable *Malone;* frail, and culpable *Collier*

---

34 SD Most editions provide an exeunt for the king and Dr Butts above and for Cranmer and the servants at the door below at this point, beginning a new scene with the SD. However, F clearly suggests the continuity of the two parts of the scene, in that the furniture for the council chamber is brought in through another doorway, followed by the councillors; the wording of the SD at 41 indicates that Cranmer has been on stage throughout and now 'approaches' the council table. The lackeys would probably go out at one door while the furniture is being brought in at the other.

34 SD.1 *under the state* Foakes asks whether the chair of state or throne might have remained on stage throughout the play. Alternatively, it

might be thrust forward from the discovery-space. 'Under' implies 'in a subordinate position to'.

38 had knowledge been informed.

43 present present time.

45–6 capable...flesh prone to, liable to the weaknesses of the flesh. See *2H4* 1.1.172–3: 'You were advis'd his flesh was capable / Of wounds and scars...' Foakes observes that much of the language of this passage comes from a speech of Bishop Stokesley to his clergy in 1530–1, reported by Halle (II, 200) and repeated by Foxe, though in a section far removed from most of the material used in the play (*Acts*, p. 959).

And want of wisdom, you that best should teach us
Have misdemeaned yourself, and not a little;
Toward the king first, then his laws, in filling
The whole realm by your teaching and your chaplains'          50
(For so we are informed) with new opinions,
Divers and dangerous; which are heresies,
And not reformed, may prove pernicious.
GARDINER Which reformation must be sudden too,
My noble lords; for those that tame wild horses               55
Pace 'em not in their hands to make 'em gentle,
But stop their mouths with stubborn bits and spur 'em
Till they obey the manage. If we suffer,
Out of our easiness and childish pity
To one man's honour, this contagious sickness,               60
Farewell all physic: and what follows then?
Commotions, uproars, with a general taint
Of the whole state, as of late days our neighbours,
The upper Germany, can dearly witness,
Yet freshly pitied in our memories.                          65
CRANMER My good lords, hitherto, in all the progress
Both of my life and office, I have laboured,
And with no little study, that my teaching
And the strong course of my authority
Might go one way, and safely; and the end                    70
Was ever to do well; nor is there living,
I speak it with a single heart, my lords,
A man that more detests, more stirs against,
Both in his private conscience and his place,

---

50 chaplains'] *Capell;* Chaplaines F

---

**50 chaplains'** Foxe's account stresses that both Cranmer and his chaplains were accused of taking part in 'pernicious' teaching. F does not use an apostrophe for the possessive plural.

**52 Divers** Various; possibly, 'opposed to the right, perverse' (*OED* sv *a* 2).

**53 pernicious** destructive, fatal.

**56 Pace 'em** Walk them in an amble.

**57 stubborn** hard or rigid.

**58 manage** handling, in the training process.

**59 easiness** indulgence.

**61 physic** medical treatment.

**62 taint** infection.

**63–5 our neighbours...memories** The up-

risings of various Protestant sects in German cities were well known at the time. Editors have pointed to an insurrection in Münzer in Saxony in 1524–5 and another by the Anabaptists in Münster in 1535 (Maxwell). Foxe mentions them in general terms as part of the accusation (*Acts*, p. 1694).

**64 upper** higher and more inland.

**68 study** effort.

**72 single heart** pure heart. 'Singleness of heart' is a biblical phrase; see Acts 2.46, Eph. 6.5.

**73 stirs** takes action.

**74 place** office.

Defacers of a public peace than I do.        75
Pray heaven the king may never find a heart
With less allegiance in it! Men that make
Envy and crooked malice nourishment
Dare bite the best. I do beseech your lordships
That in this case, of justice, my accusers,        80
Be what they will, may stand forth face to face
And freely urge against me.

SUFFOLK                Nay, my lord,
That cannot be; you are a councillor,
And by that virtue no man dare accuse you.

GARDINER My lord, because we have business of more moment,    85
We will be short with you. 'Tis his highness' pleasure
And our consent, for better trial of you,
From hence you be committed to the Tower,
Where, being but a private man again,
You shall know many dare accuse you boldly,        90
More than, I fear, you are provided for.

CRANMER Ah my good Lord of Winchester, I thank you;
You are always my good friend; if your will pass,
I shall both find your lordship judge and juror,
You are so merciful. I see your end,        95
'Tis my undoing. Love and meekness, lord,
Become a churchman better than ambition;
Win straying souls with modesty again,
Cast none away. That I shall clear myself,
Lay all the weight ye can upon my patience,        100
I make as little doubt as you do conscience
In doing daily wrongs. I could say more,
But reverence to your calling makes me modest.

GARDINER My lord, my lord, you are a sectary,

---

80 case, of] *Foakes;* case of F     92 Winchester, . . . you] *Collier;* Winchester: . . . you, F; Winchester, . . . you, *Rowe*

---

75 **Defacers** Destroyers.
   80 **of justice** out of justice, in fairness. F has no comma after 'case', and Maxwell argues that 'case of justice' means 'case where justice is involved'.
   81 **Be. . .will** Whoever they are.
   82 **urge against** accuse.
   84 **by. . .virtue** by virtue of that.
   85 **moment** importance.

93 **pass** is approved, ratified.
   94 **both** Modifies 'judge' and 'juror'. For placing, see Abbott 420–1.
   95 **end** purpose.
   96 **undoing** ruin.
   101 **do conscience** make conscience, i.e. have any scruples.
   103 **modest** temperate.
   104 **sectary** follower of a heretical sect.

That's the plain truth; your painted gloss discovers,                105
To men that understand you, words and weakness.
CROMWELL  My Lord of Winchester, y'are a little,
By your good favour, too sharp; men so noble,
However faulty, yet should find respect
For what they have been; 'tis a cruelty                              110
To load a falling man.
GARDINER                    Good master secretary,
I cry your honour mercy; you may worst
Of all this table say so.
CROMWELL                       Why, my lord?
GARDINER  Do not I know you for a favourer
Of this new sect? Ye are not sound.
CROMWELL                                    Not sound?                115
GARDINER  Not sound, I say.
CROMWELL                       Would you were half so honest!
Men's prayers then would seek you, not their fears.
GARDINER  I shall remember this bold language.
CROMWELL                                            Do.
Remember your bold life too.
CHANCELLOR                        This is too much;
Forbear, for shame, my lords.
GARDINER                          I have done.
CROMWELL                                        And I.          120
CHANCELLOR  Then thus for you, my lord; it stands agreed,
I take it, by all voices, that forthwith
You be conveyed to th'Tower a prisoner,
There to remain till the king's further pleasure
Be known unto us. Are you all agreed, lords?                         125
ALL  We are.
CRANMER     Is there no other way of mercy

119, 121 SH CHANCELLOR] *Capell;* Cham. F

105 **painted** specious, false.
105 **gloss** surface lustre.
105 **discovers** reveals.
106 **words** mere words.
112 **cry...mercy** beg your honour's pardon.
112 **worst** with the least justification.
115 **sound** orthodox, holding to the approved doctrines.

116 **honest** true, having integrity.
119 SH F has *Cham.* but this appears to be an error, since the Chancellor is the one conducting the business of the meeting. SH for 121 is similarly mistaken.

But I must needs to th'Tower, my lords?

GARDINER                                              What other
Would you expect? You are strangely troublesome.
Let some o'th'guard be ready there.

*Enter the Guard*

CRANMER                                          For me?
Must I go like a traitor thither?

GARDINER                                        Receive him,                    130
And see him safe i'th'Tower.

CRANMER                               Stay, good my lords,
I have a little yet to say. Look there, my lords;
By virtue of that ring, I take my cause
Out of the gripes of cruel men, and give it
To a most noble judge, the king my master.                          135

CHAMBERLAIN This is the king's ring.

SURREY                                          'Tis no counterfeit.

SUFFOLK 'Tis the right ring, by heaven. I told ye all,
When we first put this dangerous stone a-rolling,
'Twould fall upon ourselves.

NORFOLK                                     Do you think, my lords,
The king will suffer but the little finger                          140
Of this man to be vexed?

CHAMBERLAIN                           'Tis now too certain;
How much more is his life in value with him?
Would I were fairly out on't!

CROMWELL                                     My mind gave me,
In seeking tales and informations
Against this man, whose honesty the devil                          145
And his disciples only envy at,
Ye blew the fire that burns ye: now have at ye!

128 **strangely** extraordinarily.
128–31 Although the Chancellor has taken the
vote, it is Bishop Gardiner who takes the initiative
and tries to act swiftly without any further non-
sense from Cranmer. He is also the most reluctant
to agree to a reconciliation after the king's
intervention (203).
130 **Receive** Take.
134 **gripes** clutches.
138–9 **When…ourselves** Proverbial (see
Tilley s889), and biblical (Prov. 26–7).

142 **in value with** highly esteemed by
143 **fairly…on't** well out of it.
143 **My…gave me** I had a misgiving.
144 **tales and informations** gossip and complaints.
146 **only** In modern usage, 'only' would
precede 'the devil'.
146 **envy at** begrudge, regard with malevolent
dislike.
147 **have at ye** be prepared; warning of an
attack.

*Enter* KING *frowning on them, takes his seat*

GARDINER Dread sovereign, how much are we bound to heaven
In daily thanks, that gave us such a prince,
Not only good and wise, but most religious; 150
One that, in all obedience, makes the church
The chief aim of his honour, and to strengthen
That holy duty out of dear respect,
His royal self in judgement comes to hear
The cause betwixt her and this great offender. 155
KING You were ever good at sudden commendations,
Bishop of Winchester. But know, I come not
To hear such flattery now, and in my presence
They are too thin and base to hide offences;
To me you cannot reach. You play the spaniel 160
And think with wagging of your tongue to win me;
But whatsoe'er thou tak'st me for, I'm sure
Thou hast a cruel nature and a bloody.
[*To Cranmer*] Good man, sit down. Now let me see the proudest
He, that dares most, but wag his finger at thee. 165
By all that's holy, he had better starve
Than but once think his place becomes thee not.
SURREY May it please your grace –
KING                              No, sir, it does not please me;
I had thought I had had men of some understanding

148] *Pope;* Dread Soveraigne / How...Heaven F    **159** base] F; bare *conj. Malone*    **159–60** offences; / To me...reach. You] *Foakes;* offences, / To me...reach. You F; offences. / To me...reach; you *Rowe;* offences. / To me...reach, you *Johnson;* offences. / To me...reach you *Cam., Maxwell*    **164** SD] *Rowe;* not in F    **164–5** proudest / He,] F; proudest, / He *Collier*

**153 dear respect** zealous regard.
**155 her** i.e. the church.
**156 sudden commendations** compliments on the spur of the moment.
**159 base** Several editors have adopted Malone's conjecture 'bare', forming an image with 'thin' and 'hide'; the correction is attractive but unnecessary.
**159–60** F punctuation, with only a comma after 'offences', has provoked debate. Several have preferred to place a full stop after 'offences' and to link 'To...reach' with 'spaniel' by omitting the full stop after 'reach' (Maxwell) or by

changing it to a comma (Johnson). However, Maxwell's argument that 'To...reach' should not stand as an independent statement is weak: it provides a connection between the 'flattery' of 158 and the spaniel image that follows.
**165 He** Man. See *Shr.* 3.2.234: 'the proudest he'; other examples are fairly common. However, as Maxwell argues, a comma may have dropped out at the end of the previous line.
**166 starve** die.
**167 his place** i.e. as privy councillor. Some are attracted by F4's correction 'this place'.

And wisdom of my council; but I find none.                   170
Was it discretion, lords, to let this man,
This good man – few of you deserve that title –
This honest man, wait like a lousy footboy
At chamber door? and one as great as you are?
Why, what a shame was this? Did my commission      175
Bid ye so far forget yourselves? I gave ye
Power as he was a councillor to try him,
Not as a groom. There's some of ye, I see,
More out of malice than integrity,
Would try him to the utmost, had ye mean,            180
Which ye shall never have while I live.
CHANCELLOR                              Thus far,
My most dread sovereign, may it like your grace
To let my tongue excuse all. What was purposed
Concerning his imprisonment, was rather,
If there be faith in men, meant for his trial         185
And fair purgation to the world, than malice,
I'm sure, in me.
KING                              Well, well, my lords, respect him,
Take him and use him well; he's worthy of it.
I will say thus much for him, if a prince
May be beholding to a subject, I                      190
Am for his love and service, so to him.
Make me no more ado, but all embrace him;
Be friends, for shame, my lords. My Lord of Canterbury,
I have a suit which you must not deny me:
That is, a fair young maid that yet wants baptism;    195
You must be godfather, and answer for her.
CRANMER The greatest monarch now alive may glory
In such an honour: how may I deserve it
That am a poor and humble subject to you?

---

175 **shame** disgrace.
180 **try** put on trial; also, 'oppress' or 'afflict'.
180 **mean** means, opportunity. See *Oth.*
3.1.37: 'I'll devise a mean.'
181 **while I live** A reminder to the audience of
Cranmer's martyrdom under one of Henry's
successors, Mary.

182 **like** please.
186 **purgation** clearing from the accusation or
suspicion of guilt (Onions). The circumlocutions
of the Chancellor betray the acute embarrassment
of the councillors.
190 **beholding** indebted.
192 **ado** difficulty, fuss.

KING Come, come, my lord, you'd spare your spoons; you shall have    200
    two noble partners with you, the old Duchess of Norfolk and
    Lady Marquess Dorset: will these please you?
        Once more, my Lord of Winchester, I charge you
        Embrace and love this man.

GARDINER                      With a true heart
    And brother-love I do it.

CRANMER                   And let heaven    205
    Witness how dear I hold this confirmation.

KING Good man, those joyful tears show thy true heart;
        The common voice I see is verified
        Of thee, which says thus: 'Do my Lord of Canterbury
        A shrewd turn, and he's your friend for ever.'    210
        Come, lords, we trifle time away: I long
        To have this young one made a Christian.
        As I have made ye one, lords, one remain;
        So I grow stronger, you more honour gain.

*Exeunt*

---

**5.3** *Noise and tumult within: enter* PORTER *and his* MAN

PORTER You'll leave your noise anon, ye rascals; do you take the
    court for Parish Garden? ye rude slaves, leave your gaping.

---

205 brother-love] *Malone;* Brother; loue F; Brothers love F2    207 heart] F2; hearts F    Act 5, Scene 3  5.3]
*Scena Tertia* F; *Scene IV / Cam.*    2 Parish] F; Paris F4

---

200 **spare...spoons** The king suggests that
Cranmer would like to save the expense of
apostle-spoons, the usual gift of godparents to a
child being christened. There were twelve silver
spoons in a set, each with the figure of an apostle
on the handle.

201 **two...partners** A female child would
have two godmothers as sponsors and one godfather.

205 **brother-love** F punctuation 'Brother; loue
I do it' has prompted speculation that the compositor's MS. read 'Brother; lowe I do it' (Foakes);
'lowe' = 'lo'.

208 **voice** judgement.

210 **shrewd** malicious. The saying is taken
from Foxe: 'it came into a common proverbe:
Doe unto my lord of Canturbury displeasure or a
shrewd turne, and then you may bee sure to have
him your friend whiles he liveth' (*Acts*, p. 1691).

212 **made a Christian** christened; i.e.
baptised.

**Act 5, Scene 3**

0 SD The enthusiastic and riotous crowd which
the Porter and his Man are trying to hold back
seem to have gathered at a doorway or gate at
court through which the procession must pass on
its way back from the christening. The London
populace is brought into the play for the first time
(apart from a silent presence in 2.1), representing
the nation at large in its celebration of the new
princess, whose future is so splendidly envisioned
in Cranmer's prophecy in the following scene.

0 SD.1 **within** i.e. outside; as Maxwell says, the
usual theatrical term.

1 **leave** cease.

2 **Parish Garden** Paris Garden (both spellings
were current); a centre for bull-baiting and bear-
baiting, on the Bankside in Southwark and therefore close to the Globe theatre. Jonson character-
ises it as one of the noisiest places in London in
*Epicoene* (4.4).

2 **gaping** bawling, shouting (*OED* Gape *v* 7).

[ONE] *within* Good master porter, I belong to th'larder.

PORTER Belong to th'gallows, and be hanged, ye rogue! Is this
   a place to roar in? Fetch me a dozen crab-tree staves, and          5
   strong ones; these are but switches to 'em: I'll scratch your
   heads. You must be seeing christenings? do you look for ale
   and cakes here, you rude rascals?

MAN Pray, sir, be patient; 'tis as much impossible,
   Unless we sweep 'em from the door with cannons,                    10
   To scatter 'em, as 'tis to make 'em sleep
   On May-day morning, which will never be:
   We may as well push against Paul's as stir 'em.

PORTER How got they in, and be hanged?

MAN Alas I know not, how gets the tide in?                            15
   As much as one sound cudgel of four foot
   (You see the poor remainder) could distribute,
   I made no spare, sir.

PORTER                    You did nothing, sir.

MAN I am not Samson, nor Sir Guy, nor Colebrand,
   To mow 'em down before me; but if I spared any                     20
   That had a head to hit, either young or old,
   He or she, cuckold or cuckold-maker,
   Let me ne'er hope to see a chine again,
   And that I would not for a cow, God save her.

[ONE] *within* Do you hear, master porter?                            25

PORTER I shall be with you presently, good master puppy;
   Keep the door close, sirrah.

MAN What would you have me do?

---

3 SH ONE] *Foakes; not in* F     3 master] *Var. 1773;* M. F     14 Paul's] F4; Powles F

3 **belong to** i.e. am employed in.

5 **crab-tree staves** Staves made from the crab apple tree were proverbially hard: Tilley C787.

7–8 **ale and cakes** See *TN* 2.3.116 for a famous reference to such festive fare.

12 **May-day morning** Dawn on 1 May, a time of festivity when the young went out into the fields to gather whitethorn and other branches to decorate their doorways, also to plight troth and no doubt to make love. See Herrick's poem 'Corinna's going a-maying'.

13 **Paul's** St Paul's Cathedral.

17 **poor remainder** i.e. of a broken cudgel.

18 **made no spare** spared no one.

19 **Samson…Colebrand** Heroes renowned for their strength. Guy, Earl of Warwick, killed the giant Colebrand in a well-known legend, retold by Drayton in the Twelfth Song of *Poly-Olbion* (1613).

23 **see a chine** eat beef (?); of uncertain meaning. The connection with beef comes from 'cow' in the next line, but *OED* has a reference linking 'chine' with the back and shoulders of a man.

24 **not for a cow** Apparently a common expression of no special meaning. Foakes suggests that 'cow' may have a bawdy sense, and quotes the same phrase in a MS. play, *The Tell-Tale*.

PORTER What should you do, but knock 'em down by th'dozens? Is this Moorfields to muster in? Or have we some strange     30
Indian with the great tool come to court, the women so besiege us? Bless me, what a fry of fornication is at door! On my Christian conscience, this one christening will beget a thousand, here will be father, godfather, and all together.

MAN The spoons will be the bigger, sir. There is a fellow some-    35
what near the door, he should be a brazier by his face, for o'my conscience twenty of the dog-days now reign in's nose; all that stand about him are under the line, they need no other penance: that fire-drake did I hit three times on the head, and three times was his nose discharged against me; he     40
stands there like a mortar-piece to blow us. There was a haberdasher's wife of small wit near him, that railed upon me till her pinked porringer fell off her head, for kindling such a combustion in the state. I missed the meteor once, and hit that woman, who cried out 'Clubs', when I might see from     45

30 **Moorfields** Gardens beyond Moorgate which degenerated into a field for archers about 1498, according to Stow, *Survey of London* (ed. C. L. Kingsford, 1908, II, 76–7), cited by Wright and Maxwell.

30 **muster in** gather in for training. The citizens' militia would meet in such places, as they do at Mile-end in *The Knight of the Burning Pestle* (5.2).

31 **Indian** Indians brought back from America were in great demand among the credulous, as Trinculo observes on first meeting Caliban (*Temp.* 2.2.32–3). There was special interest in Indians because of the founding of Jamestown, Virginia, in 1608.

31 **tool** The bawdy significance of the word seems to have existed in demotic speech from very early times, and continues to this day (*OED* has only a few examples from literary sources). In *TNK* 3.5.132, the word is used to describe a part of the baboon's costume.

32 **fry of fornication** i.e. swarm of would-be fornicators (Hoeniger). 'Fry' denotes fish roe but also the young fish after hatching, and then by extension other creatures hatching out in large numbers such as bees or frogs (*OED*).

33–4 **christening…thousand** The Porter's imagery throughout centres upon sexuality; the celebration of a christening becomes the celebration of fertility.

35 **spoons** christening spoons: see 5.2.200 n.

36 **brazier** worker in brass.

37 **dog-days** The hottest and from ancient times regarded as the most unhealthy days of the year, associated with Sirius, the dog-star, when it first becomes visible before sunrise (about 11 August in the latitude of Greenwich). Of uncertain number (30–54, *OED*), they may be the days before or after this event, or both.

38 **under the line** at the equator. See quibbles on the term in *Temp.* 4.1.236–7.

39 **fire-drake** Originally the fiery dragon of legend, then a popular name for meteors, and in the seventeenth century an exploding firework (*OED*).

41 **mortar-piece** A small cannon with a large bore, pointed at a high angle, used for large projectiles.

41 **blow us** (1) blow us out of the way, (2) blow us up.

42 **haberdasher's…wit** A haberdasher was a milliner and a dealer in small wares. Both senses seem to be suggested here.

43 **pinked porringer** A hat or cap resembling a porringer (a small basin or bowl) decorated by pinking, i.e. with perforations. It had once been a hat of some fashion: see *Shr.* 4.3.63–70.

44 **the meteor** i.e. the brazier again.

45 **Clubs** Rallying cry for the apprentices either to start or to stop a fight, or to defend a citizen. See Dekker, *1 Honest Whore* 4.3.111–12 (cited *OED*).

far some forty truncheoners draw to her succour, which were
the hope o'th'Strand where she was quartered. They fell on,
I made good my place; at length they came to th'broomstaff
to me, I defied 'em still, when suddenly a file of boys behind
'em, loose shot, delivered such a shower of pebbles that I        50
was fain to draw mine honour in and let 'em win the work;
the devil was amongst 'em I think surely.

PORTER These are the youths that thunder at a playhouse, and fight
for bitten apples, that no audience but the tribulation of Tower
Hill, or the limbs of Limehouse, their dear brothers, are able    55
to endure. I have some of 'em in Limbo Patrum, and there
they are likely to dance these three days; besides the running
banquet of two beadles that is to come.

*Enter* LORD CHAMBERLAIN

CHAMBERLAIN Mercy o'me, what a multitude are here!
They grow still too; from all parts they are coming,              60
As if we kept a fair here. Where are these porters,
These lazy knaves? Y'have made a fine hand, fellows!
There's a trim rabble let in; are all these
Your faithful friends o'th'suburbs? We shall have

**46 truncheoners** apprentices carrying clubs (a coinage).

**47 Strand** The Strand was then a fashionable residential street near the Thames.

**47 was quartered** lived.

**47 fell on** attacked.

**48 to th'broomstaff** to close quarters, fighting with broom sticks or staves (*OED* cites this as earliest example).

**50 loose shot** Marksmen not attached to a company or battalion (*OED* Loose *a* 1k).

**51 fain** obliged.

**51 work** fort.

**53–4 youths...apples** The apprentices or groundlings in the public theatres.

**54–5 tribulation...Hill** trouble-makers on Tower Hill. There was a gallows on Tower Hill and crowds gathered to watch public executions. *OED* speculates that the phrase may be a cant name for a gang of such trouble-makers (*OED* Tribulation 1c).

**55 limbs of Limehouse** Alliteration, as in the previous phrase, may explain the use of the term. Limehouse was a rough dockyard town, down the Thames from the city. 'Limbs' would mean

'members' or 'parts' of a Limehouse gang, but perhaps with an echo of a popular phrase, 'limb of the devil' or 'limb of Satan', as Foakes suggests.

**56 Limbo Patrum** 'Limbo' was a slang term for prison, derived from the *limbo patrum* (or *limbus patrum*), a region on the borders of hell where the souls of the 'fathers', the just who died before the coming of Christ, awaited his coming. See Dekker, *1 Honest Whore* 4.3.83–4: '(Poh) 'Sblood, doest long to lie in limbo? / (Crambo) An limbo be in hell, I care not.'

**57–8 running...beadles** The imagery of a festive time in prison with a 'running banquet' or light refreshments at the end of it is ironic since the beadles will give them a public whipping through the streets ('running').

**62 Y'have...hand** You've made a fine success of things. The phrase is often used ironically; see Tilley H99 and compare *Cor.* 4.6.118.

**63 trim** beautiful, elegant (ironical).

**64 suburbs** Parts of London outside the city's boundaries and jurisdiction, therefore considered lawless.

> Great store of room no doubt, left for the ladies,                    65
> When they pass back from the christening.

PORTER                                                    And't please
> your honour,
> We are but men, and what so many may do,
> Not being torn a-pieces, we have done:
> An army cannot rule 'em.

CHAMBERLAIN                      As I live,
> If the king blame me for't, I'll lay ye all                           70
> By th'heels, and suddenly; and on your heads
> Clap round fines for neglect. Y'are lazy knaves,
> And here ye lie baiting of bombards when
> Ye should do service. Hark the trumpets sound,
> Th'are come already from the christening;                             75
> Go break among the press, and find a way out
> To let the troop pass fairly, or I'll find
> A Marshalsea shall hold ye play these two months.

PORTER Make way there for the princess.

MAN                                          You great fellow,
> Stand close up, or I'll make your head ache.                          80

PORTER You i'th'chamblet, get up o'th'rail,
> I'll peck you o'er the pales else.

                                                              *Exeunt*

---

**66 And't** If it.

**70–1 lay. . .heels** fetter you or put you in the stocks.

**72 Clap. . .fines** Impose large fines.

**73 baiting** worrying, harassing, like dogs baiting a bear.

**73 bombards** Leather jugs or bottles for liquor, shaped like small cannon (bombards); applied to those who drank constantly from such bottles, like Falstaff in *1H4* 2.4.497: 'that huge bombard of sack'.

**76 press** crowd.

**77 fairly** fitly, becomingly.

**78 Marshalsea** A prison in Southwark, used for debtors and those who committed offences while part of the king's household.

**78 hold ye play** keep you engaged, hold you in play.

**79–82** There is debate as to whether the Porter and his Man are addressing members of

the audience, as if they were part of the unruly crowd (so J. W. Saunders, 'Vaulting the rails', *S.Sur.* 7 (1954), 69–81) or addressing actors representing the crowd who have struggled inside through the gates.

**80 close up** close against the others (or against the wall).

**81 chamblet** Common spelling for 'camlet', a rich fabric made of silk and goat's hair, originally thought to be camel's hair.

**81 o'th'rail** on the rail, or off the rail; the contraction could be used for either expression. The rail was the low railing around the edge of the stage which some contemporary illustrations picture.

**82** Otherwise I'll pitch you over the fence.

**82 SD Exeunt** No doubt the Porter and his Man go out through the beleaguered door, beating the crowd back, and the Lord Chamberlain follows.

**5.4** *Enter Trumpets sounding: then two Aldermen,* LORD MAYOR, GARTER, CRANMER, DUKE OF NORFOLK *with his marshal's staff,* DUKE OF SUFFOLK, *two Noblemen bearing great standing bowls for the christening gifts; then four Noblemen bearing a canopy, under which the* DUCHESS OF NORFOLK, *godmother, bearing the child richly habited in a mantle, etc., train borne by a lady; then follows the* MARCHIONESS DORSET, *the other godmother, and ladies. The troop pass once about the stage, and Garter speaks*

GARTER  Heaven, from thy endless goodness, send prosperous life, long and ever happy, to the high and mighty princess of England, Elizabeth.

           *Flourish. Enter* KING *and Guard*

CRANMER [*Kneeling*]  And to your royal grace, and the good queen,
    My noble partners and myself thus pray             5
    All comfort, joy in this most gracious lady,
    Heaven ever laid up to make parents happy,
    May hourly fall upon ye!
KING                          Thank you, good lord archbishop:
    What is her name?
CRANMER                Elizabeth.
KING                        Stand up, lord.
        [*The King kisses the child*]
    With this kiss, take my blessing: God protect thee,    10

---

Act 5, Scene 4    5.4] *Scena Quarta* F; *Scene V / Cam.*    1–3 Heaven...Elizabeth] *As prose, Capell; four lines,*
*ending...Heaven / ...life / ...Mighty / ...Elizabeth* F    4 SD] *Johnson; not in* F   9 SD] *Johnson; not in* F

### Act 5, Scene 4

0 SD The location of the final scene has been variously described by editors as the palace, the court, the courtyard of the palace. Elizabethan stage practice suggests that as the Porter and the others go out by one door, the christening procession enters through the other door-way, with trumpets sounding and splendid pageantry, into a neutral area which can be envisaged as any of these places. The details of the christening celebrations and the persons involved are from Holinshed (p. 934), but there is no mention in any of the sources of Cranmer's prophecy.

0 SD.2 GARTER The Garter King-at-Arms, chief herald of the court.

0 SD.2 **marshal's staff** Staff of the Earl Marshal of England.

0 SD.3 **great...bowls** Large bowls with legs so that they stand on their own (probably of silver-gilt, as Holinshed recounts).

0 SD.5 **habited** clothed.

0 SD.6 **train...lady** i.e. the train of the infant's mantle.

1–3 The Garter's proclamation follows Holinshed and is the appropriate formula for the occasion. As Foakes notes, a similar formula was used after the wedding of Princess Elizabeth and Prince Frederick in 1613.

5 **partners** fellow godparents.

Into whose hand I give thy life.

CRANMER                                    Amen.

KING  My noble gossips, y'have been too prodigal;
 I thank ye heartily: so shall this lady,
 When she has so much English.

CRANMER                              Let me speak, sir,
 For heaven now bids me; and the words I utter          15
 Let none think flattery, for they'll find 'em truth.
 This royal infant – heaven still move about her! –
 Though in her cradle, yet now promises
 Upon this land a thousand thousand blessings,
 Which time shall bring to ripeness. She shall be        20
 (But few now living can behold that goodness)
 A pattern to all princes living with her,
 And all that shall succeed. Saba was never
 More covetous of wisdom and fair virtue
 Than this pure soul shall be. All princely graces       25
 That mould up such a mighty piece as this is,
 With all the virtues that attend the good,
 Shall still be doubled on her. Truth shall nurse her,
 Holy and heavenly thoughts still counsel her;
 She shall be loved and feared. Her own shall bless her, 30
 Her foes shake like a field of beaten corn,
 And hang their heads with sorrow. Good grows with her;
 In her days, every man shall eat in safety
 Under his own vine what he plants, and sing
 The merry songs of peace to all his neighbours.         35
 God shall be truly known, and those about her

---

17 infant – heaven...her! –] *Maxwell, after Capell;* infant, Heaven...her; F    32] *Rowe;* And...sorrow: /
Good...her F

---

**12 gossips** Originally 'godsib', one who has a
spiritual relationship to a christened child
through becoming a godparent (God-related).

**12 prodigal** generous to a fault.

**17 heaven...her** See *2H6* 3.3.19: 'O thou
eternal Mover of the heavens'.

**23 Saba** Sheba, the Queen of Sheba who
sought out Solomon in Jerusalem for his wisdom:
see 1 Kings 10.1–13. 'Saba' was a common
spelling before 1611.

**26 mould up** create (according to a pattern).

**26 mighty piece** great product or master-
piece.

**30–5** One of many visions of a golden age in

the Bible; taken from 1 Kings 4.25: 'And Judah
and Israel dwelt without fear, every man under
his vine and under his fig tree...all the days of
Solomon'; and from Micah 4.1–4 about the 'last
days' when true religion will be established by the
Lord: 'nation shall not lift up a sword against
nation, neither shall they learn to fight any more.
But they shall sit every man under his vine and
under his fig tree: and none shall make them
afraid.' The reign of Elizabeth was looked upon
as a long period of peace, and the compliment
is extended to James who saw himself as a
peacemaker.

From her shall read the perfect ways of honour
And by those claim their greatness, not by blood.
Nor shall this peace sleep with her; but as when
The bird of wonder dies, the maiden phoenix,                    40
Her ashes new create another heir
As great in admiration as herself,
So shall she leave her blessedness to one
(When heaven shall call her from this cloud of darkness)
Who from the sacred ashes of her honour                         45
Shall star-like rise, as great in fame as she was,
And so stand fixed. Peace, plenty, love, truth, terror,
That were the servants to this chosen infant,
Shall then be his, and like a vine grow to him;
Wherever the bright sun of heaven shall shine,                  50
His honour and the greatness of his name
Shall be, and make new nations. He shall flourish,
And like a mountain cedar, reach his branches
To all the plains about him; our children's children
Shall see this, and bless heaven.
KING                                    Thou speakest wonders.   55
CRANMER She shall be, to the happiness of England,
An aged princess; many days shall see her,
And yet no day without a deed to crown it.
Would I had known no more! but she must die,
She must, the saints must have her; yet a virgin,              60
A most unspotted lily shall she pass
To th'ground, and all the world shall mourn her.
KING O lord archbishop,
Thou hast made me now a man; never before

37 ways] F4; way F

40 **maiden phoenix** Elizabeth was often compared to the phoenix by the poets. The fabulous Arabian bird was the only one of its kind, and when it died it was reborn from its own ashes. Here the spirit of the phoenix is said to be reborn in James.

42 **admiration** arousing wonder.

44 **cloud of darkness** Darkness is a common metaphor in the Bible for the earth in its bondage to sin.

47 **fixed** i.e. like a fixed star.

50-2 God's promises to Abraham in Gen. 17.4-6 are suggested: 'I will make thee exceeding fruitfull, & will make nations of thee: yea, kings shall proceed of thee.' Hopes for the union of Princess Elizabeth and Prince Frederick may be combined with interest in the 'new nations' being established overseas, especially Virginia.

53 **mountain cedar** See Ps. 92.12: 'The righteous...shall grow like a cedar in Lebanon.' See also the prophecy of Ezekiel at 17.22-3: the Lord God will plant 'the toppe of this hie cedre' upon 'an hie mountain and great'; 'and it shall bring forthe boughs and beare frute, and be an excellent cedre, and under it shal remaine all birdes, and everie foule shal dwell in the shadowe of the branches thereof'.

64 **Thou...man** You have turned me into a complete man.

This happy child did I get anything.                                65
This oracle of comfort has so pleased me
That when I am in heaven, I shall desire
To see what this child does, and praise my Maker.
I thank ye all. To you, my good lord mayor,
And your good brethren, I am much beholding.                        70
I have received much honour by your presence,
And ye shall find me thankful. Lead the way, lords,
Ye must all see the queen, and she must thank ye,
She will be sick else. This day, no man think
'Has business at his house, for all shall stay:                     75
This little one shall make it Holy-day.

THE EPILOGUE

'Tis ten to one this play can never please
All that are here: some come to take their ease
And sleep an act or two; but those we fear
W'have frighted with our trumpets, so 'tis clear
They'll say 'tis nought; others, to hear the city                  5
Abused extremely, and to cry 'That's witty',
Which we have not done neither; that I fear
All the expected good w'are like to hear
For this play at this time is only in
The merciful construction of good women,                           10
For such a one we showed 'em. If they smile
And say 'twill do, I know within a while
All the best men are ours; for 'tis ill hap
If they hold when their ladies bid 'em clap.

70 your] *Theobald;* you F    76 Holy-day] F; holy day *Johnson;* holiday *Var. 1778*

65 **get** (1) gain, (2) beget.
66 **oracle of comfort** divine message of encouragement.
70 **your** As Theobald notes (with Johnson's later approval), 'the *Aldermen* never were called Brethren to the King'. Foakes observes that a final *r* in Secretary hand was often attenuated and easily missed; also, that the source in Holinshed supports 'your'.
70 **beholding** indebted.
74 **sick** unhappy.
76 **Holy-day** A holiday from business and work, but also a holy day.

**Epilogue**
5–6 **city...extremely** Satirical city comedies were becoming popular, especially in the private theatres.
7 **that** so that.
8 **expected good** hoped-for praise.
10 **construction** interpretation.
13 **ill hap** bad luck.
14 **hold** hold back.

# SUPPLEMENTARY NOTES

**1.1.78–80 and his...he papers** The F punctuation has generally been altered by editors. Pope and Johnson regarded the whole phrase 'The honourable board of council out' as parenthetical and placed the comma after 'out' rather than before it, implying that the council was not then sitting, or possibly that it was entirely neglected by Wolsey's writing of the letter. They also altered the word order of 'him in' to 'in him' so that the meaning of 'he papers' would be more clearly pointed. This version has at least the advantage of being almost intelligible when spoken by an actor. If the F punctuation is accepted, it would seem to lay stress on the pair of words 'out' and 'in', perhaps referring to the peer who is not on the duty list (out) being compelled to be on the list (in) by Wolsey's letter. Foakes's interpretation of 'out' as 'the letter once out' would surely be difficult to communicate in the theatre.

**2.1.0 SD** The use of two unnamed 'Gentlemen' here and in 4.1 as commentators on off-stage action (resembling the use of messengers in neo-classical tragedies) was regarded by Spedding as un-Shakespearean and hence one reason for assigning both scenes to Fletcher. The direct stage representation of trial scenes was undoubtedly theatrical, as Shakespeare had demonstrated in *The Merchant of Venice* and *The Winter's Tale*, and Chapman in *The Tragedy of Byron* (1608). However, the dramatic emphasis given to Buckingham's trial through its staging would have seriously undermined the effect of Katherine's appearance at the divorce hearing before the king and the cardinals in 2.4, which is of far greater importance to the design of the play. Shakespeare used similar 'messengers' to describe the recognition scene between Leontes and Perdita in the final act of *The Winter's Tale* so as not to lessen the effect of Hermione's resurrection in the climactic scene. On linguistic grounds, Hoy has attributed both 2.1 and 4.1 to Shakespeare (1962, p. 79).

**5.2.0 SD** A comparison with the source shows how the dramatist has developed his material theatrically. In Foxe, the king does not see Cranmer waiting outside the council chamber with 'pages, lackeys and servingmen' but is merely told about it by 'Dr Buts'. Nor is there any hint of eavesdropping on the council: Foxe's phrase 'But let them alone (saide the King) and wee shall heare more soone' (*Acts*, p. 1694) refers to his belief that members of the council will soon approach him with the ring he had given Cranmer. Foxe does not describe the council scene beyond stating that certain charges against Cranmer (previously outlined) were made and that Cranmer answered as the king had advised him. Foxe makes no mention of an exchange between Cromwell and Gardiner, nor does the king make a dramatic entrance: instead, the councillors seek him out. At this point, Foxe reports a severe speech from the king to his councillors in direct speech. After a few of their excuses, the king bids them be reconciled to this worthy man, but there is no mention of Gardiner's reluctance to do so.

# TEXTUAL ANALYSIS

The only text for *Henry VIII* is that printed in the First Folio of Shakespeare's plays in 1623 when Heminges and Condell included it as the last in the section of history plays. This was an appropriate place for it since it brought the long sequence to a close with the historical period closest to Shakespeare's own lifetime. The printed text is an unusually good one, showing few errors or evidences of corruption, though there are difficulties of interpretation in certain passages because of the complexity of the language.

The copy behind the Folio text was, in W. W. Greg's words, 'clearly a carefully prepared manuscript, in whose hand or hands there is no evidence to show'.[1] It seems, therefore, to have been a 'fair copy' rather than an author's 'foul papers', but whether made by a scribe or by the author (or authors) cannot be ascertained. Greg believed the copy might have been a prompt-book, but other scholars are very doubtful about this. Although acts and scenes are clearly divided, with entrances and exits marked out accurately in almost every case, some of the speech headings are confused, as with the First and Second Gentlemen in 4.1.20 and 4.1.55, and again with *Cham.* (Chamberlain) and *Chan.* (Chancellor) at 5.2.119, 121. Also there are ambiguous speech headings like *Card.* when two cardinals are on stage at the same time (2.4 and 3.1). Such confusions suggest an origin in the author's foul papers and would quickly have been put right by a book-keeper. Other evidence which tells against the prompt-book hypothesis lies in the stage directions, which are very full where pageantry is involved, drawing in some detail upon the author's reading in Holinshed. Although many of the other stage direc-tions are conventional and show no signs of a particular origin, some are clearly authorial and do not belong to a playhouse script since they are descriptive, or vague as to numbers of persons, as already remarked at p. 60 above. The fair copy, then, was probably prepared from foul papers, but the scribe – if he was a scribe – remains a ghost figure about whom we know nothing.

There is a little more evidence about the compositors who worked for Jaggard on the Folio, though the shares of individual compositors are still a matter of debate. Foakes believes that three compositors worked on *Henry VIII*: B, some of whose spelling preferences are well known, who set thirteen pages, A who set two, and a third, much less known, who set the remaining thirteen. Hinman is fairly convinced, however, that A had nothing to do with the play, and names the second compositor, who set fifteen pages, as C. Hoy and Williams denominate this second compositor X and Taylor describes him as one of Jaggard's journeymen, naming

[1] W. W. Greg, *The Shakespeare First Folio*, 1955, p. 425.

him tentatively I.[1] Hinman and Hoy note that Compositor B is inclined to alter 'ye' to 'you', a fact which has some importance in the authorship controversy. There is no correspondence, however, between the pages worked by the various compositors and the portions of the play designated as by different authors.

Apparent errors in the text may be due to a compositor's misreading of his manuscript, or to faults within the manuscript itself, but there are not a great number of these. The most obvious are such misreadings as 'commissions' for 'confession's' at 1.2.164, and 'castles' for 'cattels' (chattels) at 3.2.343. Extra words are occasionally picked up by a compositor from neighbouring lines as in 'of you, to you' at 2.3.61, or a word may be clearly omitted as in 1.2.170. It is more difficult to place the blame for obscure passages where the fault may lie in the punctuation or in the spelling, the 'he papers' passage at 1.1.78–80, for example, or the phrase 'that quarrel. Fortune, do divorce' at 2.3.14.

The text presents no great difficulties to the director or actors, apart from some obscurities of language. In Act 5 there are a few minor problems of staging. Act 5, Scene 2 begins with Cranmer unable to get past the Keeper into the council chamber; he is observed waiting among pages and servants by Dr Butts, who brings the king to the window to see him. There are no exits in the text at this point, though the king asks Dr Butts to 'draw the curtain close' at his window. The following stage direction requires that a council-table with chairs and stools be brought in, and the councillors then enter. After some preliminaries, Cranmer is called forward from the door where he has been waiting.

Although not in F, most editors (apart from Foakes) provide exits for Cranmer, the king, Dr Butts, and the servants, and begin a new scene with the entry of the councillors. However, the continuity of the action suggested by the F stage direction would not trouble an Elizabethan audience: 'outside' could be considered 'inside' a moment later.[2] A different problem arises in the following scene, that of the Porter and his Man. Stage directions of shouts from 'within' suggest a crowd that is heard but not seen. Yet at the end of the scene, after a few harsh words from the Lord Chamberlain, the Porter and his Man appear to be threatening members of the crowd who have got in: 'You great fellow / Stand close up, or I'll make your head ache.' However, these are small staging problems in a play where the major challenge lies in the organisation of dances, pageants and processions in a proper relationship to the dramatic action.

## Postscript

At a late stage in the preparation of this edition, I was allowed to see the proofs of Fredson Bowers's old-spelling edition of the play for the seventh volume in the

---

1   R. A. Foakes, 'On the First Folio text of *Henry VIII*', *SB* 11 (1958), 55–60, and Foakes (ed.), *H8*, p. xvi, n. 2; Hinman, II, 214, 217; Hoy, 1962, pp. 71–90; P. Williams, 'New approaches to textual problems in Shakespeare', *SB* 8 (1956), 3–14; G. Taylor, 'The shrinking Compositor A of the Shakespeare First Folio', *SB* 34 (1981), 103–4.
2   Greg remarks that the F stage direction is a 'clumsy procedure' and wonders if there might have been a discovery to suggest the change of scene (*The Shakespeare First Folio*, p. 425).

Cambridge edition of *The Dramatic Works in The Beaumont and Fletcher Canon*. Bowers agrees with previous scholars that the copy-text was a scribal transcript rather than foul papers or prompt-book, but that the relation of the scribal copy to other possible copies remains obscure. Bowers's thorough analysis of the work of the two compositors, B and I, reveals that a large proportion of the possible misreadings and errors occur in the work of I, possibly a journeyman. On the question of authorship, he gives less weight than does Cyrus Hoy to the appearance of 'ye' in clusters in certain scenes as evidence that Fletcher may merely have worked over or 'touched up' scenes that Shakespeare had written. Such clusters, Bowers believes, may have been due to scribal aberrations or be merely accidental. He therefore reaffirms the traditional division of the play between Shakespeare and Fletcher until there is more evidence of Shakespeare's involvement in the scenes ascribed to Fletcher.

The extensive historical collation which Bowers has provided for this play will be of particular value to scholars and students concerned with problems of conjecture and emendation.

# READING LIST

This list includes the more important books and articles referred to in the Introduction and Commentary, and may be helpful to those who wish to undertake further study of the play.

Alexander, Peter. 'Conjectural history, or Shakespeare's *Henry VIII*', *Essays and Studies* 16 (1930), 85–120
Barton, Anne. 'He that plays the king: Ford's *Perkin Warbeck* and the Stuart history play', in Marie Axton and Raymond Williams (eds.), *English Drama: Forms and Development*, 1977
Bergeron, D. M. *Shakespeare's Romances and the Royal Family*, 1985
Booth, M. R. *Victorian Spectacular Theatre 1850–1910*, 1981
Brissenden, Alan. *Shakespeare and the Dance*, 1981
Bullough, Geoffrey. *Narrative and Dramatic Sources of Shakespeare*, IV, 1962
Cox, J. D. '*Henry VIII* and the masque', *ELH* 45 (1978), 390–409
Craig, Hardin. *An Interpretation of Shakespeare*, 1948
Erdman, D. V., and Fogel, E. G. *Evidence for Authorship: Essays on Problems of Attribution*, 1966
Felperin, H. *Shakespearean Romance*, 1972
Frye, Northrop. 'Romance as masque', in C. McG. Kay and H. E. Jacobs (eds.), *Shakespeare's Romances Reconsidered*, 1978
Harris, Bernard. 'What's past is prologue: *Cymbeline* and *Henry VIII*', in John Russell Brown and Bernard Harris (eds.), *Later Shakespeare*, 1966
Knight, G. Wilson. *The Crown of Life*, 1948
Leech, Clifford. *William Shakespeare, the Chronicles*, 1962
Leggatt, Alexander. ' "Henry VIII" and the ideal England', *S.Sur.* 38 (1985), 131–43
Odell, G. C. D. *Shakespeare from Betterton to Irving*, 1921
*Revels History of Drama in English, III 1576–1613*, ed. J. Leeds Barroll, Alexander Leggatt, Richard Hosley, Alvin Kernan, 1975
Rowley, Samuel. *When You See Me You Know Me*, ed. F. P. Wilson, Malone Society Reprints, 1952
Schoenbaum, Samuel. *Internal Evidence and Elizabethan Dramatic Authorship*, 1966
Sprague, A. Colby. *Shakespeare's Histories, Plays for the Stage*, 1964
*Thomas Lord Cromwell*, in *The Shakespeare Apocrypha*, ed. C. F. Tucker Brooke, 1908
Waage, F. O. '*Henry VIII* and the crisis of the English history play', *Shakespeare Studies* 8 (1975), 297–309
Wickham, Glynne. 'The dramatic structure of Shakespeare's *King Henry the Eighth*', *PBA* 70 (1984), 149–66
Yates, Frances. *Shakespeare's Last Plays: A New Approach*, 1957